ECONOGUIDE

to

Walt Disney World®
Epcot®

UNIVERSAL STUDIOS Florida®

COREY SANDLER

LONGMEADOW
PRESS

Published by Longmeadow Press, 201 High Ridge Road, Stamford, CT 06904. All rights reserved. No part of this book may be reproduced or utilized in any form or by any means, electronic or mechanical, including photocopying, recording or by any information storage and retrieval system, without permission in writing from the Publisher.

Cover and interior design by Fred Swartz, Graphic Arts Consortium, Nantucket, MA

Library of Congress Cataloging-in-Publication Data

Sandler, Corey, 1950-
   Econoguide to Walt Disney World, Epcot and Universal Studios:
   How to save hundreds of dollars and get the most out of your trip to Central Florida /
   Corey Sandler -- 1st ed.
   p. cm.

   1. Florida--Guidebooks. 2. Orlando Region (Fla.)--Guidebooks.
   3. Walt Disney World (Fla.)--Guidebooks. 4. Epcot Center (Fla.)--Guidebooks. I. Badgett, Tom.
   F309.3.S25 1992
   917.59'24--dc20
                                           92-13597
                                             CIP

Printed in the United States
First Edition
0 9 8 7 6 5 4 3 2 1

To Willie and Tessa and Jordan and Eden and Mickey and Minnie,
without whom none of this would have been necessary.

Contents

III Universal Studios Florida

IV Sea World

V Elsewhere in Central Florida

Appendix

Coupons

Index

How to Write to the Authors

ACKNOWLEDGMENTS

Dozens of hard-working and creative people helped move our words from the keyboard to the place where you read this book now.

Thanks to Fred Swartz of Graphic Arts Consortium of Nantucket, Mass. for his design of the original book. Our appreciation goes to Jose Juliano of Universal Studios Florida for his superlative behind-the-scenes tour, and to Jerie Jones and Toni Caracciolo at Sea World and Lisa Brock at Busch Gardens.

We thank the hotels, restaurants and attractions who offered discount coupons to our readers. Special thanks go to Janice Keefe who worked long and hard in the Word Association offices to collect and process the discount coupons. Thanks, too, to Dan Keefe, our official golf pro.

At Longmeadow Press, we thank Dan Bial for originally buying the book and Pam Altschul Liflander for continuing the series. We appreciate the agentry of Amy Davis and Bill Gladstone of Waterside Productions.

And finally, we thank you for buying this book. We hope you find it of value; please let us know how we can improve the book in future editions.

Corey Sandler
Word Association, Inc.
P.O. Box 2779
Nantucket, MA 02584

Introduction

Welcome to the 1994 edition of The Econoguide to Walt Disney World, Epcot and Universal Studios. We've designed this book as a guide to getting the most for your money and your time on vacation.

In addition to detailed "insider" tours of the major attractions of Central Florida, you'll find dollar-wise advice on air travel, renting a car, finding a room, meals and the all-important details of admission tickets. We've updated the book with the latest excitement at the parks, including the spectacular new "Jaws" ride at Universal Studios.

And there is a new set of money-saving discount coupons at the back of the book. Use just *one* of the nearly 100 coupons and you will save the cost of this book; use a few and you can save hundreds of dollars.

Looking for a vacation spot? Walt Disney World and the surrounding area is the number one tourist draw in the nation.

Need a place to stay? They've got nearly 20,000 rooms inside the boundaries of the park.

Hungry? No problem–nearly every type of restaurant you can imagine can be found somewhere in Walt Disney World. If you get the midnight munchies, Walt's crew will be glad to bring a Disney pizza to your door.

It all started with an amusement park primarily aimed at youngsters, but nearly every expansion since then has been aimed at expanding its base to adults.

When Disney saw how water parks were siphoning some dollars from the pipeline, Disney built River Country. When the competitors tried to fight back, along came the spectacular Typhoon Lagoon.

Were you planning to visit Sea World? Why, when Disney has built The Living Seas at Epcot?

Is the lure of Universal Studios strong? Not to worry–you can keep your dollars in the park at the Disney-MGM Studios theme park.

We know what the kids want, but is Dad's idea of a dream vacation a week of golfing or Mom's seven days on the tennis courts? Walt Disney World offers all of this in one place. You don't even have to leave Walt Disney World to go to a movie, get a haircut or visit a travel agency to extend your stay.

About the only things missing—so far—are blimp rides, miniature golf and a zoo, although there's a 9-hole executive golf course in and among the large courses at Walt Disney World and a petting zoo at Mickey's Starland, and more flight simulators than are owned by the world's airlines.

We think Walt Disney World may be the best-designed, best-run and most satisfying tourist attraction on this planet. And you have the right to spend your time and money as carefully as possible. That's what this book is all about.

Now a word about independence: That other book about Walt Disney World, the one with "The Official Guide" stamped on its cover, is an impressive collection of material. But, in our humble opinion, it suffers from a fatal closeness to its subject: it is prepared with the Walt Disney Company. We suspect that explains why it cannot find anything less than wonderful to say about anything within the boundaries of Walt Disney World, and why it almost ignores the world outside.

In that Official Book, there is not a single mention of Universal Studios, Sea World or Busch Gardens. This is not because they are unworthy of mention, or that visitors to Walt Disney World don't visit those attractions and others. The reason for their absence is the fact that the Walt Disney Co. does not profit from them.

The authors of this book have no connection with Walt Disney World, Universal Studios, Sea World, Busch Gardens or *any* of the other attractions written about here. Similarly, there is no financial interest in *any* of the discount coupons published within the book.

Our profit comes from you, the readers of this book, and it is you we hope to serve as best we can.

From Your World to Disney World

CHAPTER 1
When and How:
We Already Know Where and Why

Here are two days at Walt Disney World:

JULY 4. It wasn't exactly the flight you wanted. However, you're grateful for the privilege of forking over $840 for a coach seat in the jammed cabin of the wide-body jet. All of the rooms inside the park – at $240 per night – are sold out, but you were lucky enough to pay just $100 for a very ordinary hotel room that is a 20-minute bumper-to bumper drive from the parking lots.

According to the tram driver, you are parked in the same county as the Magic Kingdom, although you're not really sure. When you get to the ticket booths, there's a 30-minute wait just to get on the monorail to the entrance turnstiles.

Once inside, you sprint to Tomorrowland to find that the line for Space Mountain includes what seems like the entire population of Manhattan or Boston. And you'd better plan on showing up for lunch at 10:45 and dinner at 4:30 if you hope to find a table at the lowliest overpriced burger stop. But there are always the cooling thrills at Typhoon Lagoon, right? Yes, but the line to the top of the Humunga Cowabunga speed slide stretches back to Philadelphia.

MARCH 20. It seems like it's just your family and a crew of stewardesses, stretched out across the empty seats in the warm sun at 30,000 feet. Even nicer, you only had to pay $298 for a low-season excursion fare. Your ordinary hotel room cost you $29.95 (you could have rented one within the park for as little as $90) and the highway to the park was empty.

The monorail stood empty and waiting for you at the transportation center. Your leisurely walk to Space Mountain puts you into a 10-minute queue; later in the day you could skate onto a rocket car without breaking stride.

Take your pick of restaurants, and feel free to take a break in the afternoon and run over to Typhoon Lagoon; temperatures often reach 80 degrees and the lagoon is like a semi-private tropical island.

Do we have to point out which trip is likely to be more enjoyable?

OUR GUIDING RULE

The basic Econoguide strategy to getting the most out of your trip to Central Florida is this:

Go when most people don't;
stay home when everyone else is standing in line.

Specifically, we suggest you try to come to Florida when school is in session, and in the weeks between holidays: between Labor Day and Thanksgiving; between Thanksgiving and Christmas; between New Year's Day and President's Week; between President's Week and Spring Break/Easter; between Easter and Memorial Day.

We're not just talking about the crowds at Walt Disney World, Universal Studios, Sea World and elsewhere in central Florida. We're also talking about the availability of discount airline tickets, off-season motel rates and restaurant specials.

You'll find the lower prices when your business is needed, not when the "No Vacancy" lamp is lit. The best deals can be found in "low" season or the "shoulder" season midway between the least crowded and busiest periods.

This doesn't mean you can't have a good time if your (or your children's) schedule requires you to visit at high season. We'll show you ways to save money and time any time of the year.

A CENTRAL FLORIDA VACATION CALENDAR

JANUARY 🚶

(Semi-private. Warmer than Boston. Room rates at Low Season.)
When the kids go back to school and most of the adults go back to work after the Christmas-New Year's holiday, attendance drops off sharply. The second week of January through the first week of February is usually the second least crowded period of the year, with attendance averaging about 25,000 visitors per day at Walt Disney World. You'll be able to walk right onto most major rides and attractions. Room rates are at their lowest level.

FEBRUARY *first ten days* 🚶 🚶

(Moderate crowds. Warm but not hot. Room rates at "shoulder" level.)
Early February is a period of average attendance, reaching 30,000 to 35,000 daily visitors.

FEBRUARY *holiday period* 🚶 🚶 🚶

(Heavy crowds for holiday week. Room rates at High Season level.)
President's Week (celebrated in many school districts in and around the period from Feb. 12 to Feb. 22) is a time of fairly heavy attendance, up to about 45,000 daily visitors.

KEY: 🚶 = SEMI-PRIVATE   🚶 🚶 = MODERATE CROWDS

🚶 🚶 🚶 = HEAVY CROWDS   🚶 🚶 🚶 🚶 = ELBOW-TO-ELBOW

MARCH ⚊⚊

(Back to moderate attendance. Thermometer nudges into the 80s. Room rates at "shoulder" level.)

Attendance falls off to moderate from the end of February through the first week of April, averaging about 35,000 visitors. There are days in early March when you will have the parks to yourself, but at other times you will join thousands of college kids on early Spring Break or baseball fans drawn south for Spring Training. Nevertheless, this is not a bad time to come to Florida—with luck you will run into 80-degree water park weather.

APRIL ⚊⚊⚊

(The Easter Parade can get pretty thick. Consistent 80-degree weather. Room rates at High Season.)

The second and third weeks of April are among the most crowded times of the year, with Easter visitors and Spring Break students clogging the turnstiles at rates of up to 60,000 per day.

MAY ⚊⚊

(Moderate attendance, swimming weather and shoulder rates.)

Another relatively quiet period, from the end of April through the first week of June. Expect average attendance of 30,000 to 35,000 per day.

JUNE TO AUGUST ⚊⚊⚊

(Lots and lots of company. Hot sun and High Season rates.)

Just after Memorial Day, the throngs come. And stay. Crowds of about 60,000 per day can be expected from the first week of June through the third week of August. Room rates are at High Season for the entire summer. Temperatures average in the 90s and you can expect a few torrential downpours or steady rains.

SEPTEMBER TO MID-NOVEMBER ⚊

(Theme park heaven: no lines, no crowds, Low, low rates. Temperatures still high.)

Where have all the tourists gone? On the day after Labor Day, the turnstiles slow to a crawl, averaging about 20,000 visitors per day. Room rates reach bottom, too. The weather is quite good, although the occasional tropical storm or hurricane can dampen a few days here and there. The parks generally close at 6 p.m. or 7 p.m., but the lack of lines should allow you to see everything you want in the daylight.

NOVEMBER ⚊⚊⚊

(Merchants give thanks for the huge crowds at Thanksgiving. Rates at High Season.)

The one-week period around Thanksgiving brings a brief return to "No Vacancy" at motels and in attraction lines. Average attendance is about 55,000 visitors.

DECEMBER *up to Christmas Holiday* 🧍

(Mickey can get lonely at times like these, and hotels will almost pay you to come and stay.)

This is it: the Secret Season. From after Thanksgiving until the day Christmas vacation starts is *the* quietest time of the year for a visit. Attendance levels average 15,000 to 20,000 per day, and lines are rare. Room rates are rock-bottom, too.

DECEMBER *Christmas Holiday* 🧍 🧍 🧍 🧍

(Your sisters and cousins and aunts will all be on line, in front of you. You may need a loan for the super-High Season room rates.)

The Christmas-New Year's holiday is the most crowded, least time-efficient time to visit Central Florida. You'll be shoulder-to-shoulder with an average of 75,000 to 80,000 other visitors each day at Walt Disney World, with large crowds and long lines at Universal Studios, Sea World and other area attractions. The crowds can become so large that some of the parks actually close the gates by mid morning. Don't feel too bad if you're shut out; you could be inside. On line. You cannot count on temperatures warm enough for swimming, either. Room rates are at their highest levels, too. It's a festive, happy time, but frankly, we'd rather be alone or close to it. If you must go, be sure to arrive at the park early and follow the Power Trip plan for your best chance.

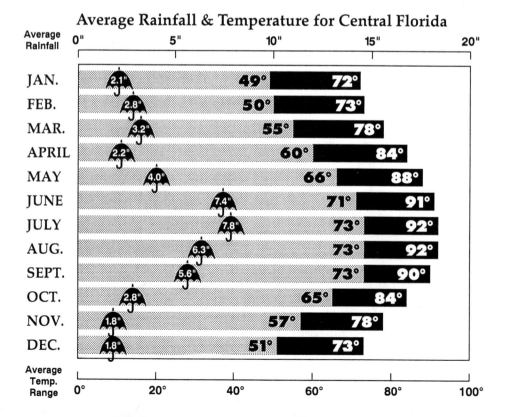

Average Rainfall & Temperature for Central Florida

Average Rainfall	0"	5"	10"	15"	20"
JAN.	2.1"		49°	72°	
FEB.	2.8"		50°	73°	
MAR.	3.2"		55°	78°	
APRIL	2.2"		60°	84°	
MAY		4.0"	66°	88°	
JUNE		7.4"	71°	91°	
JULY		7.8"	73°	92°	
AUG.		6.3"	73°	92°	
SEPT.		5.6"	73°	90°	
OCT.	2.8"		65°	84°	
NOV.	1.8"		57°	78°	
DEC.	1.8"		51°	73°	
Average Temp. Range	0°	20°	40°	60°	80°	100°

The Best Day to Go to the Park

When Mommy, Daddy, Junior and Missy arrive in Orlando on Sunday (the most common arrival date) for a week's visit (the most common length of vacation) the first place they will go, on Monday, is the Magic Kingdom. Epcot comes next, then the Disney-MGM Studios. The remainder of the week is usually given over to other area parks and attractions.

So, we feel the best plan for your visit is to adopt what we call a **Contrarian View.** In other words, go against the common logic which says, "We came here for the Magic Kingdom and that's where we'll go first."

MAGIC KINGDOM AND EPCOT	GO	DON'T GO
	Friday	Monday
	Sunday	Tuesday
	Saturday	Wednesday
	Thursday	

DISNEY-MGM STUDIOS	GO	DON'T GO
	Sunday	Wednesday
	Friday	Tuesday
	Saturday	Thursday
	Monday	

UNIVERSAL STUDIOS AND OTHER AREA ATTRACTIONS	GO	DON'T GO
	Sunday	Thursday
	Friday	Wednesday
	Monday	Saturday
	Tuesday	

Here is one schedule you might want to consider if you are visiting Central Florida during one of the busy times of the year:

The Econoguide
Contrarian Schedule

SATURDAY	SUNDAY	MONDAY	TUESDAY
Arrive in Orlando Visit water parks, smaller attractions or dinner theaters	Magic Kingdom, Disney-MGM Studios or Universal Studios	Universal Studios or Disney-MGM Studios	Sea World, beach, golf, water parks or other attractions.

WEDNESDAY	THURSDAY	FRIDAY	SATURDAY
Busch Gardens, Space Center, Cypress Gardens	Epcot Center	Magic Kingdom	A second chance at the park of your choice before heading home

Orlando Area

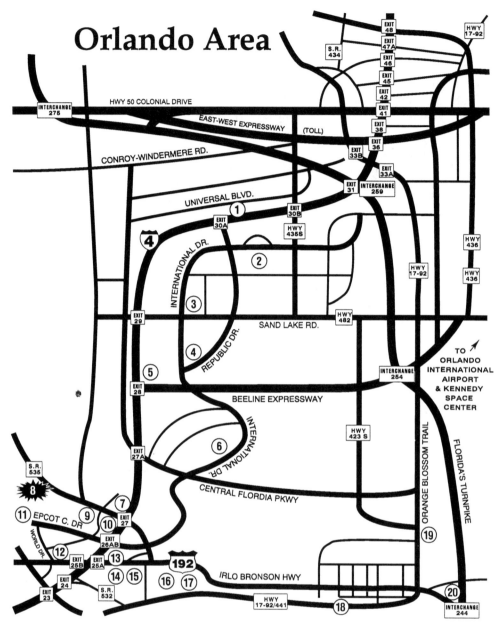

1 Universal Studios
2 Wet 'n Wild
3 Fun 'n Wheels
4 Mercado
5 Orange County Civic/
Convention Center
6 Sea World
7 Crossroads
8 **Magic Kingdom**
9 Walt Disney World Village &
Pleasure Island

10 Typhoon Lagoon
11 Epcot Center
12 Disney-MGM Studios
13 Water Mania
14 Old Town
15 Fort Liberty
16 Alligatorland Zoo
17 Medieval Times
18 Kissimmee Airport
19 Gatorland Zoo
20 Houston Astros Training Camp

Chapter 2
How to Buy the Lowest-cost Airline Ticket and Protect Yourself from the Uncertainties of Modern Travel

This chapter is being written at 31,000 feet, headed southbound from Boston to Orlando on a jumbo jet. The cost of the seat was $298.

The businessman across the aisle will suffer through the same mystery meal, watch the same crummy movie and arrive in Orlando at the same millisecond we do – and pay $804 for his ticket.

But we're not even the winner in the airline ticket sweepstakes. The couple in front were happily bumped off the previous flight because of overbooking and are discussing where to use the two free round-trip tickets they received in compensation. And up front in first class—where the food is ever so slightly better–a family of four is traveling on free tickets earned through Mom's frequent flyer plan.

In today's strange world of air travel, there is a lot of room for maneuvering for the dollarwise and clever traveler. You can pay an inflated full price, you can take advantage of the lowest fares or you can play the ultimate game and parlay tickets into free travel. In this chapter, we'll show you how to do each.

In mid-1992, American Airlines led a revolution in ticket pricing which holds the potential to greatly simplify air fare, if it holds. We're not so sure that competition won't begin the cycle of complexity again.

There are three golden rules to saving hundreds of dollars on travel: Be flexible, be flexible and be flexible.

• Be flexible about when you choose to travel, and visit Walt Disney World during the off-season or low-season when airfares, hotel rooms and other attractions offer substan-

The best policy. Consider buying trip cancellation insurance from a travel agency, tour operator or directly from an insurance company (ask your insurance agent for advice.) The policies are intended to reimburse you for any lost deposits or prepayments if you must cancel a trip because you or certain specified members of your family become ill. Read the policy carefully to understand the circumstances under which the company will pay.

Take care not to purchase more coverage than you need; if your tour package costs $5,000 but you would lose only $1,000 in the event of a cancellation, then the amount of insurance required is just $1,000. Some policies will cover you for health and accident benefits while on vacation, excluding any preexisting conditions.

tial discounts. We've described the off-season in the previous chapter.

• Be flexible about the day of the week you travel. In many cases, you can save hundreds of dollars by changing your departure dates one or two days in either direction. Ask your travel agent or airline reservationist for current fare rules and restrictions.

> The days of lightest air travel are generally mid week, Saturday afternoons and Sunday mornings.
>
> In general, you will receive the lowest possible fare if you include a Saturday in your trip, buying what is called an **Excursion Fare.** Airlines use this as a way to exclude business travelers from the cheapest fares, assuming that business people will want to be home by Friday night.

• Be flexible on the hour of your departure. There is generally lower demand–and therefore lower prices–for flights that leave in the middle of the day or very late at night.

• Be flexible on the route you will take, or your willingness to put up with a change of plane or stopover. Once again, you are putting the law of supply and demand in your favor. A direct flight from Boston to Orlando for a family of four may cost hundreds more than a flight that includes a change of planes in Raleigh, N.C. before proceeding to Orlando.

> Don't overlook the possibility of flying out of a different airport, either. For example, metropolitan New Yorkers can find domestic flights from LaGuardia, Newark or White Plains. Suburbanites of Boston might want to consider flights from Worcester or Providence as possibly cheaper alternates to Logan Airport.

• Plan way ahead of time and purchase the most deeply discounted advance tickets, which usually are non-cancelable. Most carriers limit the number of discount tickets on any particular flight; although there may be plenty of seats left on the day you want to travel, they may be offered at higher rates.

• In a significant change, in 1992, most airlines modified "non-refundable" fares to become "non-cancelable." What this means is that if your plans change or if you are forced to cancel your trip, your tickets retain their value and can be applied against another trip, usually for a fee of about $25 per ticket.

• Or, conversely, you can take a big chance and wait for

Double indemnity.
Your homeowner's or renter's insurance policy may include coverage for your possessions while you travel, making it unnecessary to purchase a special policy. Check with your insurance agent.

the last possible moment, keeping in contact with charter tour operators and accepting a bargain price on a "leftover" seat and hotel reservation. You *may* also find that some airlines will reduce the prices on leftover seats within a few weeks of departure date; don't be afraid to check regularly with the airline, or ask your travel agent to do it for you. In fact, some travel agencies have automated computer programs that keep a constant electronic eagle eye on available seats and fares.

• Take advantage of special discount programs like Senior Citizens clubs, military discounts or offerings from organizations to which you may belong. If you are in the over-60 category, you may not even have to belong to a group like AARP; simply ask the airline reservationist if there is a discount available–you may have to prove your age when you pick up your ticket or boarding pass.

If you are traveling to a convention that happens to take place in Orlando, you may be able to get in on a discount negotiated by the group with a particular airline. This was one area in which *some* airlines announced changes in mid-1992. They eliminated convention and corporate discounts, and in some cases ended senior discounts. By mid-1993 many such special programs were back on the books in one form or another.

• Consider doing business with a discounter, known in the industry as consolidators or less flatteringly, as "bucket shops." Look for their ads in the classified sections of many Sunday newspaper travel sections. These companies buy the airlines' slow-to-sell tickets in volume and resell them to consumers at rock-bottom prices. Be sure to study and understand the restrictions; if they fit your needs and wants, this is a good way to fly.

• A bit more in the shadows are ticket brokers who specialize in the resale of frequent flyer coupons and other free or almost-free tickets. Are you willing to take a small financial risk with the chances of saving hundreds or even thousands of dollars on a long trip?

Although most airlines attempt to prohibit the resale or transfer of free tickets from the original "owner" to a second or third party, the fact is that very rarely are they successful in preventing such re-use. (When is the last time you were asked for some proof of identity in boarding a domestic air flight?)

Funny hat fares. In fact, you may not have to have any affiliation at all with a convention group in order to take advantage of special rates, if offered. All the airline will ask is the name or number of the discount plan for the convention; the reservationist is almost certainly not going to ask to see your union card or funny hat.

Check with conventions and visitors bureaus at your destination to see if any large groups are travelling when you plan to fly. Is this sneaky and underhanded? Yes. But we think it is sneaky and underhanded for an airline to charge hundreds of dollars more for the seat to the left and right of the one we're sitting in.

Finding a bucket shop. Look for ads for ticket brokers and bucket shops in places like the classified ads in *USA Today*, the "Mart" section of the *Wall Street Journal* or in specialty magazines like *Frequent Flyer*.

*Be sure to read and understand the terms of your con-
tract with the broker, and pay for your ticket with a credit card, if possible.*

YOUR CONSUMER RIGHTS

The era of deregulation of airlines has been a mixed
blessing for the industry and the consumer. After a period of wild competition based mostly on price, we now are
left with fewer, huge airlines and a dizzying array of con-
fusing rules.

The U.S. Department of Transportation and its Federal
Aviation Administration still regulate safety issues, over-
booking policies, baggage limits and no-smoking rules.
Almost everything else is between you and the airline.

Policies on fares, cancellations, reconfirmation and check-
in requirements, compensation for lost or damaged baggage or for delays all vary by airline. Your rights are limited and defined by the terms of the contract you make with
an airline when you buy your ticket. You may find the contract included with the ticket you purchase, or the airlines
may "incorporate terms by reference" to a separate document which you will have to request to see.

Whether you are buying your ticket through a travel agent or dealing directly with the airline, here are
some important questions to ask: Is the price guaranteed or can it change from the time of the reservation
until you actually purchase the ticket?

Can the price change between the time you buy the
ticket and the date of departure?

Is there a penalty for cancellation of the ticket?

Can the reservation be changed without penalty, or
for a reasonable fee? And, ask your travel agent the
following:

Is there anything I should know about the financial
health of the airline offering me this ticket?

Are you aware of any significant threats of work stop-
pages or legal actions that could ruin my trip?

OVERBOOKING

Overbooking is a polite industry term that refers to the
legal business practice of selling more than an airline can
deliver. It all stems, alas, from the unfortunate habit of many
travelers of neglecting to cancel flight reservations that will
not be used. Airlines study the patterns on various flights
and city pairs and apply a formula that allows them to sell

Checking in again.
Having a boarding pass
issued by a travel agent
is not the same as
checking in at the air-
port; you'll still need to
show your ticket at the
counter so that the
agent knows you're
there.

more tickets than there are on the plane in the expectation that a certain percentage will not show up at the airport.

But what happens if all passengers holding a reservation do show up? Obviously, the result will be more passengers than seats, and some will have to be left behind.

The involuntary bump list will begin with the names of passengers who are late to check in. Airlines must ask for volunteers before bumping any passengers who have followed the rules on check-in.

Now, assuming that no one is willing to give up his or her seat just for the fun of it, the airline will offer some sort of compensation–either a free ticket or cash, or both. It is up to the passenger and the airline to negotiate an acceptable deal.

The U.S. Department of Transportation's consumer protection regulations set some minimum levels of compensation for passengers who are bumped from a flight due to overbooking.

If a passenger is bumped involuntarily, the airline must provide a ticket on its next available flight. Unfortunately, there is no guarantee that there will be a seat on that plane, or that it will arrive at your destination at a convenient time.

If a passenger is bumped involuntarily and is booked on a flight which arrives within one hour of the original arrival time, no compensation need be paid; if the airline gets the bumpee to his or her destination more than one hour, but less than two hours after your scheduled arrival, the traveler is entitled to receive an amount equal to the one-way fare of the oversold flight, up to $200; if the delay is more than two hours, the bumpee will receive an amount equal to twice the one-way fare of the original flight, up to $400.

It is not considered "bumping" if a flight is cancelled because of weather, equipment problems or the lack of a flight crew. You are also not eligible for compensation if the airline substitutes a smaller aircraft for operational or safety reasons, and if the flight involves an aircraft with 60 seats or less.

HOW TO GET BUMPED

Why in the world would you *want* to be bumped? Well, perhaps you'd like to look at missing your plane as an opportunity to earn a little money for your time instead of an

Kids in mid-air. If you are flying with children, discuss with your airline or travel agent any special needs you might have. These might include a request for a bulkhead seat to give children a little extra room for fidgeting (although you will lose the storage space underneath the seat in front of you) or special meals (most airlines offer a child's meal of a hot dog or hamburger on request, which may be more appealing to a youngster than standard airline fare).

Be sure to pack a special bag for young children and carry it on board the plane. Extra diapers in the baggage compartment won't help you at all in an emergency at 25,000 feet. Include formula, food and snacks as well as a few toys and books to occupy young ones.

Changes in altitude at takeoff and landing may cause some children discomfort in their ears. Try to teach them to clear their ears with an exaggerated yawn. Giving children bubble gum or sucking candy, or a bottle for babies, can help, too.

annoyance. Is a two-hour delay worth $100 an hour to you? How about $800 for a family of four to wait a few hours on the way home–that will pay for a week's hotel plus a meal at the airport.

If you're not in a tremendous rush to get to Orlando–or to get back home–you might want to volunteer to be bumped. We wouldn't recommend doing this on the busiest travel days of the year, or if you are booked on the last flight of the day, unless you are also looking forward to a free night in an airport motel.

COMPLAINT DESK

The skies may be friendly and the airline may be doing what it does best, but we don't know of a single frequent flyer who doesn't have a horror story or two about air travel.

Unfriendly skies.
To register a complaint with your air carrier, send a letter to their customer service department.

Whatever the problem, your first step should be to try and resolve it directly with the airline. They're the ones who have the power and the money to make you happy, and they are sometimes quite accommodating.

Most airlines and some large charter operations have customer service agents on duty at the airport; they are usually able to take care of some problems immediately, reissuing tickets for missed connections, giving travel vouchers or hotel coupons in certain circumstances. Present your case firmly but politely, and be specific (and reasonable) about what you want from the airline. If you are a member of an airline's frequent flyer club or other such special program, it doesn't hurt to mention that.

If you cannot resolve the matter at the airport, be sure to keep all documentation from your flight, including tickets, boarding passes and baggage checks; obtain receipts for any hotels, meals or taxicabs you were obliged to use because of the problem. Write down the name of the customer service agent you spoke to, and then send a carefully phrased (polite, but firm) letter to the office of the airline in question. Include in your letter a specific request for what you would like them to do; be reasonable.

BELLY-UP

What happens if the airline goes bankrupt between the time you buy your ticket and you return from your trip? That's not an idle question in these difficult economic times.

Although in the past, some or all of the surviving airlines have honored tickets from failed carriers, there is no guarantee of that in the future. Some carriers, seeking to reassure ticket buyers even as the business pages report their possible bankruptcy, have created escrow accounts to repay any customers who might be stranded.

In either case, you could still end up losing a fair amount of money if your trip is interrupted very close to departure, with too little time to purchase a deep-discount fare. The worst possible situation would arise if the airline went out of business in the middle of your trip, forcing you to buy a replacement one-way ticket on short notice.

How do you protect yourself? First of all, read the newspapers and consult with a capable travel agent. The shaky status of Eastern Airlines, Pan American, Midway Airlines and other recent casualties were obvious in the months before their fall.

Secondly, and most importantly, buy your ticket with a credit card. When you do so, you are making a contract with the bank or company that issues the card and not the airline itself. Under terms of the U.S. Fair Credit Billing Act, you are entitled to a prompt refund—from the card issuer—if a product is not delivered as promised.

If you have paid by check—or even worse, by cash—you must apply for a refund from the carrier. It might be necessary to file a claim in a bankruptcy court as an unsecured creditor, which may or may not turn out to be a satisfactory conclusion to your dream vacation.

National Organizations For complaints about charter companies, several national industry groups say they will accept and respond to complaints in writing about members of their organizations:

U. S. Tour Operators Association 211 East 51st St., Suite 4B New York, NY 10022

American Society of Travel Agents Consumer Affairs Department P.O. Box 23992 Washington, DC 20026-3992

Association of Retail Travel Agents 25 South Riverside Avenue P.O. Box 388 Croton-on-Hudson, NY 10525

TOUR PACKAGES AND CHARTER FLIGHTS

Tour packages and flights sold by tour operators or travel agents may look similar, but the consumer may end up with significantly different rights.

It all depends whether the flight is a "scheduled" or "non-scheduled" flight. A scheduled flight is one that is listed in the Official Airline Guide and available to the general public through a travel agent or from the airline. This doesn't mean that a scheduled flight will necessarily be on a major carrier, or that you will be flying on a 747 jumbo jet; it could just as easily be the propeller-driven pride of Hayseed Airlines. In any case, though, a scheduled flight does have to meet stringent federal government certification requirements.

In the event of delays, cancellations, or other problems with a scheduled flight, your recourse is with the airline.

A non-scheduled flight is also known as a charter flight. The term "charter" is sometimes also applied to a complete

Second chance. Tour cancellations are rare. Most tour operators, if forced to cancel, will offer another package or other incentives as a goodwill gesture. If a charter flight or charter tour is cancelled, the tour operator must refund your money within 14 days.

Drop us a card. Keep in touch with your travel agent or tour operator. In many cases they can anticipate major changes before departure time and will let you know. And, many operators will try hard to keep you from demanding a refund if you find a major change unacceptable. They may offer a discount or upgrade on a substitute trip or adjust the price of the changed tour.

package that includes a non-scheduled flight, hotel accommodations, ground transportation and other elements.

Charter flights are generally a creation of a tour operator who will purchase all of the seats on a specific flight to a specific destination, or who will rent an airplane and crew from an air carrier.

Charter flights and charter tours are regulated by the federal government, but your rights as a consumer are much more limited than those afforded to scheduled flight customers.

WRITTEN CONTRACTS

You wouldn't buy a hamburger without knowing the price and specifications (two all-beef patties on a sesame seed roll, etc.) Why, then, would you spend hundreds or even thousands of dollars on a tour and not understand the contract that underlies the transaction?

When you purchase a charter flight or a tour package you should review and sign a contract that spells out your rights. This contract is sometimes referred to as the "Operator Participant Contract" or the "Terms and Conditions." Look for this contract in the booklet or brochure that describes the packages; ask for it if one is not offered. The proper procedure for a travel agent or tour operator to follow requires that they wait until the customer has read and signed the contract before any money is accepted.

Remember that the contract is designed mostly to benefit the tour operator, and each contract may be different from others you may have agreed to in the past. The basic rule here is: **if you don't understand it, don't sign it.**

Depending on your relative bargaining strength with the provider, you may be able to amend the contract so that it is more in your favor; be sure to obtain a countersignature from an authorized party if you make a change in the document, and keep a signed copy for yourself.

TOUR CANCELLATIONS

A charter flight or charter tour may be cancelled by the tour operator for any reason up until 10 days before departure. This may happen if not enough travelers buy the flight or tour. This is a risk you agree to in exchange for the low fare.

Although the operator can get off more-or-less scot free if a trip is cancelled, not so the traveler. If you cancel, expect to pay a penalty; the closer to the scheduled date of departure, the more that is at risk. Sometimes there is no refund within a few days before departure. If you or the tour operator find a substitute to take your place, you are entitled to a full refund minus a small administrative fee.

PRICE AND ITINERARY CHANGES

The tour operator can increase the cost of your trip or make changes to the itinerary. However, on a charter flight or charter tour, the tour operator cannot increase the price less than 10 days prior to departure and major changes entitle you to cancel your trip and receive a full refund if the changes are not acceptable to you.

Major alterations include:

- Changes in departure or return cities;
- Changes in departure or return dates, unless the date change results from a flight delay which the tour operator had no knowledge of until two days prior to the scheduled departure date;
- Price hikes of more than 10 percent;
- Changes in hotels, unless the tour operator has reserved the right in the contract to substitute other hotels of comparable value; and
- A departure delay of more than 48 hours. Changes not considered major include the substitution of aircraft or airline, or modifications to aircraft routing.

THE BEST WAY TO BOOK A PACKAGE OR CHARTER FLIGHT

If possible, use a travel agent–preferably one you know and trust from prior experience. In general, the tour operator pays the travel agent's commission. Some tour packages, however, are available only from the operator who organized the tour; in certain cases you may be able to negotiate a better price by dealing directly with the operator, although you are giving up one layer of protection for your rights.

Pay for your ticket with a credit card; this is a cardinal rule for almost any situation in which you are prepaying for a service or product.

Realize that charter airlines don't have large fleets of planes available to substitute in the event of a mechanical problem or an extensive weather delay. They may or may not be able to arrange for a substitute piece of equipment from another carrier.

If you are still willing to try a charter after all of these warnings, make one more check of the bottom line before

Lug-it-yourself. If you are using a scheduled airline to connect with a charter flight, your baggage will not be automatically transferred. You must make the transfer yourself.

Delays may be costly. Charter and tour flights operate independently of other flights. If you are on a trip that combines scheduled and non-scheduled flights, or two unrelated charter flights, you may end up losing your money and flight because of delays.

It may make sense to avoid such combinations for that reason, or to leave extra hours or even days between connections. Some tour operators offer travel delay insurance that pays for accommodations or alternative travel arrangements necessitated by certain types of delays.

you sign the contract. First of all, is the air travel less expensive than the lowest non-refundable fares from a scheduled carrier? (Remember that you are, in effect, buying a non-refundable fare with most charter flight contracts.)

Have you included taxes, service charges, baggage transfer fees or other charges the tour operator may put into the contract?

Is the savings significantly more than the 10 percent the charter operator may boost the price without your permission? Do any savings come at a cost of time? Put a value on your time.

And finally, don't buy a complete package until you have compared it to the a la carte cost of such a trip. Call the hotels offered by the tour operator, or similar ones in the same area and ask them a simple question: "What is your best price for a room?" Be sure to mention any discount programs that are applicable, including AAA or other organizations. Do the same for car rental agencies and place a call to Walt Disney World and any other attractions you plan to visit to get current prices.

And, of course, don't overlook the discount coupons for hotels, motels, restaurants and attractions that are included in this book–that's why they're there.

CHAPTER 3
How to Sleep and Eat for Less

NEGOTIATING FOR A ROOM

Notice the title of this section: we didn't call it "buying" a room. The fact of the matter is that hotel rooms, like almost everything else, are subject to negotiation and change.

Here is how to pay the highest possible price for a hotel room: Walk up to the front desk without a reservation and say, "I'd like a room." Unless the "No Vacancy" sign is lit, you're going to pay the "rack rate," which is the published maximum nightly charge.

Here are a few ways to pay the lowest possible price:

1) Before you head for your vacation, spend an hour on the phone and call directly to a half dozen hotels that seem to be in the price range you'd like to spend. (We recommend membership in AAA, and use of their annual Tour Books as *starting points* for your research.)

Start by asking for the room rate. Then ask them for their *best* rate. Does that sound like an unnecessary second request? Trust us, it's not: we can't begin to count the number of times the rates have dropped substantially when we ask again.

[True story: I once called the reservation desk of a major hotel chain and asked for the rates for a night at a Chicago location. "That will be $149 per night," we were told. "Ouch," I said. "Oh, would you like to spend less?", the reservationist asked. I admitted that I would, and she punched a few keys on her keyboard. "They have a special

Here's my card.
Membership in AAA brings some important benefits for the traveler, although you may not be able to apply the club's usual 10 percent discount on top of whatever hotel rate you negotiate. (It doesn't hurt to ask, though.) Be sure to request a Tour Book and Florida and Orlando maps from AAA, even if you plan to fly to Florida; they are much better than the maps given by car rental agencies.

Weekly, not weakly.
Are you planning to
stay for a full week?
Ask for the weekly rate.
If the room clerk says
there is no such rate,
ask to speak to the
manager: he or she
may be willing to shave
a few dollars per day
off the rate for a long-
term stay.

Clearing the air. If you
don't indulge, ask for a
Non-Smoking Room at
check in. The air will be
somewhat cleaner and
furniture somewhat
fresher.

promotion going on. How about $109 per night?," she asked.

[Not bad for a city hotel, I reasoned, but still I hadn't asked the big question. "What is your best rate?", I asked. "Oh, our best rate? That would be $79," said the agent.

[But, wait: "Okay, I'll take it. I'm an AAA member, by the way." Another pause. "That's fine, Mr. Sandler. The nightly room rate will be $71.10. Have a nice day."]

When you feel you've negotiated the best deal you can obtain over the phone, make a reservation at the hotel of your choice. Be sure to go over the dates and prices one more time, and obtain the name of the person you spoke with and a confirmation number if available.

2) When you show up at your hotel on the first night stop and look at the marquee outside and see if the hotel is advertising a discount rate. Most of the hotels in the Walt Disney World area adjust their prices based on attendance levels at the park. It is not uncommon to see prices change by $10 or more over the course of a day.

Here's where you need to be bold. Walk up to the desk as if you *did not* have a reservation, and ask the clerk: "What is your best room rate for tonight?" If the rate they quote you is less than the rate in your reservation, you are now properly armed to ask for a reduction in your room rate.

Similarly, if the room rate advertised out front on the marquee drops during your stay, don't be shy about asking that your charges be reduced. Just be sure to ask for the reduction *before* you spend another night at the old rate, and obtain the name of the clerk who promises a change. If the hotel tries a lame excuse, like "That's only for new check-ins," you can offer to check out and then check back in again. That will usually work; you can always check out and go to the hotel across the road that will usually match the rates of its competitor.

3) And here is the way to make the most informed choice, in the Low Season only. Come down without a reservation, and then cruise one of the motel strips like I-192 (Irlo Bronson Highway) or International Drive. Check the outdoor marquees for discount prices and make notes. Find a phone booth and make a few phone calls to the ones you found attractive. Once again be sure to ask for the best price. The later in the day

you search for a room, the more likely you are to find a hotel ready to make a deal.

DIALING FOR DOLLARS BY TELEPHONE

As we cited in our "True Story," you must be aggressive in representing your checkbook in negotiations with a reservation agent. Sometimes, you will also need to be persistent.

Condé Nast Traveler magazine conducted a survey in 1991 of hotel rates and found wide discrepancies between the prices quoted by central toll-free services, by a clerk called directly at a particular hotel and by a travel agent. The survey was decidedly indecisive: no one source consistently yielded the lowest prices.

The magazine's recommendation: use the services of a travel agent you trust, and request that the agent verify the lowest rate with a direct call. The agent can check the computer first and then compare that rate against the hotel's offer.

EATING FOR LESS

As a tourist magnet, the Orlando area offers just about every type of restaurant from fancy to ordinary, from American to European to Asian. (The largest single collection of foreign restaurants, of course, can be found within the World Showcase pavilions of Epcot Center.) But the emphasis seems to be on "family" restaurants. If there is a single major franchise fast food restaurant in America that is not represented in the Orlando area, we don't know about it.

The biggest collections of fast food restaurants can be found on I-192 (Irlo Bronson Highway) and International Drive. If you're into grease, you can probably find seven different McDonald's or Burger Kings or Pizza Huts for a week's stay.

Somewhat unique to the South are the "all you can eat" buffets which usually offer breakfasts in the range of $2 to $5, lunches from $4 to $8 and dinners from $6 to $12. Chains include Ponderosa Steak House, Sizzler, Shoney's and Gilligan's.

We are partial to the Sizzler's buffet bar, which includes salad, pasta, chicken wings and a touch of dessert. Another good deal is the Olive Garden Italian restaurant chain, where moderately priced meals come with a regularly replenished salad bowl.

I-192 is a many-named splendor. I-192 bears several different names in its traverse from I-27 west of the park to and through downtown Kissimmee. For much of its length near the park, it is called Irlo Bronson Memorial Highway. (Bronson was a prominent local politician and developer.) Near Kissimmee it is called Vine Street; past Kissimmee toward St. Cloud it is called 13th Street. Some segments are also called Space Coast Highway.

You can call it 192 anywhere and people will know what you mean.

Secret stock of rooms. Delta Airlines is the "official" airline of Walt Disney World, and as a result has quite a few rooms at park hotels allotted to it. You may be able to save money on rooms, or at least get into otherwise sold-out hotels by purchasing an air-room package from Delta.

WHERE SHOULD YOU STAY?

Except for the busiest days of the year–Christmas through New Year's and the Fourth of July among them–you're not going to have *any* trouble locating a place to stay in the Orlando-Kissimmee area. In fact, the biggest problem facing most visitors is choosing among the various places to stay.

In this chapter, we'll offer a tour of the main hotel areas in and around Walt Disney World. We'll work our way from the Orlando International Airport in toward Walt Disney World.

How should you choose a place to stay? We'd suggest you start by deciding on a price range you'd be willing to pay. Few would argue with the statement that some of the most exciting and most convenient hotels are to be found within the Walt Disney World park boundaries, but this comes at a not insignificant premium. Following are some ranges for low season rooms; high season rates can be as much as double:

$25 to $60 per night.
East and West of I-4 on I-192.
(The further east and west you go–up to about eight miles from I-4), the lower the prices. South Orange Blossom Trail area. Downtown Orlando.

$50 to $100 per night.
International Drive. (Some lower.)
Apopka-Vineland Road area.
Orlando International Airport.

$90 to $300 per night.
Walt Disney World.

As you can see, the room rates are pretty self-selecting for location, and to a large extent, the quality of the room. Next you can make decisions on extras including special recreational facilities.

ORLANDO INTERNATIONAL AIRPORT AREA

The airport is located about 30 minutes away from Walt Disney World. If your plane arrives late, or if you are preparing for an early morning departure, you might want to consider staying near the airport. Room rates for "name" hotels are higher than those in the tourist areas of Kissimmee; expect to pay $60 to $125 per night in low season and from $70 to $150 per night in high season.

The closest airport to your airline's arrival gate doesn't even require you to leave the airport. The **Hyatt Airport** hotel was scheduled to open in mid-1992, in the main airport building.

Other hotels nearby to the airport can be found along Semoran Blvd. (S.R. 436), which leads into Frontage Road and McCoy Road, two service roads that parallel the Bee Line Expressway (Route 528).

On Semoran Blvd., look for **Park Suite Airport, Holiday Inn Airport** and **Radisson Airport.** Frontage Road hotels include **Courtyard by Marriott Airport, Sheraton Airport** and **Penta Hotel Airport.** On McCoy Road, you'll find **Econo Lodge Orlando Airport** and **Days Inn Airport.**

Less than a mile north of the airport on Semoran Blvd. is an office park and hotel complex that includes: the **Holiday Inn-Orlando International Airport** on T.G. Lee Blvd. and **Guest Quarters Suite Orlando** and **Orlando Airport Marriott** on Augusta National Drive.

Moving west from the airport you are heading for the South Orange Blossom Trail area.

SOUTH ORANGE BLOSSOM TRAIL/
SAND LAKE ROAD/FLORIDA MALL AREA

Near the intersection of the Bee Line Expressway and the combined Route 17-92 and 441–which is better known as the South Orange Blossom Trail–you will find a collection of more than a dozen brand-name motels. The further north you travel, toward Orlando, the more likely you are to find lower-priced locally owned motels. (You'll also find some "adult" bookstores and strip joints.)

We are not in any way recommending this area as an attractive place. Rumor has it that there once was grass in the neighborhood. This is strictly a place to sleep, with the exception of the intersection of South Orange Blossom Trail with Sand Lake Road (S.R. 482). Here you will find the Florida Mall, with shopping, movie theaters and chain restaurants. Sand Lake connects to the east with McCoy Road and runs directly into the airport.

Nightly rates in this area range from about $40 to $100 in off season and $50 to $150 per night in high season. Some of the national chain hotels on South Orange Blossom Trail between the Bee Line and Sand Lake Road include **Days Inn Midtown, Comfort Inn, Holiday Inn-Central Park, La Quinta Motor Inn-Florida Mall, Quality Inn**

Wrong numbers. Be sure you understand the telephone billing policy at the motel. Some establishments allow free local calls, while others charge as much as 75 cents for such calls. (We're especially unhappy with service charges for 800 numbers.) Be sure to examine your bill carefully at checkout and make sure it is correct.

We strongly suggest you obtain a telephone credit card and use it when you travel; nearly all motels tack high service charges on long distance calls.

Executive Suites, Ramada Inn South, LaQuinta Inn, Sheraton Plaza Hotel. Howard Johnson's Airport and **Travelodge.**

INTERNATIONAL DRIVE (FROM SEA WORLD TO UNIVERSAL STUDIOS)

The next major stop on our tour is the International Drive area, a 5-mile uninterrupted stretch of every national hotel and restaurant chain you've ever heard of, and some you probably haven't. This road serves no purpose other than tourism; it's a convenient midway location for the visitor looking to explore in all directions. Room rates run from about $50 to $100 in low season.

One end of International Drive begins south of the Bee Line Expressway at the entrance to Sea World. From there it wanders more or less northerly to pass by the Orange County Convention and Civic Center, the Mercado shopping area, across Sand Lake Road (S.R. 482), in front of Wet 'N Wild and then heads east across Kirkman Road near the main entrance to Universal Studios Florida.

International Drive is, then, just minutes from Sea World, Universal Studios, Wet 'N Wild and half a dozen other smaller attractions. There are restaurants of all descriptions on the road, as well. The road is about a 15-minute drive south to Walt Disney World or north to Orlando.

Hotels south of the Bee Line near Sea World include the **Stouffer Resort** on Sea Harbor Drive and **Lexington Hotel Suites, Wynfield Inn** and **Sheraton World** on Westwood Blvd.

North of the Bee Line, International Drive includes several internationally named hotel circles. Off Hawaiian Court, look for **Days Inn, Rodeway Inn** and **Red Roof Inn.** On the other side of International Drive, across from the Civic Center, are the **Peabody Orlando** and the **Heritage Inn,** two of the fancier hotels on the road. Next to the Civic Center is a **Clarion Hotel.**

Off Samoan Court is the **Quality Inn Plaza.** The next group of lures includes the King Henry's Feast dinner theater and Caruso's Palace, a garish Italian restaurant that seems transplanted from Las Vegas.

In the stretch that includes Austrian Court and Jamaican Court, extending to Sand Lake Road, you will find **Park Suites International Drive, Gold Star Inn, Summerfield Suites Hotel, Courtyard by Marriott, Radisson Inn,**

Fairfield Inn, Ramada Inn Plaza, Embassy Suites, Inns of America, Howard Johnson's and Marriott.

North of Sand Lake, hotels include Quality Inn, The Enclave Resorts, Ramada Hotel North, Days Inn, Lakefront Inn and Holiday Inn. At this point, you will be across the road from Wet 'N Wild. Area hotels include International Inn, Rodeway Inn, Las Palmas, Continental Plaza and Knights Inn.

Just before Kirkman Road, look for American Way on the left side, home to Super 8 Motel, International Gateway Inn, Orlando Sunshine Resort, Comfort Inn Wet 'N Wild and Quality Resort.

Enough already? Almost. To get to Universal Studios, you'll need to turn left onto Kirkman Road. Several newer motels can be found along Kirkman, including Days Inn, Howard Johnson's Florida Center, Twin Towers and Delta Court of Flags. And there are also hotels on nearby Turkey Lake Road, including a Comfort Suites and Sonesta Villa Resort.

I-192/IRLO BRONSON MEMORIAL HIGHWAY/ VINE STREET KISSIMMEE

Katella Avenue which fronts on the main entrance to Disneyland in California, was Walt Disney's worst nightmare. It's an unending stretch of unattractive hotels, miniature golf courses and fast food restaurants.

When Disney began secretly buying up tens of thousands of acres of central Florida swamp and cypress grove in the 1960s, it was with the intention of shielding his new park deep within a green barrier. There was to be no Katella Avenue at Walt Disney World.

And, in fact, Disney was successful. The Magic Kingdom, Epcot Center and the Disney-MGM Studios theme parks and all of the other attractions in the park seem to exist in a world unto themselves. There are, of course, tens of thousands of hotel rooms within the park as well as places to eat for all guests and day visitors, but the sheer size of the park swallows them up and hides them from sight of each other.

But, of course, the Walt Disney Company cannot own *every* square mile of Florida, even if they wanted to. There are two places where Disney meets the real world: at Apopka-Vineland Road (S.R. 535) and at I-192.

Most of the hotels and attractions on 192 can be found

Safety first. The small safes available in some hotels can be valuable to the traveler; be sure to inquire whether there is a service charge for their use. We've been in hotels that apply the charge regardless of whether we used the safe or not; look over your bill at check-out and object to any charges that are not proper. In any case, we'd suggest that any objects that are so valuable that you feel it necessary to lock up should probably be left home alone.

The real Old Town.
Orlando was established as a campground for soldiers during the Seminole Indian War of 1835 to 1842 and then continued as a trading post. The war resulted in the removal of most native Americans in Florida to reservations in Oklahoma.

The Orlando Metropolitan Area was the seventh-fastest growing area in the country, according to the 1990 Census. Its population grew 53 percent since 1980, to 1,072,748. The city itself includes 54 lakes.

between I-4 and I-441 (Main Street / South Orange Blossom Trail) in Kissimmee. I-4 at I-192 actually lies within the southern end of the huge Walt Disney World property. The undeveloped Disney land here is set aside as a nature preserve, and not incidentally serves as a buffer to keep development away from the main entrance to the park.

West of I-4, toward I-27, is the less popular side of 192, although a number of newer hotels have been built in the area. Room rates at low season range from as low as $29 at I-27, to about $75 per night. Hotels in this area often include the label "Main Gate" or "West Gate" in their name, and include: **Ramada Resort Main Gate, Holiday Inn Main Gate West, Hilton Inn Gateway, Econolodge Hawaiian Main Gate, Quality Inn Main Gate West, Motel 6 Main Gate West, Knights Inn Main Gate, Wilson World Main Gate, Radisson Inn Main Gate, Comfort Inn Main Gate, Howard Johnson's, Days Inn West Gate, Best Western West Gate, Econolodge West Gate, Quality Inn Main Gate, Sheraton Lakeside Inn, Travelodge Main Gate West** and **Ramada West Gate.**

The busier side of 192 runs about 10 miles from I-4 east to Main Street in Kissimmee. The area closest to I-4 is often call "Main Gate East." Near I-4 you will find attractions including Arabian Nights, Old Town, Fort Liberty and Water Mania. Between the intersection of S.R. 535 and Kissimmee is Xanadu, Medieval Times, Fun 'N Wheels and the Kissimmee Municipal Airport. A few miles past South Orange Blossom Trail and just short of the intersection with the Florida Turnpike is the Osceola County Stadium, the Spring Training home of the Houston Astros.

APOPKA-VINELAND ROAD/CROSSROADS/ WORLD CENTER

The "back door" to Walt Disney World can be found off S.R. 535, Apopka-Vineland Road. Here Hotel Plaza Blvd. leads into the Disney Hotel Plaza area, Disney Village and Pleasure Island. Further along the road are the entranceways to the Magic Kingdom, Epcot, Disney-MGM Studios and the other attractions within the park.

In this area is the huge **Orlando World Center**, off S.R. 536 in Orlando. The hotel includes 1,503 rooms and suites, an 18-hole golf course, several large pools and tennis courts. Other area hotels on S.R. 535 include the **Holiday Inn Lake Buena Vista, Hawthorne Suites, Days Inn Resort, Compri, Radisson Inn, Park Square Inn, Comfort**

Inn, **Howard Johnson's, Blue Tree Resort** and **Embassy Suites.**

HOTELS WITHIN WALT DISNEY WORLD

Within Walt Disney World are three clusters of hotels and resorts. Reservations can be made through travel agencies or through the Disney central travel desk at (407) 934-7639. The hotels include:

MAGIC KINGDOM RESORT AREA

Disney Contemporary Resort. Is it a hotel with a monorail running through the middle, or a monorail station with a hotel surrounding? Either way, it's a most unusual setting and just a mouse trot from the main gate of Walt Disney World. The resort includes 1,052 rooms, a health club, marina and pool. Note that not all of the rooms are in the A-shaped main building with the monorail station, but may be located in the less-spectacular annex buildings along the lake. Transportation to the parks is by monorail, water taxi and bus. Room rates began at $180 in 1992.

Contemporary life. The Contemporary Hotel is an attractive lure, what with its monorail station within the lobby. However, only about half of the hotel's rooms are within the main tower, and they are the highest priced at the resort; the remainder are in the much more ordinary North and South Gardens wings.

Disney's Grand Floridian Beach Resort. An opulent new resort along the shores of Seven Seas Lagoon with its own monorail station, it is a mixture of Victorian elegance and modernity in white and coral trim–in typical Disney fashion, it is much prettier than a hotel you might find in the "real" world. The spectacular five-story Grand Lobby is topped by stained glass skylights. Some of the rooms include quirky dormers and turrets as well as balconies with close-up views of the Magic Kingdom. Five restaurants include the fancy **Victoria and Albert's** and **Garden View Lounge** where afternoon tea is served daily. The resort includes 901 rooms, a health club, tennis courts, marina, white sand beach, pool and a kid's club. Transportation to the parks is by monorail, water taxi and bus. The parking lot is across the road. Room rates began at $220 in 1992.

Disney's Polynesian Resort. A Disneyfied version of Hawaiian Island architecture and landscaping, including palmlined walkways and tropical gardens, two exotic swimming pools and a station on the monorail. Native island dancers perform at the nightly **Polynesian Revue** dinner show; there are four other restaurants in the complex. The resort includes 855 rooms in island-style longhouses, plus a marina, pools and a kid's club. Transportation to the parks is by monorail, water taxi and bus. Room rates began at $180 in 1992.

A change of name. The Disney Inn used to be called the Golf Resort, but the name—and little else—was changed for marketing purposes.

Quick tickets. Guests in hotels within Walt Disney World can purchase tickets—at regular prices—at guest services desks within their hotels, saving a few minutes of waiting at the park.

The Disney Inn. Situated between two PGA tour golf courses (probably the only ones in the world with sand traps shaped like Mickey Mouse) this small, rustic resort also includes the **Diamond Mine Recreation Center** with swimming pools and tennis courts. Food service includes **The Garden Gallery,** which features a breakfast buffet as well as a full menu. The small resort includes 288 rooms, a health club, tennis courts, golf courses and a pool. Rooms are within low, informal villas. Transportation to the parks is by bus. Guests can also walk past greens and flamingoed lakes to the Polynesian Resort and its monorail station. Room rates began at $175 in 1992.

Disney's Fort Wilderness Resort and Campground. Park your camper, pitch a tent or rent one of Disney's Fleetwood Trailer Homes, complete with air conditioning, television, telephone, kitchen and daily housekeeping service. All campsites at the secluded 740-acre site include electrical hookups, water and a charcoal grill; most have sanitary hook-ups. Comfort stations, a trading post and shower and laundry facilities are nearby. The resort includes recreational facilities such as a petting farm, horseback trail rides, fishing, canoeing and biking. Nearby are Disney's two newest golf courses, Osprey Ridge and Eagle Pines. Also close by is **River Country** and **Discovery Island.** In the center of the resort is **Pioneer Hall,** which includes the **Hoop-Dee-Doo Musical Revue,** an all-you-can-eat Wild West dinner show. Other places to eat include **Crockett's Tavern** and the **Trail's End Buffeteria.** The resort includes 784 campsites and 408 rental trailers, tennis courts, marina and a pool. Transportation to the parks is by bus, tram and water taxi. Campsite rates started at $30 and trailer homes at $165 in 1992.

EPCOT RESORT AREA

Disney's Yacht and Beach Club Resorts. A pair of attractive resorts nearby to Epcot Center and the Disney-MGM Studios Theme Park. The Yacht Club is the more formal of the two, made to appear like a New England grand hotel. Both hotels share **Stormalong Bay,** a fantasy lagoon filled with pools and water activities including bubble jets and a whirlpool. A fleet of boats are available for rent, too. Food service includes a nightly New England-style clambake. Restaurants include the **Cape May Cafe,** and an old-fashioned soda parlor. The Yacht Club includes 635 rooms and the Beach Club an additional 580; also offered are a health club, tennis courts, marina, beach, pool and a kid's club. The resorts are within walking distance of the new International Gateway entrance to Epcot Center; other transportation to the parks is by tram, water taxi and bus. Room rates began at $195 in 1992.

Walt Disney World Dolphin and **Walt Disney World Swan.** Why not have a gigantic triangular hotel with a huge dolphin's head on top, or a rounded building graced by a pair of tremendous swans? This is Walt Disney World, after all. Two of the most distinctive hotels of the park face each other across a large grotto pool with a waterfall and whirlpools. The Dolphin, operated by Sheraton, includes **Harry's Safari Bar & Grille** offering seafood and beef, **Sum Chow's** Oriental restaurant, **Ristorante Carnevale** for Italian specialties, the **Coral Cafe** buffet, the **Tubbi Checkers Buffeteria** and the **Cabana Bar and Grill.** Next door at the Swan (operated by Westin Hotels and Resorts) you will find the Italian eatery **Palio,** as well as the **Garden Grove Cafe** and **Kimonos,** an Oriental lounge and sushi bar.

The Dolphin offers 1,509 rooms, with 1992 prices starting at $185; the Swan has 758 rooms, with 1992 prices starting at $180. The resorts include a health club, tennis courts, marina, beach, pool and a kid's club. Epcot is within walking distance; transportation to the parks includes tram, water taxi and bus.

Disney's Caribbean Beach Resort. One of the best bargains within the park, the sprawling resort spreads across five "villages" named after Caribbean islands–each colorful village has its own pool and beach. In addition, the five communities are linked to **Old Port Royale,** which lies along **Barefoot Bay.** Within the port is a food court with a wide range of fast food choices; outside is a large swimming pool that includes a fort with water slides. Guests can also rent a bike or boat. And, there is **Parrot Cay,** a children's playground on a small island. The resort includes 2,112 rooms, a marina, beach and pool. Transportation to the parks is by bus. Room rates began at $85 in 1992.

DISNEY VILLAGE RESORT AREA

Disney's Port Orleans Resort. A recreation of the French Quarter, packed with charming detail. The new resort's swimming pool is located at **Doubloon Lagoon,** a sea-serpent

Babysitter club. Guests at hotels at Walt Disney World can hire an in-room babysitter by consulting with Guest Services or the In-Room-KinderCare Learning Center.

water slide. Restaurants at **Port Orleans Square** include Cajun specialties. The resort includes 1,008 rooms, a marina and a pool. Transportation to the parks is by water taxi and bus. Room rates began at $85 in 1992.

Disney's Village Resort. A collection of light and open townhouses and multi-level villas in the woods near the Disney-MGM Theme Park and Epcot Center. Most rooms include refrigerators, and villas include fully equipped kitchens. Nearby is the **Lake Buena Vista Golf Course**, six lighted pools, tennis courts and a marina. The resort includes 585 units, a health club, tennis courts, marina, golf and pools. Transportation to the parks is by bus. Room rates began at $175 in 1992.

Disney's Vacation Club Resort. One of the newest resorts at Walt Disney World, units range from studios that sleep four to one, two and three-bedroom and Grand Villas with beds for as many as 12. The homes are on the **Lake Buena Vista Golf Course.** The resort includes a health club, tennis courts, marina and pool. Transportation to the parks is by water taxi and bus. Room rates began at $180 in 1992

Disney's Dixie Landings Resort. A bit of the old South, this is another in Disney's more affordable new resorts. The buildings are styled after plantation mansions and low bayou homes. A food court is offered at a central marketplace and at **Bayou Bill's Cafe.** The resort includes a marina and pool. Transportation to the parks is by water taxi and bus. Room rates began at $85 in 1992.

DISNEY HOTEL PLAZA

Seven hotels built and operated by major (non-Disney) hotel companies are clustered near the Disney Village Marketplace and Pleasure Island. Guests can drive or use Disney buses to the park. These are high-quality but very standard hotels, without the fanciful touch of Disney-owned properties.

Buena Vista Palace. A 27-story lakeside tower including nine restaurants, a **Recreation Island** with three pools. The resort includes more than 900 rooms and suites, a health club, tennis courts and pools. Room rates began at $130 in 1992. (407) 827-2727 or (800) 327-2990.

Grosvenor Resort. A lakeside tower with 628 rooms that includes a large recreation facility including tennis and handball courts, a children's playground and heated swimming pools. **Baskerville's**, a British-themed restaurant is modeled after Sherlock Holmes' 221B Baker Street home in London; next door is **Moriarty's**, a pub named after the great detective's arch nemesis. Room rates began at $115 in 1992. (407) 828-4444 or (800) 624-4109.

Guest Quarters Suite Resort. Each one- or two-bedroom suite includes a refrigerator and small wet bar and the 229-room hotel offers a pool and tennis. Room rates began at $165 in 1992. (407) 934-1000 or (800) 424-2900.

Hotel Royal Plaza. This 396-room hotel includes four restaurants and lounges with nightly entertainment, a pool and recreation center and tennis courts. Room rates began at $140 in 1992. (407) 828-2828 or (800) 248-7890.

Howard Johns on Resort Hotel. A family-oriented hotel with a 14-story central atrium, 323 rooms and swimming pools. Room rates began at $115 in 1992. (407)-828-8888 or (800) 223-9930.

The Hilton. A large resort and conference center, it includes nine restaurants and lounges, two pools, an outdoor spa, Youth Hotel and access to Disney golf courses. Room rates began at $179 in 1992. (407) 827-4000 or (800) 782-4414.

Travelodge Hotel. A lakeside hotel with a Caribbean flavor and a roof-top nightclub. Room rates began at $85 in 1992. (407) 828-2424 or (800) 348-3765.

WHY STAY AT A HOTEL WITHIN WALT DISNEY WORLD?

The hotels within Walt Disney World are among the most attractive, most imaginative places to stay at any major tourist area we know of. They offer all sorts of extras not available outside of the park, and quite a few conveniences.

However, all of this comes at a price. The lowest rates at Walt Disney owned or operated hotels, or those operated by major chains on the park property, generally start at around $100 per night in low season, which is the high end of most off-site hotels. It is up to you to decide what value to place on the extras that come with your higher room rates; **you should also consider the possibility of obtaining similar special treatment outside the park.** (We heard of one family that booked perfectly nice rooms a few miles outside of the park and used the money they saved to engage limousine service to and from the park.)

Insider advantages to guests at Walt Disney World Resorts include:

Complimentary use of the Walt Disney World transportation system, including monorail, bus, ferryboat and launch transportation to the parks, avoiding crowded parking lots.

Advance reservations for dining, Disney Dinner Shows and Disney Character Breakfasts.

Preferred access to tee times on all five championship golf courses. Also available are horseback riding, swimming, tennis, health clubs and other facilities.

CHAPTER 4
Cars, Buses and Monorails

Central Florida is one of the most popular tourist destinations in the United States, and millions of visitors fly to Orlando International Airport and then rent a car for use during their stay. In the best sense of capitalism, this has resulted in a tremendously competitive market; there is a huge supply of rental vehicles in the Orlando area and some of the lowest prices of anywhere in the nation.

You will find, of course, the major rental companies like Avis, Budget, Hertz and National. You will also find very large operations by companies like Alamo and General. And there are also more than a few rental agencies that operate only in Florida.

Your travel agent may be of assistance in finding the best rates; you can make a few phone calls by yourself, too. Rental rates generally follow the same Low-Shoulder-High Season structure. We have obtained rates as low as $59 a week for a tiny subcompact (a convertible, no less) in low season.

Be aware that the least expensive car rental agencies usually do not have their stations at the airport itself. You will have to wait for a shuttle bus to take you from the terminal to their lot, and return the car to the outlying area at the end of your trip. This may add about 20 to 30 minutes to your arrival and departure schedule.

The Orlando airport imposes a fee on rentals (6 percent in 1993), and the State of Florida adds a daily surcharge ($2.05 in 1993.)

Pay attention, too, when the rental agent explains the gas tank policy. The most common plan says that you are

Credit cars. Although it is theoretically possible to rent a car without a credit card, you will find it to be a rather inconvenient process. If they cannot hold your credit card account hostage, most agencies will require a large cash deposit-perhaps as much as several thousand dollars-before they will give you the keys.

Extra miles. Don't let it force you to pay too much for a rental car, but all things being equal, use a rental agency that awards frequent flyer mileage in a program you use.

A bad policy. Car rental companies will try–with varying levels of pressure–to convince you to purchase special insurance coverage. They'll tell you it's "only" $7 or $9 per day. What a deal! That works out to about $2,500 or $3,330 per year for a set of rental wheels. And the coverage is intended primarily to protect the rental company and not you.

Check with your insurance agent before you travel to determine how well your personal automobile policy will cover a rental car and its contents. And we strongly recommend you use a credit card that offers rental car insurance; such insurance usually covers the deductible below your personal policy. The extra auto insurance by itself can usually more than pay for an upgrade to a "gold card" or other extra service credit card.

The only sticky area comes for those visitors with a driver's license but no car, and therefore no insurance. Again, consult your credit card company and your insurance agent.

expected to return the car with a full tank; if the agency must refill the tank, you will be billed a service charge plus what is usually a very high per-gallon rate.

Other optional plans include one where the rental agency sells you a full tank when you first drive away, and takes no note of how much gas remains when you return the car. Unless you somehow manage to return the car with the engine running on fumes, you are in effect making a gift to the agency with every gallon you bring back.

We prefer the first option, making a point to refill the tank on the way to the airport on getaway day.

Do you need to rent a car? In a word, maybe.

Here's how to do without a car: First of all, you can take a taxi, bus or limousine service from the airport to your hotel. Some of the larger hotels outside of Walt Disney World offer free scheduled van service from the airport; be sure to figure the value of such service (about $50 round trip) as a reduction in the true cost of the hotel room.

Secondly, we would recommend that car-less visitors stay at a hotel that offers free or reasonably priced shuttle service to Walt Disney World as well as Universal Studios, Sea World or anywhere else you would like to visit during your stay. The schedule of such shuttles should be an important element of your decisionmaking. Does the hotel offer a single ride in the morning to the Transportation and Ticket Center and a single pick-up at night? Is the arrival time at Walt Disney World early enough for you to make the best use of your day? What happens if you want to come home early?

Obviously, if you are staying within Walt Disney World, you will have immediate access to the immense Walt Disney Transportation System, including monorails, buses, trams and water taxis that connect to every corner of the park. However, you will *not* find transportation to places outside of Walt Disney World.

The advantage of renting a car is this: You are not held hostage to someone else's schedule or definition of a Walt Disney World-centered vacation trip. If you are staying within the park, you are able to leave to go Universal Studios or Busch Gardens for the day; you can also go to dinner at a restaurant that doesn't have little mouse ears on the paper napkins. You can also come and go between the parks and your hotel with ease; guests at Disney-owned or operated hotels are given a pass to drive through the parking tollbooths without paying.

If you are staying outside of the park, you can set your own schedule for coming and going. And, you will be able to drive to restaurants outside of the parks and away from your hotel, which may also save you money.

Our recommendation is that you do rent a car. If your budget is very tight, we'd suggest you reduce the amount of money you pay for your hotel by staying a little further away from one of the parks. Use the money you save to purchase freedom on wheels.

WALT DISNEY WORLD BUS ROUTES

Here are the bus routes operated by Walt Disney World Transportation. If there is not a bus from where you are to where you want to get, the solution is usually to ride to the Transportation and Ticket Center (TTC) at the Magic Kingdom and make a transfer there. For information, call Transportation Operations at (407) 824-4457.

Fast food. One advantage to bringing a car to the park is the chance to save a bit of money and get a more relaxed, better meal by ducking out of the park at lunch and visiting a decent buffet or menu restaurant; come back to the park for some evening rides and the fireworks. (Be sure to get your hand stamped when you leave the park *and* hold on to your ticket stub—both are needed for readmission on the same day. Your parking receipt is also valid for re-entry to any of the parking lots.)

BLUE — Fort Wilderness ✳ TTC

GREEN — Disney Inn ✳ Polynesian Inn ✳ TTC
Magic Kingdom (during park hours)

GOLD — Contemporary Resort ✳ TTC
Polynesian Resort
Grand Floridian Beach Resort

STW
Gold & Black — Contemporary Resort ✳ Fort Wilderness
Disney-MGM Studios Theme Park
Pleasure Island (6 p.m. to 2 a.m.)

STE
Gold & Black — Contemporary Resort ✳ Fort Wilderness
Disney-MGM Studios Theme Park
Pleasure Island (6 p.m. to 2 a.m.)

EC
Blue & White — Epcot Center
Disney-MGM Studios Theme Park

MK — TTC ✳ Disney-MGM Studios Theme Park

TTC ✳ Disney Village Marketplace
Pleasure Island (after 6 p.m.)
Typhoon Lagoon ✳ Epcot Center

Red & White

Disney Village Hotel Plaza
Magic Kingdom (Proper I.D. required)

Red & White

Disney Village Hotel Plaza
Epcot Center (Proper I.D. required)

Red & White

Disney Village Hotel Plaza
Disney Village Marketplace
Pleasure Island (Proper I.D. required ;
route begins at 6 p.m.)

Red & White

Disney Village Hotel Plaza
Disney-MGM Studios Theme Park
(Proper I.D. required)

Green & Gold

Disney Village Resort
Magic Kingdom (during park hours)
TTC (before the Magic Kingdom
opens and after the Magic Kingdom closes)

Green & Gold

Disney Village Resort ✳ Epcot Center
Disney Village Marketplace

Green & Gold

Disney Village Resort
Disney Village Marketplace
Pleasure Island (after 6 p.m.)

Orange & White

Caribbean Beach (Old Port Royal)
Typhoon Lagoon
Disney Village Marketplace
Pleasure Island (after 6 p.m.)

Caribbean Beach ❋ Magic Kingdom
(during park hours) ❋ TTC
Orange & White (before Magic Kingdom opens and
after Magic Kingdom closes)

 Caribbean Beach ❋ Epcot Center

Orange & White

 Caribbean Beach
Disney-MGM Studios Theme Park
Orange & White

 Caribbean Beach Internal Circulation Route

 Walt Disney World Swan
Walt Disney World Dolphin
Purple & Gold Magic Kingdom (during park hours)
TTC (before Magic Kingdom opens
and after Magic Kingdom closes)

 Epcot Center Resorts ❋ Typhoon Lagoon
Disney Village Marketplace
Purple & Gold Pleasure Island (after 6 p.m.)

 Fort Wilderness Internal Route:
Settlement Transportation Circle
All Trailer Loops ❋ Camping Loops
Reception Outpost

 Fort Wilderness Internal Route:
Settlement Transportation Circle
Camping Loops ❋ Creekside Meadow

 Fort Wilderness Internal Route:
River Country ❋ Day Visitors
Parking Area

Front seat drivers.
There is one row of
seats in the front cab
with the driver of the
monorail. Ask one of
the attendants to place
you there for an inter-
esting and different per-
spective; you may have
to let a train pass by if
there are many people
waiting on line.

Beam me aboard. The
term monorail comes
from the fact that there
is just one rail for the
train–a large concrete
"beamway" that
includes the electrical
power for the 250-
passenger trains. Each
day, Disney's system
transports an average
of 80,000 visitors.
There are 14 trains for
the 13.7 miles of track.

ALL ABOARD THE MONORAIL

The sleek Walt Disney World Monorail system appears
to be the solution to transportation problems of the present and future; in fact, though, using it can be about as
thrilling as a broken-down Long Island Railroad com-
muter train at rush hour.

There are three "loops" of track in the Disney system,
each served by its own set of monorail trains. In order to
transfer from one loop to another you must exit the monorail and move to another platform and another train.

Loop A: From the Transportation and Ticket Center
to main gate of the Magic Kingdom. Non-stop service to and from the parking lot, moving in a counterclockwise direction around Seven Seas Lagoon.

Loop B: A local train, running from the Transportation
and Ticket Center in a clockwise direction around Seven
Seas Lagoon. The first stop from the TTC is the
Polynesian Village Resort, then the Grand Floridian
Beach Resort, the Magic Kingdom, the Contemporary
Resort Hotel and back to the TTC. If you are staying
at the Contemporary, the closest hotel to the Magic
Kingdom itself, you will still have to go the long
way around the loop.

Loop C: From the TTC to Epcot Center and back.

So, let's say you're staying at the Polynesian Village
Resort and want to get to Epcot. You've got to get on
Loop B and go all the way around the lake and back to the
TTC, which was next door to your starting place. Then you've
got to exit the train, go down one ramp and up another
and board a Loop C train.

And, no, there are no direct buses from the Polynesian
(just one example) to Epcot. There are buses to the TTC,
where you can change to another bus to Epcot. And, if you
want to go to Disney-MGM Studios, Typhoon Lagoon or
another part of the park, the bus to the TTC transfer point
is the only way to get there.

We hate to say it, but your own personal pollution-
generating, fossil-fuel eating rental car will be much more
convenient if your tour plans are at all ambitious.

CHAPTER 5
You've Got to Have a Ticket

As if you don't already face enough decisions–dates, airlines, hotels and more–there is also the matter of those little pieces of cardboard called admission tickets. Actually, they're not all that little: a family of four visiting Walt Disney World for a week could easily spend (are you ready for this?) something like $800 for daily tickets.

But, like everything else we write about in this Econoguide, there are various ways to analyze the available options. The very best thing you can do is to sit down with a calendar *before* you leave for Florida and chart out a schedule. Then, study the available ticket packages to find the one that fits your plans best. And don't overlook the money-saving strategies we discuss here–or the discount coupons for Universal Studios, Busch Gardens and other attractions you'll find in the back of this book.

WALT DISNEY WORLD TICKET PLANS

All ticket prices and limitations listed here were in effect in mid-1993 and are subject to change. Tax is not included.

One-Day Ticket. Good in one park only. You will be allowed to exit and return to the park on the same day–be sure to have your hand stamped–but cannot go to another park or ride the monorail or bus system to another park.

Four-Day Passport. Good in all three parks for any four days. You can go from one park to another on the same day–be sure to have your hand stamped. The four passes do not have to be used consecutively, and are valid forever. Includes unlimited use of Walt Disney World transportation system.

**Walt Disney World
1993 Prices**

ONE-DAY PASS
Adult $35 plus tax
Child $28 plus tax
(Ages 3 to 9.)

**FOUR-DAY
SUPER PASS**
Adult $125
Child $98

**FIVE-DAY
SUPER DUPER PASS**
Adult $170
Child $135

ANNUAL PASSPORT
Adult $199 first year;
Child $174 first year

PLEASURE ISLAND
$13.95 plus tax after 7
p.m.; includes admission
to all clubs and perfor-
mances. Children under
the age of 18 must be
accompanied by a par-
ent, and will not be
allowed in all clubs.

**TYPHOON LAGOON
ONE-DAY TICKETS**
Adult $20.50
Child $16.50

**RIVER COUNTRY
ONE-DAY TICKET**
Adult $13.25
Child $10.50

DISCOVERY ISLAND
Adult $8.50
Child $4.75

Five-Day Super Pass. Good in all three parks for any five days. You can go from one park to another on the same day-be sure to have your hand stamped. The five passes do not have to be used consecutively, and are valid for-ever. Also valid for admission to Typhoon Lagoon, River Country, Discovery Island and Pleasure Island, for seven days from the first use of the pass. Also includes unlimited use of Walt Disney World transportation system.

AN ECONOGUIDE TO DISNEY TICKETS

Which of the three types of tickets should you buy? There is no one answer, because no two families follow the same schedule on a trip to Central Florida.

Obviously, if your plans call for a full week's stay and you plan to visit every corner of the park–from the Magic Kingdom to Epcot to MGM Studios to Pleasure Island at night and Typhoon Lagoon, River Country and Discovery Island on hot afternoons, then the 5-Day Super Pass makes the most sense, representing potential savings of $68.75 or more over the cost of individual tickets. (Or more? To begin with, you can visit multiple parks on the same day with a multi-day pass; with the 5-day pass you can also make unlimited, repeat visits to the water parks and Pleasure Island.)

If you are in town for a weekend and plan only a two or three-day visit, you'll probably want to buy just single admission tickets.

Now, here's a more complex decision: suppose you plan to visit Disney theme parks for four days and also want to go to Typhoon Lagoon, Pleasure Island, Discovery Island or River Country or all of them during your stay. It *may* make more sense to buy a five-day pass. Add up the value of admission to the secondary parks you will visit and subtract them from the cost of the pass. And then con-sider saving or re-selling the unused fifth theme park ticket before you leave.

RESELLING UNUSED TICKETS

Disney tickets are marked "Non-refundable" and "Nontransferrable." This means that you cannot resell any unused tickets to the company. (No refunds are given because of rain, even at the water parks). It also theoreti-cally means that you cannot resell or even give your unused ticket to another person. However, your name does not appear on the ticket and there is no way at present for

Disney to enforce the company's ban on transfer.

Here are some of the ways visitors to Walt Disney World make use of extra tickets on a multiple-day pass:

1) Put the tickets away in a safe deposit box for a later visit. They bear no expiration date. **Advantages:** ticket prices go up, not down, and you may end up saving a few dollars the next time you come to Orlando. **Disadvantages:** you could lose the ticket, and your 9-year old will require an adult ticket on his next birthday, too.

2) Bring the tickets home and give or sell them to friends planning a visit to the park.

3) Resell them at a slight discount to visitors you may meet at your hotel or at a restaurant. It probably would not be best to draw a lot of attention to yourself by trying to make such a sale near the ticket lines on Walt Disney World property.

4) Resell them at a larger discount to one of the many ticket brokers you will find inside the lobbies of outside the-park hotels and along the major hotel and restaurant strips including I-192 and International Drive. In mid-1992, we were offered $20 for each adult ticket and $15 for each child's ticket.

BUYING DISCOUNT TICKETS

Yes, you can get Disney tickets for wholesale. But it takes a bit of doing. There are two routes to discounts: an unofficial, unauthorized path and an official way.

First the **official** ways:

1) Book an all-inclusive hotel and park admission package from the Walt Disney Company. Packages include the top-of-the-line "World Adventure", "Grand Plan" and "Admiral Plan" packages, which offer rooms, tickets, use of recreational facilities and breakfast, lunch and dinner every day at the hotel or within the parks. Other plans that exclude some or all meals are "Family Vacation Fun", "Festival Magic", "Resort Romance" and "Camping Adventure." Be sure to figure the true value of the package. Ask for the regular room rate, and then add in the value–to you–of recreation and meals to determine if there is a real discount.

2) Book a hotel and admission package from one of the hotels outside of the park. Again, find out the

A mark, a yen, a buck or a pound. Disney ticket sellers will be happy to take cash, traveler's checks, personal checks with ID, American Express, Master Card and Visa credit cards.

Lines at the ticket booths are usually within reasonable limits within half an hour before and after opening time; lines will build at mid-morning to as much as 15 minutes. You can save some time by purchasing tickets at all Disney-owned or operated hotels and many large area resorts.

regular hotel charge to determine if your admission tickets are being offered at a discount.

3) Use an admission pass discount such as the **Magic Kingdom Club,** described below.

4) Look for very occasional promotions by the Walt Disney Company through some of the official tourist agencies in the Orlando area. For example, the Orlando/Orange County Convention & Visitors Bureau, which operates an office at 8445 International Drive, offers an off-season discount booklet that in 1992 included a $5 discount on 5-Day Super Passes only. Write to the bureau at P.O. Box 690355, Orlando, FL 32869.

Now, a few **unofficial** ways.

1) Buy your tickets from one of the official tourist and convention offices. They *may* have discount tickets directly from Walt Disney World, or they may have some tickets that have come through the gray market such as extra supplies from hotel packages.

2) Buy your tickets from one of the ticket brokers along tourist roads described above. You'll likely be offered passes at 10 to 20 percent off the list price. Their sources include hotel packages as well as any tickets they may have bought from visitors. Be sure to examine the tickets carefully to make sure they are valid. The safest way to pay for anything is with a credit card, next safe is with a personal check and least safe is with cash.

3) You will also see ticket booths that offer "free" attraction tickets. Trust us–in case this is news to you–there is no such thing as a free lunch, or a free ticket to Walt Disney World. What these places are doing is fronting for a vacation timeshare or condominium sale. You'll be offered a free ticket as payment for sitting through a sales pitch. We've endured this a few times, and found that several hours of sometimes high-pressure sales presentations is not worth the payback, unless you are seriously considering a real estate purchase. And if you are, be sure to have a heart-to-heart conversation with your accountant or financial advisor *before* you sign any contract.

MAGIC KINGDOM CLUB GOLD CARD

One option to consider is membership in the **Magic**

Kingdom Club. For $49 for a two-year membership, card holders receive discounts of $5 to $8 off multi-day passes at Walt Disney World and lesser discounts on one-day tickets to the Magic Kingdom, Epcot, Disney-MGM Studios, Typhoon Lagoon, River Country, Pleasure Island and Discovery Island. (The card is also worth $2 off a day pass and $4 off a two-day pass at Disneyland in California.)

By our calculations, that's not such a great deal for the tickets alone. If a family of four makes two four- or five-day trips to Walt Disney World in a two-year period, the total discount would be $40, which is less than the price of the membership.

But, there are other discounts that come with the card that make it more attractive: up to 30 percent savings at selected Walt Disney World resorts (15 percent at the Disneyland Hotel in Anaheim); discounts on car rentals and air fare, a two-year subscription to *Disney News* magazine, and a newsletter, a tote bag, key chain and luggage tag and more.

The Magic Kingdom Club is also offered to owners of Walt Disney Co. stock–even a single share.

For information, call (800) 248-2665 or write to Magic Kingdom Club Gold Card, P.O. Box 3850, Anaheim, CA 92803-3850.

DISNEY DINNER SHOWS

The dinner shows at Walt Disney World resorts generally require advance reservations and purchase of tickets.

Polynesian Revue. At Luau Cove, Disney's Polynesian Resort. An all-you-can-eat feast including ribs, chicken, MahiMahi and drinks, accompanied by island dancers and acts. Seatings at 6:45 p.m. and 9:30 p.m. Adults $32.86, Junior (12-20) $25.44, and Child (3-11) $16.96. All prices plus tax and gratuity.

Broadway at the Top. At the Top of the World restaurant at Disney's Contemporary Resort. Show tunes plus appetizer, entree, dessert and non-alcoholic beverage. Seatings at 6 p.m. and 9:15 p.m. Adults $44.50, and Child (3-11) $19.50. All prices plus tax and gratuity; evening dress is suggested.

Hoop-Dee-Doo Musical Revue. At Pioneer Hall at Disney's Fort Wilderness Resort and Campground. A Western singing and dancing show, featuring all-you-can-

Home delivery. Tickets can also be purchased by mail by sending a check, made payable to the Walt Disney World Company, Box 10030, Lake Buena Vista, FL 32830-0030. Mark the envelopes "Attention: Ticket Mail Order" and include an additional $2 for the privilege. Allow as much as six weeks for processing. We'd advise calling Walt Disney World to check if ticket prices have changed: (407) 934-7639.

eat chicken, ribs and corn. Seatings at 5 p.m., 7:15 p.m. and 9:30 p.m. Adults $34.98; Juniors $26.50, and Children (3-11) $18.02.

Walt Disney World

Introduction

WHICH WALT DISNEY WORLD
DO YOU HAVE IN MIND?

* The world of Mickey and Minnie and Alice and Dumbo and the Enchanted Tiki Birds?[1]

* The only place on the planet where China touches Norway and where you can drive among dinosaurs?[2]

* The home of R2D2, Humphrey Bogart, the Alien and Kermit the Frog?[3]

* The stately adult pleasure dome of Merriweather A. Pleasure, where you can boogey (almost) all night?[4]

* The watery wonderland of Humunga Kowabunga or Whoop 'N Holler Hollow?[5]

* The campfire sing-along at the trading post?[6]

* The home of Moe, Larry, Curly and hundreds of other trained and untrained parrots, peacocks and tortoises?[7]

* A place with five championship-level golf courses, including two stops on the PGA Tour?[8]

* The home port of the largest private flotilla in the world, bigger than many navies?[9]

Oh, that Disney World. Let's define a few terms here at the start:

Walt Disney World is the huge entertainment complex that includes within it The Magic Kingdom, Epcot Center and the Disney-MGM Studios Theme Park as well as Pleasure Island, Typhoon Lagoon, River Country, Discovery Island, the six Disney golf courses, Disney Village and the hundreds of Disney-oper-

1 The Magic Kingdom.

2 Epcot Center.

3 Disney-MGM Studios.

4 Pleasure Island.

5 Typhoon Lagoon and River Country

6 Fort Wilderness.

7 Discovery Island.

8 Disney Inn, Bonnet Lakes and Lake Buena Vista.

9 The Walt Disney World marinas.

One if by monorail. Although the monorail may look speedy, in truth it is only about a minute or two faster than the ferryboat in getting from the Transportation and Ticket Center to the Magic Kingdom. And the two ferryboats can carry about three times as many passengers as one monorail train. So, if the line for the monorail is lengthy, go by sea.

ated and Disney licensed hotels and restaurants within the property lines of the World.

Our goal in this, the largest section of the book, is twofold: first to break down the huge World into smaller and more understandable pieces, and secondly, to put them back together again in a way that shows how to get the most out of it.

There are six chapters in this section:

* The Magic Kingdom;
* Epcot Center;
* The Disney-MGM Studios;
* The other Walt Disney World parks, including Typhoon Lagoon, River Country, Discovery Island and Pleasure Island;
* Golfing with Mickey and other sports and recreation, and
* Learning adventures.

We'll begin each of the first three chapters with our list of "Must-See" attractions and the exclusive "Power Trip" tour. We hope you'll take the time to read the chapters before you go, and once again when you're in Florida.

GETTING TO THE PARK

The idea behind the Walt Disney World transportation system was a good one–getting to the Magic Kingdom should be a magical experience. When you leave your car you should be in an entirely different world.

"We'll have visitors park all the way on the other side of a large lagoon and then let them take an exciting monorail ride or a soothing ferryboat to the main gate," the planners said. "By the time they're in the park, they'll completely forget about the outside world.

So far, so good, but let's consider how it works out more than 20 years after the planners made their drawings.

First you park way out in East Overshoe, practically the next county. Then you must walk to the central aisle of the parking lot and wait for a gigantic snake-like tram to take you to the Transportation and Ticket Center. You'll have to show your ticket to the attendant there and then choose between a monorail or a ferryboat ride around or across the Seven Seas Lagoon to the main gates.

Total time from parking to your first step onto Main Street is about 30 minutes at the start of the day;

Commuting from Epcot. If your plan for the day calls for a start at the Magic Kingdom and ends with a special dinner at Epcot, you might try this strategy: arrive early at Epcot and park there. Ride the monorail to the transfer point at the Transportation and Ticket Center and pick up the monorail to the Magic Kingdom. Then reverse that route in the afternoon and you will be able to stay as late as you want at Epcot and pick up your car there.

as much as 45 minutes at peak periods from about 10 a.m. to noon when there are long lines at the monorail or ferryboat.

At the end of the day, you'll have to reverse the process. And you *did* remember where you parked your car, right?

There's no easy way around the process for most visitors to The Magic Kingdom staying outside of the park. The situation is very different at Epcot Center and Disney-MGM Studios, where you can park and walk or take a single short tram ride to the gates.

FROM WITHIN WALT DISNEY WORLD

One of the advantages of staying at a hotel within Walt Disney is the availability of Disney's own bus, monorail and boat fleet. Disney operates more than 125 buses over 125 miles of paved roads in the park. And the 750 watercraft of Walt Disney World qualify as the fifth largest Navy in the world.

The buses go directly to the entrance of the Magic Kingdom, Epcot and MGM Studios. Similarly, the boat services from some Disney hotels go directly to the Magic Kingdom or to the back door International Gateway entrance to Epcot. Visitors staying at a Disney hotel with a monorail stop have direct service only to the Magic Kingdom; you'll have to transfer at the TTC to an Epcot train if that is your destination.

The principal transportation system at the Magic Kingdom-and one of the most famous-is the Mark IV Monorail system, which links the Magic Kingdom and the Transportation and Ticket Center, and a second route that runs from the Ticket Center to Epcot Center. A local version of the Magic Kingdom loop stops at several of the major hotels within the park.

Back of the bus. Can you park at a Disney hotel parking lot and ride a monorail, boat or bus directly to one of the parks? The answer is yes . . . and no. In theory, you must have a guest ID card to ride one of the internal modes of transport. However, cards are not always asked for, and Disney does encourage guests at Walt Disney World to sample the restaurants and shops at its hotels in the afternoon and evening and at those times cards are not requested. Disney also quietly sells a daily transportation ticket, priced in 1992 at $2.50.

MUST-SEES

Space Mountain
(Tomorrowland)

It's a Small World
(Fantasyland)

Mickey's House & Starland Show
(Mickey's Starland)

The Haunted Mansion
(Liberty Square)

Pirates of the Caribbean
(Adventureland)

Jungle Cruise
(Adventureland)

Big Thunder Mountain Railroad
(Frontierland)

Splash Mountain
(Frontierland)

Tom Sawyer Island
(Frontierland)

THE POWER TRIP

ADULTS AND TEENS.

Join the gate-opening sprint to Space Mountain in Tomorrowland for an eye-opening start to your day. When you're back on Earth, hop the Skyway for a lift to the far end of Fantasyland.

Walk to Splash Mountain and Big Thunder Mountain Railway and ride both.

Backtrack to the Haunted Mansion in Liberty Square for a howl. Then walk across the top of Frontierland and down into Adventureland to ride Pirates of the Caribbean.

You have now completed five of the most exciting and most crowd-drawing attractions for older visitors. At this point, we'd suggest changing direction and walking in a clockwise direction back toward Tomorrowland; visit any other ride that appeals to you as you go: stop in at the rarely crowded but very worthy Magic Journeys in Fantasyland and American Journeys in Tomorrowland. If you have the time, come back for a ride after dark on Thunder Mountain Railway–it's a whole other experience after the sun goes down.

CHILDREN (AND PARENTS UNDER THEIR CONTROL.)

Head left from Main Street and enter Adventureland. Ride Pirates of the Caribbean and the Jungle Cruise.

Walk into Frontierland and (depending on the ages and inclinations of the children) ride Splash Mountain and Big Thunder Mountain Railway. Resist the temptation to take the raft to Tom Sawyer Island at this time.

Enter Liberty Square. Ride The Haunted Mansion if your children don't mind a few hundred Disney spooks.

At Fantasyland, visit It's a Small World and (if absolutely necessary) ride Dumbo, the Flying Elephant. The lines for Grand Prix Raceway and 20,000 Leagues Under the Sea will probably have built up to 30 or more minutes by now; we'd suggest skipping them on the Power Tour and coming back some other morning or evening.

Escape to Tomorrowland, bypassing Mickey's Starland for the moment. Ride StarJets and (if the children are up to it, and if the lines are of a reasonable length) Space Mountain. Then visit American Journeys.

Now you are free to reverse direction and explore the less-crowded rides. We recommend families next visit Mickey's House & Starland Show in Mickey's Starland, Cinderella's Golden Carrousel in Fantasyland, the raft ride to Tom Sawyer Island in Frontierland, and The Hall of Presidents in Liberty Square for children studying American history.

CHAPTER 6
The Magic Kingdom

Once upon a mouse, back in 1928, Walter Elias Disney created the character of Mickey Mouse for a short cartoon called "Steamboat Willie."

Everything else has been built upon the slender shoulders of the cute little rodent, along with his gal Minnie and buddies Donald, Daisy, Snow White and a cast of thousands of other cartoon and movie favorites.

Disney, who set up a little park alongside his first movie studios to entertain visitors, expanded his world considerably with the opening of Disneyland in California in 1955. Although much has changed in the nearly 40 years since Disneyland was first planned, the basic structure of that park, and all that have followed, is the same.

Today, breathes there a man, woman, girl, boy or mouse who has not dreamed of visiting The Magic Kingdom? The entertainment vision of Walt Disney–along with the incredible marketing skills of the company he left behind–have made Disney's parks and symbols probably the world's best-known popular icons. You can see Mickey Mouse t-shirts on the streets of Moscow, Epcot towels on the beaches of the Caribbean, Minnie dresses on the boulevards of Paris and Roger Rabbit hats worn in the alleys of Tokyo.

In 1992, Euro Disneyland near Paris joined the three other parks–Disneyland, Walt Disney World and Tokyo Disneyland–on the global map. An expansion of the California empire and other foreign parks are on the drawing boards as you read this book.

In Florida, by far the largest of all of the Disney parks,

Oui, Oui, Monsieur Mickey. The newest Disney theme park (joining Disneyland, Walt Disney World and Tokyo Disneyland) is Euro-Disneyland, which opened in April of 1992 in Marne-laVallé, 20 miles east of Paris. The large park, in a former beet field, cost $4 billion to construct. When a studio tour opens about 1995, the park will cover an area equal to about 20 percent of the city of Paris.

According to Disney executives, Paris will become a "side trip" for millions of foreign tourists who will come to France to meet Mickey. The company expects crowds of at least 11 million in its first years.

Although the park will be instantly recognizable to any Disney veteran

Oui, Oui... Cont.

(including Sleeping Beauty's Castle and Big Thunder Mountain), there are some new European themes for some familiar attractions. While Tomorrowland stresses space tech-nology at the American parks, Euro-Disneyland's Discoveryland emphasizes the works of Leonardo da Vinci (including the dramatic "Orbitron") and European fantasists such as Jules Verne and H.G. Wells. Hotels within the Disney boundaries, though, definitely take on an American theme. Major ones include The Disneyland Hotel and Newport Bay Club. The Hotel Cheyenne is like a Western movie, while the Hotel Santa Fe features Tex-Mex food and an active volcano. The Hotel New York has Disneyfied skyscrapers and a skating rink. And there's even a uniquely American campground, Camp Davy Crockett. High season room rates will be roughly comparable to American parks. Admission tickets in 1992 cost 225 francs (about $40) for adults and 150 francs (about $28) for children.

the empire sprawls across miles of land and includes three major theme parks and half a dozen other attractions. However, it is still The Magic Kingdom–home of Fantasyland, Adventureland, Frontierland and Tomorrowland–that is what visitors think of when they first set out for Orlando.

In this section, we'll offer the Ultimate Unauthorized Tour of The Magic Kingdom, area by area. We'll tell you which rides are "must-sees" and which ones are not worth crossing the road for if they are blessed with lengthy lines. We'll sample all of the restaurants of the park. And we'll pass along inside information that we trust will add to your fun.

MAIN STREET USA

Somewhere, someplace at some time, there was an America like this. It's a place of small stores with friendly proprietors, where the streets are clean and the landscape neat and where a scrap of paper never lingers on the ground.

At the start of your visit to the Magic Kingdom, think of Main Street USA as an interesting place to walk through on the way to somewhere else. Come back later to browse, shop or eat; if you are following our advice, you will have arrived early at the park with a specific destination in mind.

But when you do come back, marvel in the attention to detail of the storefronts and interior decorations of the shops. Most of the names on the second story windows are those of former and present Disney employees responsible for creation or maintenance of the park.

Main Street is the place to be if you are a serious parade fan; the entertainment begins at the railroad station just inside the gates. You can, though, also see the parades near Cinderella Castle and on the streets of Frontierland, both of which are nearer the major attractions of the park.

Walt Disney Railroad. A pleasant way to tour the park (our favorite way to end a day), these real steam engines take passengers on a 1¹/₂ mile, 15-minute circuit of the park.

Walt Disney was a railroad nut, even running a small-scale system in his own backyard. The four engines that are part of the Magic Kingdom's rolling stock were built in the United States but spent much of their working lives in Mexico's Yucutan Peninsula, hauling sugar cane. The wheels, side rods and other major parts of the engines are original, although the boilers and cabs have been rebuilt. Originally constructed to burn coal or wood and later converted to oil, the steam engines are now powered by diesel fuel.

The "Lilly Belle," named for Disney's wife, was built in 1928, coincidentally the same year Mickey Mouse made his screen debut. Also on the tracks is the "Roy O. Disney," named for the boss' brother, the "Walter E. Disney," named for the man himself, and the less-often seen "Roger Broggie," christened after a longtime Disney employee and friend.

Walt Disney Story. We wouldn't go here first, but this small museum and movie theater is worth a stop later in the day for adults who want to remember Walt Disney and older children who want to learn about his history and how Mickey, Minnie, Disneyland and Walt Disney World came to be.

Main Street Cinema. What else would you expect to be playing in the moviehouse on Disney World's main drag but continuous Disney cartoons? Among the biggest treats are those that reach back to the dawn of Disney, like "Steamboat Willie," the first Mickey Mouse movie.

Penny Arcade. Disney has brought together a marvelous collection of antique games and amusements, including *penny* hand-crank movies, an old Wurlitzer PianOrchastra mechanical orchestra from the 1920s, fortune-telling machines like the one from "Big" and mechanical baseball games. In the back of the arcade are some of the most impressive modern machines.

Main Street Vehicles. Old-fashioned cars, horse-drawn trollies and fire engines move slowly down Main Street to Cinderella Castle.

TOMORROWLAND

Every Disney visitor with a bit of spunk—and their mom and dad—has got to visit Tomorrowland at least once to catch a rocketship to Ryca 1 on the ride known as Space Mountain.

When Tomorrowland was originally conceived, it was as a showcase of the future. Unfortunately, what was once the future is now the present. Most of the attractions in Tomorrowland, with the singular exception of Space Mountain, seem stuck somewhere in the 1970s. A major reconstruction is planned for later this decade.

WOW Space Mountain. The big enchilada, the highmost high, the place where hundreds of Magic Kingdom visitors have dropped their eyeglasses, cameras and hairpieces. It is also one of the most popular of all of the attractions at

Harmony Barber Shop. Not quite a "Shave and a haircut, two bits," but that's the general idea. It's a real old-timey barbershop, and you can get your ears lowered for about $12.50 or a shave for about $8. A barbershop quartet entertains within and outside the shop from time to time.

Other barbershops—as well as beauty shops—can be found within Disney's Contemporary Resort and Disney's Polynesian Resort.

House of Magic. A good collection of little gifts, including some of the least expensive toys in the park. The only place in the Magic Kingdom where you can get fake broken eggs, squirting nickels and pocket noisemakers.

Under construction. Disney's plans include a complete redevelopment of the somewhat dated and tired Tomorrowland, around 1996. Current plans call for the area to be renamed Discoveryland; possible rides and attractions include **Alien Encounter** as well as rides featuring time travel, teleportation and a journey into the creative future vision of author Jules Verne.

Left, right, up, down.
Check out the world of
transportation at the
right corner of the
Space Mountain build-
ing near the Carousel
of Progress. In one
spot you can see the
Disney steam train, the
modern monorail and
the electric WEDway
cars. To your left is the
aerial skyride and the
earthbound Grand Prix
raceway. And then
think of the rocket ships
on rails within the
mountain.

**Mickey'll take
Manhattan.** The Magic
Kingdom opened on
Oct. 1, 1971. Walt
Disney World includes
28,000 acres or some
43 square miles of
land, making it about
the size of San
Francisco or twice the
size of Manhattan.

The Magic Kingdom
occupies about 107
acres. (By way of com-
parison, Disneyland
occupies just 80 acres
in California.) Epcot
Center occupies about
260 acres (including a
40-acre lake) and the
Disney-MGM Studios
sprawl over some 135
acres.

Just 5,000 acres of
Walt Disney World land
are considered devel-
oped, and Disney has
set aside a permanent
wildlife conservation
area of some 8,200
acres.

Walt Disney World (and at the similar–but not identical–ride at Disneyland.)

Space Mountain is a masterpiece of Disney imagineering,
merging a relatively small and slow (top speed of about 28
mph) roller coaster with an outer space theme. The small cars
zoom around indoors in near-total darkness, the only light
coming from the projected images of stars and planets on the
ceiling. The ride is a triumph of scene-setting, the amusement
park equivalent of a big-budget movie's special effects. The
cars feel like they are moving much faster than they are
because you have no point of reference in the dark.

The waiting line for Space Mountain wends its way
through an imaginative maze designed to make visitors
feel like they truly are embarking on an intergalactic journey. You'll walk through corridors decorated with satellite pictures of other planets, pass through beams of
pulsating light and then descend a walkway into a busy
launching pad packed with technicians and engineers
loading spacecraft–including yours.

As you wait in the launching pad, the excitement growing in the pit of your stomach, look around at some of the
fantastic details. The control room has television monitors
that view the interior of the ride for safety checks; a computer controls the passage of the cars on the two mirror-
image tracks. Overhead, a projector paints the pictures of
huge rolling asteroids. You will not be the first to observe
that they look like close-ups of chocolate chip cookies; Disney
has never revealed its recipe.

Professional Space Mountain riders–and there are tens
of thousands of them–will argue over which seat affords
the best ride. The last row of seats seems to benefit from
a "whip" effect as the cars make sharp turns; we prefer the
very front row, where you don't have the back of someone else's head to mar the illusion of space travel and there
is a terrific blast of onrushing air as you move on the
track. At busy times, you probably will not be able to
cajole an attendant into allowing you to select the seat of
your choice; late at night or on the occasional slow day you
might be in luck.

Do keep a hand on your personal belongings; wrap
camera and purse straps around your feet and make sure
that children are properly placed beneath the restraining
bar. (Disney launch technicians will double-check the
safety arrangements, too.)

Now, speaking of waiting lines: they can easily extend to 90 minutes or more on a busy afternoon. The general rule to avoid long lines at the Magic Kingdom especially applies here. Get to the ride when the gates first open and you may be able to stroll right on board; or come back to the ride at the end of the day. Another somewhat quiet time is during the dinner hour, from about 6 to 7 p.m.

If you go to the effort to get to the park before the official opening, walk up Main Street as far as you are allowed. On most mornings, Disney attendants hold back the early crowd at a rope near the walkway to the Tomorrowland Terrace restaurant. When the rope drops, walk, trot or sprint (your choice) to Space Mountain. Walking easily on a low-season day, it took 25 minutes from the drop of the rope to the moment we were seated in our space rocket, including an easy 15-minute wait.

The ride is about 3 minutes in length. If both tracks are operating and the doors are open, a crowd backed up to the front door means a wait of about one hour; sometimes, though, attendants will build up the line outside while the inside queues clear out. This is often done at the end of the day to discourage huge crowds as closing hour approaches.

Children under three cannot ride Space Mountain and those under seven must be accompanied by an adult; all riders must be at least 44 inches tall, and pregnant women and others with back or health problems are advised against riding.

Space Mountain, along with other major rides like Thunder Mountain Railroad, offers a "switch off" arrangement if not all of the people in your party want to ride the coaster, or if you are traveling with a child too young or too small to ride. Inform the attendant at the turnstile at the launching area that you want to switch off; one parent or adult can ride Space Mountain and change places with another at the exit.

Mission to Mars. It was originally called Mission to the Moon, which gives you an idea of just how old the concept and design is for this rather primitive simulation. You'll sit in a high-angled circular auditorium, looking down on a screen in the floor or up at smaller screens around the edges–kind of like a view from the cheap seats of a baseball stadium. The seats tilt and shake a little, which is fun, but the total experience is rather lame when compared to the exhibits at Epcot or MGM Studios.

Hal, Mickey-san. If ever proof was required of the global impact of American popular culture, it came with the opening of Tokyo Disneyland in 1983. The park, which is owned by a Japanese company under license to Disney, is located six miles outside of Tokyo. It includes familiar Disney attractions as well as new shows such as **Pinocchio's Daring Journey, The Eternal Seas** and **Meet the World.**

Instead of Main Street, U.S.A., you'll find **World Bazaar** as the gateway to Adventureland, Fantasyland, Tomorrowland and Westernland. Adventureland attractions include the **Jungle Cruise, Enchanted Tiki Room** and **Pirates of the Caribbean.** In Westernland you'll find the **Mark Twain Riverboat, Tom Sawyer Island, The Golden Horseshoe Revue** and **Country Bear Jamboree,** among other lures.

Hai, Mickey-san.
Cont

Fantasyland includes the new Pinocchio ride, plus **It's a Small World, Haunted Mansion, Snow White's Adventure** and the **Mickey Mouse Revue.** There are also venerable favorites like **Dumbo, the Flying Elephant** and **Cinderella's Golden Carousel.** Tomorrowland includes yet another **Space Mountain** as well as **Meet the World,** an attraction based on Japanese history and the country's influence on the rest of the world.

Closing time. Closing time varies according to the season, and is sometimes adjusted from day to day based on attendance patterns. Check at the park for details. The announced Closing Time is actually a relative thing, usually meaning the time when the last person is allowed to join a ride line. The parks themselves are cleared out about an hour or so after then, and the final bus or other transportation to parking lots or hotels leaves about 90 minutes after closing time.

The good news is that there rarely is a line to get into this 18-minute attraction (including a preflight); the bad news is that this is a mission that deserves to have been scrubbed. If you're tired, it's a place to sit down and get out of the sun or rain; the kids might enjoy the vibrating seats.

Circlevision 360 "American Journeys." A spectacular travelogue of these United States, from the glaciers of Alaska to the beaches of Hawaii to a Cape Kennedy blastoff to New York's Statue of Liberty, this is an often-overlooked gem. A short sequence on board a whitewater rafting expedition brings many viewers close to instant seasickness. Nine projectors send images to huge screens that encircle the audience.

The same technique was used for the spectacular "Wonders of China" film shown in Epcot at the China Pavilion and "O Canada" at the Canada Pavilion, also not to be missed.

The large theater swallows crowds quickly—there are no seats within, and so all must stand through the 20-minute show. Only rarely will lines be larger than the capacity of the theater for the next show.

Dreamflight. One of the newest attractions at Tomorrowland, it nevertheless suffers from some of the "blahs" of much of the area. The ride combines some attractive sets and scenery with short snippets of spectacular film.

The purpose of the ride is to emphasize the thrill and history of flight, but this exhibit doesn't have a dream of surpassing any of the technology shows at Epcot. The best effect in the ride is a rather simple one: rotating light beams within a fog tunnel to simulate high speed.

Still, it's a pleasant way to get off your feet for a while and there is rarely a line for this 6-minute ride.

WEDway PeopleMover. 20-passenger cars circle slowly above Tomorrowland, taking a quick peek into a part of Space Mountain (a good way for the faint of heart to get some idea of what the excitement is about). The PeopleMover is a pet project of the Magic Kingdom, demonstrating an unusual means of propulsion—the linear induction motor. The track and the car form a motor together, as magnetic pulses pull the car down a flat coil.

There is rarely a significant line for this 10-minute ride, which we found to be about 7 minutes too long. Still, it's a seat and a bit of a view. WED, in case you didn't realize it, are Walt's initials.

StarJets. A basic amusement park ride with two-passenger rockets and an up/down lever. The ride is a favorite of many youngsters–they love that lever. It spins–a bit dizzily for some–high above the Space Bar restaurant, giving a neat view of Tomorrowland. Nowhere near as threatening (to some) as Space Mountain, it nevertheless is not for people with fear of heights.

The line for the 90-second ride varies greatly; we'd recommend coming back another time if there are more than 30 or 40 people ahead of you.

Carousel of Progress. This ride, originally presented by General Electric at the 1964-1965 World's Fair in New York, tells the story of how (surprise, surprise) electricity has been a wonderful thing for American consumers. It's interesting, but no great shakes. Be sure to check out GE's Horizons exhibit at Epcot, which is considerably more current and entertaining.

There's rarely a line for this 18-minute show in which the theater seats revolve around a stationary central core populated by some of the more primitive Disney Audio-Animatronic robots at the park; school age youngsters may be fascinated, and older viewers nostalgic. The best seat is down front in the center of the auditorium. Note the eyes on the various robot dogs in each scene. And, in this day of political correctness, it is worth noting that the carousel is an all-white middle class world, and one in which dad is still the indisputable king of the castle.

Skyway. Entrance to the aerial tramway that runs to Fantasyland. Passengers must exit at Fantasyland, although it is a simple matter to go down the stairs and back up again to return to Tomorrowland if you desire. Lines for the 5-minute show are rarely longer than a few minutes. The trip is especially dramatic in the evening.

Grand Prix Raceway. All kids we know dream of getting behind the wheel of Daddy's car; most adults we know dream of taking a spin around a Grand Prix race course. Perhaps that's why this attraction, which doesn't have much to do with Tomorrowland that we can think of, is such a popular destination. Adults, alas, will probably find the trip rather boring; children will beg for another go around the course.

There are four parallel tracks of about a half-mile each, and the little race cars have real gasoline engines that will

Lost and found. A family of four touring Walt Disney World for four days and not losing at least one backpack, two sets of sunglasses and three hats is unlike any we know. On the day of a loss, check at City Hall in the Magic Kingdom or Guest Services at Epcot or the Disney-MGM Studios. After a day, items are taken to a central lost and found at the Transportation and Ticket Center.

It's your dime, Mickey. Disney is part owner of the telephone company (Vista-United Telecommunications) that serves the nearly 20,000 telephones in the Magic Kingdom. That might explain why Mickey Mouse appears on the cover of the fat phone books for Lake Buena Vista and environs.

propel them forward at up to a sluggish 7 mph. The steering gear works, too, allowing the driver to move the car left and right down the course–although there is a center rail that will keep the car from completely leaving the track.

Children must be at least 52 inches tall to ride in one of the cars alone–otherwise their feet won't reach the gas pedal. Mom or Dad, though, can sit alongside and press the pedal while junior happily steers.

Waiting lines can reach to nearly an hour on the most crowded days; visit the track early or late to make the best use of your time.

FANTASYLAND

This is the stuff of young dreams: Cinderella's castle, Dumbo, Peter Pan, Alice in Wonderland, Snow White and the toy riot of It's A Small World. Fantasyland is a bright and cheerful place, decorated in splashes of color and sprinkled with snippets of song.

Mad Tea Party. A Disney version of a rather common amusement park ride, in which circular cars move around a track and also spin around on platforms. (If it sounds dizzying, that's because it is: the very young and others with sensitive stomachs or ears might prefer the Carrousel across the way. However, the riders have some control over how fast the cups spin; grab hold of the wheel in the center of the cup and don't let go for the least movement.)

At Fantasyland, the ride has been designed like a scene from Disney's classic 1951 film, "Alice in Wonderland." Our favorite part is the drunken mouse who pops out of the teapot in the center.

The ride itself is only about 90 seconds long; the wait can be much more than that. We'd recommend hopping on board only if lines are short.

20,000 Leagues Under the Sea. We love the idea of a submarine ride, but if that's what you are looking for this is not a very fine example. Actually, Disney put a great deal of effort into this attraction, including the construction of a fleet of 61-foot-long subs and creation of a large lagoon filled with fish, giant clams, coral, icebergs, caves and more–all of it fake. Oh, did we neglect to mention the lost city of Atlantis and the polar ice cap?

The attraction is loosely based on the Jules Verne book of the same name, and in particular the 1954 Disney movie. And despite repeated warnings from those in the know, it

Tall tale. Cinderella Castle is 189 feet tall–nine feet higher than Spaceship Earth in Epcot. (The castle at Disneyland in California, by the way, is called Sleeping Beauty Castle and is much smaller, with towers rising just 71 feet.)

Vacancy. Way up top in the steel and fiberglass walls of Cinderella's Castle is an apartment originally intended for use by members of the Disney family. As far as we are aware, it's not for rent, even on New Year's Eve when the nearest available room may be in Philadelphia.

Lockers. Store extra clothing and other items at one of the coin-operated lockers beneath the Main Street Railroad Station and at the Transportation and Ticket Center.

is one of the more popular attractions of the park.

Passengers clamber down ladders into the narrow confines of the sub and sit alongside underwater windows; some riders may find the loading and unloading very difficult.

The 8½-minute ride moves rather slowly and loading is even slower; long lines build up by midday and may not disappear at all until late. Personally, we'd rather watch the plastic grass on Main Street grow . . .

Mr. Toad's Wild Ride. Not all that wild, but a rather entertaining ride based on one of Disney's more obscure films, "The Adventures of Ichabod and Mr. Toad," which was in turn loosely based on the book, "The Wind in the Willows."

You will ride in an antique car on the road to Nowhere in Particular, crashing through fireplaces, into a chicken coop and on a railroad track headed straight for an oncoming locomotive. It's light enough fare for most children, although the very young might become a bit scared by the day-glo devils and the somewhat loud sound effects. Adults will find this 2-minute ride among the more ordinary at the Magic Kingdom; we'd recommend against joining a midday line unless a youngster is in charge.

Snow White's Adventures. The sign over the door actually reads, "Snow White's Scary Adventures," which is a bit of a tipoff to the fact that this ride emphasizes the grimmer parts of the Grimm Brothers fairy tale, as presented in Disney's 1938 animated movie. This place can't hold a fading candle to the spooks in The Haunted Mansion across the way in Liberty Square, but there are a few skeletons and a wicked witch who will jump out a few times. Some very young children may be scared by the effects.

The ride is about 2½ minutes in length, and lines at midday can reach to an hour. That's longer than we would want to wait; go early or late or not at all.

Magic Journeys. A special movie that explores a child's fantasies in an extraordinary 3-D world of nature, fantasy and civilization. Originally shown at Epcot, it was moved out of Journey into Imagination when Michael Jackson's Captain EO began its run there.

Before the main feature, visitors will stand to watch Walt Disney's only 3-D movie starring its famous cartoon characters. **Working for Peanuts,** an 8-minute short made in 1953, stars Donald Duck and Chip and Dale. You will

Under foot. Among the most amazing wonders of the Magic Kingdom is one that most visitors never see. Below your feet are nine acres of underground "utilidor" corridors hiding the sewers, water pipes, air conditioning, electrical cables, communications links and garbage collection facilities. There is also an extensive system of tunnels allowing employees to come and go within the park virtually unseen; have you ever wondered why you have never seen Mickey walking to work, or seen a Mike Fink keelboat captain strolling through Tomorrowland?

About that trash: as you might expect in a Magic Kingdom, Disney does not use an ordinary garbage truck. Refuse is sucked to a central collection point through a huge network of pneumatic tubes.

be loaned a pair of polarized 3-D glasses that will bring the cartoon off the screen and into your lap. The film itself actually demonstrates why pure cartoons are not particularly well suited to three-dimensional adaptations; what we see is a flat background, a flat foreground, flat characters and the occasional flat special effect launched out toward your head–peanuts, mostly.

But it is Magic Journeys that truly demonstrates the art. An early scene seemingly places you literally in the middle of a sea of flowers, and goes on from there to outer space, an indoor circus and a marvelous sequence involving a kite that hovers out over the audience like a fluttering butterfly. Some youngsters might be a bit upset by a short sequence involving bats and witches, but the overall effect of this journey is warm wonder.

There is almost never a line for the two films, which add up to about 30 minutes; it's a great place to rest weary feet or get out from the sun or rain.

Dumbo, the Flying Elephant. Once again, Disney has taken a very ordinary amusement park ride and made it something special, at least for little visitors. Riders sit within fiberglass flying elephants that can move up and down as they circle around a mirrored ball and a statue of Timothy Mouse, the little guy who becomes Dumbo's manager in the classic Disney animated movie.

This ride has a tremendous draw for young children; even more unhappily, it is also one of the slowest-loading attractions in the park. By midday, lines can reach to an hour for the 90-second ride. If your kids insist on an elephant-back ride, head for Dumbo early or late in the day.

Cinderella's Golden Carrousel. One of the few mostly "real" things in this world of fantasy, the carrousel dates back to 1917. Many of the horses are hand-carved originals, although the herd has been augmented with some fiberglass replicas. No two of the horses are identical. The musical organ, which plays selections from Disney hit movies, is an Italian original.

The lines for the two-minute ride ebb and flow; we'd suggest you wait for the times when you can walk right on board.

WOW It's a Small World. Every little girl's wildest dream: a world of beautiful dancing dolls from all over the world. There is nothing to get your heart beating here, but even the most cynical–including little boys and adults–will probably find something to smile about in this upbeat boat ride. We especially enjoy the Audio Animatronic can-can dancers.

This 11-minute ride was originally designed for the 1964-65 World's Fair in New York, but unlike the Carrousel of Progress, the Small World ride has timeless appeal.

The boats are large and the lines move pretty quickly (if two queues are being formed, the line to the left moves a bit faster), but we'd advise coming to this attraction early or late in the day. Children who like this ride will probably also enjoy the Rivers of Time ride at the Mexican pavilion of Epcot.

Peter Pan's Flight. A mellow excursion into some of the scenes from Disney's version of the story of the little boy who doesn't want to grow up. Riders sit in a small pirate ship that suspends them a foot or so off the floor. Everyone's favorite scene is the overhead view of London by night, which does a pretty good job of simulating Peter's flight. The ride was under reconstruction in the spring of 1992, with promises of new joys.

Skyway. The Fantasyland entrance to the aerial tramway, which returns to Tomorrowland; it's a great way to get a glimpse of the north end of the park. Passengers must exit at Tomorrowland, although it is a simple matter to go down the stairs and back up again to return to Fantasyland if you desire. Lines for the 5 minutes show are rarely longer than a few minutes. The trip is especially dramatic in the evening; time your voyage properly and catch an aerial view of the nightly parade.

MICKEY'S STARLAND

Walt Disney World, Disneyland and the entire Disney empire was in fact built from the ears of the most famous rodent of all, but until 1989 Mickey didn't have a place of his own. In that year, Disney honored the mouse's 60th (!) birthday with the first new area at Walt Disney World since its opening.

Mickey's Hollywood Theatre, Mickey's House & Starland Show, Magical TV World, Mickey Mouse Club Funland Tent and **Mickey's Dressing Room.** If you have kids, or ever were one, then there's not a whole lot of doubt about this: you've got to visit Mickey Mouse's house.

There are no outerspace roller coasters or multimillion dollar water slides at Mickey's Starland; instead we have

Meeting places. Try not to select the front of Cinderella Castle as a meeting place for groups that go their own way within the park. This location can become quite crowded during the daily parades and other events. Instead, choose the back side of the castle near the carousel or a landmark off the parade route.

Art gallery. Disneyana Collectibles, between Walt Disney Story and Tony's Town Square Cafe, offers rare and not-so rare memorabilia, including animation art. More animation is for sale at shops in the Disney-MGM Studios park.

Child under tow. On a crowded day, it is possible to lose sight of your children from time to time. Discuss with them beforehand a place to meet if you get separated; you can also obtain name tags to place on your children at City Hall or the Baby Center next to the Crystal Palace. Disney employees are well trained on how to deal with a lost child; track one down for assistance.

The Baby Center is specially designed to assist in nursing or changing infants; most other rest rooms throughout the parks have some accommodation to this need. The Baby Center also offers for sale emergency rations of Similac, Isomil and Enfamil formula, replacement pacifiers and bottles and diapers. Strollers are available for rent beneath the railroad overpass at the entrance to the Magic Kingdom.

the sort of giddy happiness that has sustained the mouse's popularity for all of these years. Disney also uses the area to present and promote some of its newer cartoon stars, including Rescue Rangers, Tale Spin and DuckTales.

You'll explore Mickey's house from corner to corner–he has some great remembrances scattered about, including souvenirs of his greatest films, songs and TV shows. From the house you'll head into the Magical TV World for a rollicking live stage presentation starring the Mick and some of his favorite cohorts including the ultimate cheapskate Scrooge McDuck, the world's worst pilot Launchpad McQuack and the silliest rescuers we know, Chip and Dale.

The show will obviously appeal most to youngsters up to about the awkward teens; adults will find it a pleasant 15 minute diversion.

From the show, it's on to the Mickey Mouse Club Funland tent, packed with a bunch of neat and silly buttons to push and games to play.

Ah, but the best is yet to come for those in the know. After the show, move through the tent, head outside and to the right to Mickey's Hollywood Theater. There–thrill of thrills–you can enter into Mickey's dressing room for a semi-private photograph and autograph session.

Note that Mickey's dressing room is small, and only a few people are let in at one time; to avoid wasting a lot of time in line, we suggest you either head immediately for his door after the show, or go to the petting farm and wait for the shortest lines between shows.

Grandma Duck's Farm. A Disney-clean petting zoo, including occasional appearances by Minnie Moo, a white cow with (natural, we're told) black markings in the shape of mouse ears. There is also a charming kid-sized maze of bushes and shrubs.

Walt Disney World Railroad. The vintage railroad that circles the Magic Kingdom has a station here at the back of Starland. The next stop is Main Street, and the third stop is in Frontierland.

LIBERTY SQUARE

A peaceful laid-back corner of America, home of the Presidents (robotically assisted), a festive riverboat (which runs on underwater tracks) and a haunted mansion (which is too creepy to pass by without a tour.) The square is also home to a massive live oak tree festooned with 13 lanterns–one for each of the 13 original colonies–like the Liberty Trees used as political statements in pre-Revolution times.

⭐ **The Haunted Mansion.** Scare yourself silly in this masterpiece of an attraction with some of the most sophisticated special effects at Walt Disney World. The experience begins in the graveyard waiting line; before you let the tombstones make you feel too creepy, stop and read some of the inscriptions. They're a howl!

Once you are admitted to the mansion itself, you will be ushered into a strange room with an interesting visual trick–is the ceiling going up or the floor going down? Either way, the portraits on the wall are a real howl. The attendants, dressed as morticians, play their roles well–we've tried our best over the years to make them crack a smile, without any success.

You'll enter onto a moving set of chairs and settle in for a tour through a house that is in the control of the largest collection of spooks this side of the CIA. We've ridden the ride many times, and see something different each time. Among the best effects are the dancing ghouls at the dinner party, the moving door knockers and the face within the crystal ball.

This ride is probably the single best combination of Disney Audio-Animatronics, moviemaking and scene-setting at the Magic Kingdom.

Some very young children may become a bit scared, although most kids of all ages can see the humor amongst the ghouls. And speaking of humor, stop to read the inscriptions on the tombs at the exit.

Lines for this show vary greatly; the best time to visit is early or late in the day. Try not to join the crowds streaming toward the mansion's door each time the Hall of Presidents lets out or the riverboat arrives. The ride lasts about nine minutes, including a two-minute pre-show.

The Hall of Presidents. A living history lesson featuring some of Disney's best Audio-Animatronic robots. The show is derived from the hit Illinois pavilion at the 1964-1965 New York World's Fair, which startled fairgoers when a seated Abe Lincoln wearily came to life to address the audience. In the Magic Kingdom version of the show, all 41 American presidents are represented on stage. They respond to their names in a grand roll call and then sit and fidget or whisper to each other while Abe conducts the meeting.

The flag-waving show and a spectacular film that pre-

Tomb with a view. Our favorite Haunted Mansion tombstones include: "Dear Departed Brother Dave. He Chased a Bear into a Cave"; "Here Rests Wathel R. Bender. He rode to glory on a fender", and "Here Lies Good Old Fred. A Great Big Rock Fell on his Head."

More favorites, from the cemetery at the exit of the ride: Bluebeard's tomb reads, "Here lyeth his loving wives. Seven winsome wives, some fat some thin. Six of them were faithful, but the seventh did him in." Other pun-full names on the wall include Paul Tergyst, Clare Voince, Metta Fisiks and Manny Festation.

Heritage House. This hideaway store offers an interesting collection of old maps and historical documents reprinted on parchment for about $1 apiece.

cedes the robotics may have particular appeal to school children studying American history. Others may enjoy the technical artistry of the robots, and some may enjoy studying the details of the costumes on each of the chief executives.

We found the American Experience show at Epcot to be superior.

The show takes about 20 minutes; the 700-seat auditorium quickly eats up waiting lines and the maximum wait should be no more than two shows, or about 40 minutes.

Liberty Square Riverboat. One of the most nearly real of all of the exhibits at the Magic Kingdom, The Richard F. Irvine is a true steam-powered sidewheeler. Built at Walt Disney World for the ride, it circles the half-mile Rivers of America attached to an underwater rail. The ride itself is no great shakes, but is a pleasant reprieve on a hot day. The Mike Fink Keelboats and Davy Crockett's Explorer Canoes make the same circle and see the same simulated Old West sights.

The ride takes about 16 minutes; lines rarely extend beyond a full boat load, so your waiting time should be 16 minutes or less.

Mike Fink Keelboats. Small riverboats that follow the same circuit as the Riverboat, a bit faster. Mike Fink, by the way, was a riverboat captain of legend who had an adventure with Davy Crockett. The small boats here, the Bertha Mae and the Gullywhumper, take about 10 minutes for a circuit. Because of the small capacity of the boats, we'd advise against joining a long line if there is one; we'd also suggest against duplicating a trip on the keelboats and one on the riverboat.

ADVENTURE LAND

Ahoy, mateys: welcome to a most unusual corner of Central Florida, where you will find a Caribbean Island, an African veldt, a South Pacific bird tree and more. Adventureland includes some of the most dramatic landscaping touches in the Magic Kingdom and the most popular band of Pirates since Penzance.

WOW **Pirates of the Caribbean.** Yo, ho, yo, ho . . . one of Disney's very best. After an approach through a dank dungeon waiting area, you'll settle into a broad-beamed boat for a cruise into the middle of a pirate raid on a Caribbean island town.

We especially like the moonlit battle scene as your boat

Shiver me timbers. Some young children may be scared by the simulated cannon fire and the skulls and bones that are fairly liberally strewn about in some of the caves of **Pirates of the Caribbean.** And some adults may find bones of their own to pick–things like the depiction of women as objects for sale at auction and a hint of racism. However, the ride just might offer an opportunity to discuss such unhappy elements of history with youngsters.

passes beneath the guns of two warring ships; cannonballs will land all around you in the cool water. Pay attention, too, to the jail scene where a group of pirates try to entice a mangy dog to bring them the key. The ride includes a wondrous collection of Audio-Animatronic humans and animals, including robotic chickens and pigs.

In any case, Pirates of the Caribbean is a masterpiece of Disney artistry. You don't want to miss this one!

Lines can become quite long at midday; head for this popular trip when the park first opens, or in late afternoon. The waiting area is mostly under cover, which makes it a good place to be in the rain or a very hot day. The ride itself takes about seven minutes.

Swiss Family Treehouse. This is one of those "no accounting for taste" attractions—you'll either love it or hate it, probably depending upon how deeply the story of the Swiss Family Robinson is engraved upon your memory. Actually, this attraction is a remembrance of the 1960 Disney movie version of the classic novel "Swiss Family Robinson", written by J.D. Wyss and completed by his son Johann Rudolf Wyss in 1813.

The treehouse winds up and across a Disney simulation (constructed of sculpted concrete and steel) of a banyan tree. There's a bit of climbing of stairs and a few ropewalk bridges, and on a busy day, your view may be mostly the backside of the tourist in front of you. It takes five to ten minutes to walk up, through and down the tree; incredibly, there can sometimes be lengthy lines for the privilege; if there's a line and you're determined to climb this tree, come back late in the day.

Jungle Cruise. Another Disney classic, this is an escorted boat tour through a simulated wild kingdom that somehow stretches from the African veldt to the Amazon rain forest to the Nile valley and the jungles of southeast Asia.

You'll see some of Disney's most famous special effects, like the automated hippos who lurk just below the water's top and the cavorting elephants who will spray water from their trunks. The shores are lined with robotic zebras, lions and giraffes. The best part of the ride is the hokey but still entertaining patter of the tour guides in pith helmets—it's a punster's heaven. ("Be sure to tell all your friends about Jungle Cruise," our guide told us. "It cuts down the lines." He also apologized for some of the worst one-liners: "I'd tell funnier jokes, but they have to be Disney-approved.")

Money, money. If you run out of cash on vacation (hardly an inconceivable prospect) there are branches of SunBanks on Main Street in the Magic Kingdom, inside the gates of Epcot Center and across the road from the Disney Village Marketplace. The banks will exchange foreign currency, sell cashier's checks and money orders and issue cash advances from bank credit cards. A SunBank automatic teller machine is located at the entrance plaza of Disney-MGM Studios.

**Thunder Mountain
Railroad** at night is like
another ride altogether.
Like Space Mountain,
the fun is increased
because the darkness
hides the track ahead
of you.

Amateur gardeners may be thrilled by the amazing collection of plants, flowers and trees–most of them real–that Disney groundskeepers manage to keep alive.

The ride is just short of ten minutes; the line to get on board, alas, can sometimes wind around and around the corral for more than an hour. Go early or late on busy days.

Tropical Serenade. The home of the Enchanted Tiki Birds, a collection of more than 200 wise-cracking, wing-flapping automatic winged creatures, along with a collection of singing flowers, totem poles and statues. Your hosts are Jose, Michael, Pierre and Fritz.

Tropical Serenade is among the strangest of all of the attractions at the Magic Kingdom, and you've got to be in exactly the right frame of mind to enjoy the show. The birds were among Disney's first attempts at Audio-Animatronics, representing the state of the art as it existed around 1963 when a very similar show was introduced at Disneyland.

We know some young children who have been absolutely enchanted by the birds; the very young and the cynical need not apply.

There is rarely much of a line to get into the 17-minute show; for us, the very best thing about this show is that it takes place in a dry, air-conditioned theater.

FRONTIERLAND

Almost anything goes in this wild western corner of the Magic Kingdom, home of Davy Crockett, Tom Sawyer, a bunch of vacationing bears, a runaway mining train and the park's newest, wettest and wildest big splash.

WOW **Big Thunder Mountain Railroad.** One of the best rides at the park, it is at the same time much more than and much less than it appears.

Big Thunder is a Disneyfied roller coaster, one of only three "thrill" rides in the park (along with Space Mountain and the new-for-1993 Splash Mountain.) As roller coasters go, it is fairly tame, with about a half-mile of track and a three minute ride with a few short drops and some interesting twists and turns. But in the Disney tradition, it is the setting and the attention to detail that make this one of the most popular places to be.

You will ride in a runaway mining train up through a quaking tunnel, across a flooding village and back down around and through a 197-foot-high artificial mountain.

The mountain is bedecked with real mining antiques from

former mines out West. Look, too, at the Audio-Animatronic animals, birds and an old coot of a miner in a bathtub as you zoom by.

Picking the right time to visit the railroad can make a real difference at this very popular attraction; waits of more than an hour are common at midday in the busy season.

The line outside, near the rafts to Tom Sawyer Island, is only a small portion of the waiting area. There is a large upper corral and a winding path down through the mining station to the railroad. The shortest lines can be found early in the day or just before dinnertime; the ride takes on a very different feeling at night, and true fans should experience it then as well as during the day.

Children under 7 must be accompanied by an adult; no one under 40 inches is allowed to ride.

WOW Splash Mountain. Disney's "highest, scariest, wildest and wettest" attraction opened at the end of 1992, next to Big Thunder Mountain Railroad.

The ride includes four lifts and five drops, with the biggest plunging about 50 feet at a 45-degree angle and a top speed of about 40 miles per hour. Unlike most other such rides, the drops have no water in them, allowing the eight-passenger log-like cars to fall faster and smoother without hydroplaning. The big drop, visible to the crowds along the Rivers of America in Frontierland, will make it appear as if the log car has fallen into a pond and below its surface. Actually, riders will barely be splashed.

Some of the best special effects take place within the mountain, with a story based on Disney's classic "Song of the South" cartoon, made in 1946. The ride follows Brer Rabbit as he tries to outwit Brer Fox and Brer Bear on a wild journey to the Laughin' Place. The end of the ride arrives with the singing of the most famous song from that film, "Zip-A-Dee-Doo-Dah."

We fully expect Splash Mountain to become as big a magnet for crowds as Space Mountain–an inside source told us that the queue area, which is open to the elements, is set up for crowds in a two-hour wait.

WOW Tom Sawyer Island. Another essential, at least for the youngsters, is the raft ride over to this little island in the middle of the Rivers of America. Based vaguely upon Mark Twain's classic book, you'll find dark caves, water-wheels, a barrel bridge and a rope bridge to bounce on;

Mirth control. The population of the greater Orlando area grew from 453,270 to more than 1.1 million from 1970 to 1990. In the same period, air traffic exploded from 1 million annual passengers to more than 17 million.

Just before Walt Disney World opened in 1970 there were about 6,000 hotel rooms in the area; in 1990, there were more than 70,000 rooms with an average occupancy rate of 84 percent.

at the far end of the island is a little bridge to Fort Sam Clemens, where kids can scramble around the parapets and fire air guns at passing sidewheelers.

The little snack bar at the fort sells, along with beverages, a most unusual fast food: whole sour pickles.

Parents will appreciate the space to let their children burn off a bit of energy after standing in lines all day; be advised, though, that it is fairly easy to misplace a youngster in one of the simulated caves or a trail. Make arrangements with children on a meeting place if you become separated.

Lines for the raft rarely require more than 10 minutes waiting. The island closes at dusk.

Country Bear Vacation Hoedown. Also known as The Country Bear Jamboree, this is a doggedly cute show starring some 20 robotic bears of various sizes, shapes and personalities, full of corny jokes and strained puns. (Where else but at a Disney park could you possibly expect to see a trio of bears named Bubbles, Bunny and Beulah singing a bowdlerized Beach Boys hit, "Wish They All Could Be California Bears"?)

For our money, we find this 15-minute attraction just barely (sorry) easier to take than the Enchanted Tiki Birds; youngsters and fans of Disney Audio-Animatronics will probably want to argue strongly in its favor. And, the Hoedown is a very popular show, despite our opinion. The best time to visit is early, late or during one of the parades. The best seats are at the very front or back of the hall.

Frontierland Shootin' Arcade. A durn-fancy shooting gallery, sort of a live video game and not like any other shooting gallery you have seen at a country fair. Players aim huge, real buffalo rifles at a Disney replica of an 1850s frontier town. The rifles fire infrared beams at targets on tombstones, clouds, banks, jails and other objects; direct hits make the targets spin, explode or otherwise surprise.

To use the rifles you must pay an additional charge for a specific number of "bullets."

Diamond Horseshoe Jamboree. Disney's squeaky-clean version of a Western Dance Hall revue is a lot of fun for young and old, although it can be a bit of a hassle to work into a tight schedule.

There are pretty can-can girls, corny comics and strolling musicians to entertain visitors of all ages. (The show is similar to the Hoop-Dee-Doo Musical Revue, presented at the Fort Wilderness Campground; seeing both would be a bit of overkill. Hoop-Dee-Doo extends to almost two hours, and the food offerings are quite a bit more adventuresome.)

The show itself is about 30 minutes in length; you'll need to arrive 30 to 45 minutes before showtime to make your way to your seat and place orders for drinks or sandwiches (strictly optional, although it may be difficult to prevent kids from badgering you for something at the table.) And, admission to the show is by reservation only; you'll need to stop by the booth in front of Disneyana Collectibles on Main Street to select one of the five or six shows available each day. Do so early.

The best way to maximize your day and include the Jamboree in your schedule would be to plan your lunch or dinner to coincide with a show.

EATING YOUR WAY THROUGH THE MAGIC KINGDOM

There are three types of restaurants at the Magic Kingdom: Overpriced and bad; overpriced and barely acceptable, and overpriced and almost good.

We'd recommend that you not consider meals to be an important part of your experience at the Magic Kingdom; save your time and money for one of the somewhat better Epcot Center or Disney-MGM Studios restaurants or for an evening outside of the Disney borders.

You do, though, have to eat. Disney has a rule against bringing your own sandwiches or other food into the park. You certainly can pack a baby's formula and in dozens of visits we have never seen an attendant search a backpack or shoulder bag for tuna fish on rye.

If you don't pack your own, it is possible to pick and choose among the offerings at the park. Disney does offer a few non-standard and more healthy offerings, like pasta salads, turkey burgers and smoked turkey legs at some of its stands. Nevertheless, each year guests at Walt Disney World eat more than 7 million hamburgers, 5 million hot dogs, 5 million pounds of french fries, 265,000 pounds of popcorn and 46 million Cokes.

We include general price ranges in our listings and mention specific prices for some items. Pricing on food–as on everything–is subject to change. All food establishments within Disney World offer soft drink at prices ranging from $1.40 to $1.65.

Nee how-ma, Mickey syen-sheng. After an absence of several years following a dispute over alleged piracy of its trademarks, the Walt Disney Co. announced in 1992 its intention to re-enter the Chinese market. Disney expects to manufacture a range of products including clothing, shoes and schoolbags in Guangzhou, China to sell at a chain of 20 "Mic-Kids" retail outlets; plans call for as many as 300 stores by 1995. As much as 70 percent of the products made using cheap labor in China will be exported to Disney outlets around the world.

Future plans include the return of the Chinese-language "Mickey and Donald Show" and a possible theme park in southern China by the end of the century.

KEY

¶¶ = FAST FOOD

Y = PUB

🏠 = FULL-
SERVICE
RESTAURANT

MAIN STREET, U.S.A.

¶¶ Main Street Wagons. Located throughout the Main Street area. Espresso, capuccino, soft drinks. Hot dogs and baked goods. Fresh fruit and vegetables, priced from $1-$3. We particularly like the fruit wagons which offer fruit drinks ($1.50) and assorted fruit cups served in tall, plastic soda glasses ($3) and various fresh fruits and vegetables. A few umbrella-shaded tables are available on East Center Street beside the Main Street Market house.

¶¶ Main Street Bake Shop. On Main Street near the Plaza Ice Cream Parlor. Unusual baked goods and beverages, $2-$4. Cookies about $1. Watch cookies made from scratch through the large window fronting on Main Street. There is a small seating area inside the pleasant, floral decorated shop, but most customers take their goodies to go, either to sit at one of the nearby umbrella tables or to carry with them as they move deeper into the park.

Very crowded at opening time, this shop is popular for breakfast sweets and coffee. Check out the oversize iced and glazed doughnuts and sweet rolls. A separate cookies and pastries line is available to the right of the entrance if that is all you want.

¶¶ Plaza Ice Cream Parlor. Near Main Street Bake Shop, across from Refreshment Corner. Lines can be long in this pleasant, old-fashioned ice cream shop, but they move rather quickly. About $2 for most items.

¶¶ Refreshment Corner. At the top end of Main Street. Hot dogs, soda, soft drinks and coffee. Attractive red and white umbrella tables on a sunny patio. A good place for a quick snack, or a drink and a rest. Don't encourage the birds to beg for food; they'll try anyway.

🏠 The Crystal Palace. At the top of Main Street, toward Adventureland. Breakfast, lunch and dinner. Salads, prime ribs, broiled chicken, fish, pasta, $7-$15. Child's pasta, chicken or hot dog plate, $4-$6.

The building is a replica of the Crystal Palace, built for the first International Exhibition in Victorian London in 1851. The atmosphere is bright and airy with floral designs in a Victorian "gazebo" setting. A wrap-around veranda, cooled with fans, provides outdoor seating. Look up to see stained and cut glass in three domes overhead. Two covered waiting areas; some seating available while you wait for a table.

🏠 **Tony's Town Square Restaurant.** Just inside the entrance gate to the right, next to Disneyana Collectibles and near The Walt Disney Story. Italian food, steaks, seafood, hamburgers and salads, $15-$21; appetizers $3-$8. Breakfast, lunch and dinner; Reservations recommended.

The restaurant is modeled after the cafe in Disney's classic "Lady and the Tramp" movie. Seating for about 200. For starters try the fresh melon with prosciutto or fried calamari with marinara sauce, each under $5. Entries include sirloin steak with lobster and pasta ($21), seafood linguine ($20), and seafood grill ($19).

🏠 **The Plaza Restaurant.** At the top of main street toward Tomorrowland. Gourmet hamburgers, soups, sandwiches and salads. Lunch and dinner. $7-$9. Child's peanut butter, miniburger or hot dog about $3.50.

This pleasant 19th-century-style dining room offers table service inside and bright yellow and white umbrella tables outside. Inside, the room is large bright and airy; period mirrors, imitation gas lamps and carpeting enhance the elegant setting. In addition to Reuben sandwiches and burgers ($8.50), the Plaza offers a chef's salad or a fruit salad for about $8.

ADVENTURELAND

🍴 **Adventureland Veranda.** At the east end of Adventureland, near the Swiss Family Treehouse. Oriental entrees and sandwiches, hamburgers, hot dogs in South Seas setting, $3-$5.50. Child's menu, $3. Lunch and dinner.

Americanized Oriental cuisine in a series of open dining rooms stirred by hanging fans. Medium-sized round tables seat four. A covered outdoor dining area is also available. For a light meal, try egg rolls or fried rice a la carte ($3). For the children, select from fried chicken strips or hot dog basket ($3). Teriyaki steak sandwich ($5.50), fruit salad ($5.25), and polynesian chicken sandwich ($5), round out the menu. For dessert, try Key Lime Pie ($2).

🍴 **Sunshine Tree Terrace.** At the North end of Adventureland, behind the Enchanted Tiki Birds' Tropical Serenade. Citrus drinks, frozen yogurt, shakes and desserts, $2-$3.

A quick stop for a light snack or drink. Try citrus swirl yogurt cups at $1.75, shakes ($2.25), and root beer floats ($2.75). A few umbrella tables give you a place to rest while you snack.

KEY	
🍴	= FAST FOOD
⑂	= PUB
🏠	= FULL-SERVICE RESTAURANT

|¶|| **El Pirata Y El Perico.** Across from the Pirates of the Caribbean. Tacos, nachos, hot dogs and more, $4-$5. Child's box lunch, $3.50.

Mexican decor, offering tacos, salads and hot dogs. Notice the interesting lanterns, stucco walls and tile floors, but be ready for a noisy atmosphere when you dine indoors. The covered patio is a better choice. We like the taco salad at $4.50.

|¶|| **The Oasis.** In the center of Adventureland, near Bwana Bob's. Soft drinks and snacks. A thatched-roofed shack with bamboo seating.

|¶|| **Aloha Isle.** Between the Adventureland Veranda and the Egg Roll Wagon. Pineapple and fruit drinks, $1.75. Try fresh pineapple spears for under $1, or raspberry/vanilla swirl for $1.75; a variety of tall fruit drinks.

|¶|| **Egg Roll Wagon.** Outside Adventureland Veranda, next to Aloha Isle. Egg rolls and more egg rolls, $2. A variety of traditional and unusual egg rolls, including pork, shrimp, pizza and oriental cheese, about $2. No seating.

FRONTIERLAND

|¶|| **Pecos Bill Cafe** and **Mile Long Bar.** Just past the Country Bear Vacation Hoedown. Burgers, chicken barbecue and hot dogs, $5. Western saloon atmosphere in the side-by-side restaurants that share a common menu. Look carefully at the animals mounted on the wall; they're talking and singing robots.

The chicken and bean salad ($5.75) is a good burger alternative, but if hamburger fits your fancy, try the Pecos Bill Trail Bacon Cheeseburger Basket, $5.25. Barbecue chicken sandwiches are $5.

|¶|| **Westward Ho.** Across from the Mile Long Bar. Chips, cookies and drinks, $1-$3. Walk-up refreshments for carry along snacks. A Mickey Mouse mug filled with the soft drink of your choice is $3.

|¶|| **Turkey Leg Wagon.** Directly across from the Country Bear Vacation Hoedown. Smoked turkey legs, $3. Walk-up, takeout service for huge smoked turkey legs–just follow the smell to the end of the line. As you carry along one of these interesting treats, watch out for sea gulls; they'll sometimes fly right at the turkey leg trying to take a bite out of it!

LIBERTY SQUARE

¶| Columbia Harbour House. On Liberty Square across from Ichabod's Landing. Battered shrimp and chicken, cold sandwiches, pasta salads, salads. Lunch and dinner, $3-$6. Children's menu includes chicken sandwich or hot dog, $3.50-$4.

Seafood dining in seafaring atmosphere. Multiple small rooms break up the dining area. The dark, cool decor provides a comfortable respite from the sun. Larger tables seat 6 to 8. A few, small, semi-private dining rooms accommodate groups.

For an unusual appetizer or full meal, try the clam chowder served inside a large, round loaf of dark bread. When the chowder is gone, you can eat the bowl ($3). A filling fruit plate is about $5.25, and apple cobbler or chocolate and banana cream pies for dessert are about $2.

¶| Sleepy Hollow. On Liberty Square near the Hall of Presidents. Disney Handwiches, hot dogs, chicken salad, snacks, beverages, $3-$4.

Light fare in an early American decor. Notice the interesting wooden ceiling and plate rail displaying antique bottles, plates, and vases. The attractive blue and white tile floor enhances the early American atmosphere. Round tables and some picnic-style benched tables, some open and some covered. A pleasant "outdoor-indoor" dining area is under the brick-walled arbor.

Disney Handwiches–an innovative one-handed sandwich that consists of a long roll hollowed out and filled with a variety of goodies and wrapped in a paper cover–filled with chicken salad or vegetables, and a quarter-pound hot dog are the main menu items. Cinnamon rolls and cookies are available for after-meal treats.

🏛 Liberty Tree Tavern. Next to Diamond Horseshoe Jamboree. Sandwiches, salads, beef, chicken, seafood, salads, $7-$13.50. Reservations recommended; request a seating time at the door.

Sit-down dining in a colonial atmosphere with a lot of interesting details including maple bench seats, fireplaces, and simulated peg flooring. A variety of sandwiches is available from $7-$10. Seafood and other entrees from $9.50-$13.50. A chilled seafood platter offers an interesting alternative to hot food, $8.50.

¶| Liberty Square Wagon. On the walkway between Columbia Harbour House and The Hall of Presidents.

KEY

¶| = Fast Food

Y = Pub

🏛 = Full-Service Restaurant

KEY

[YI] = FAST FOOD

[Y] = PUB

[▲] = FULL-
      SERVICE
      RESTAURANT

Baked potatoes with toppings and beverages, $2-$3.

In an area where sandwiches and other fast foods average about $5, the potato wagon is a popular alternative for a filling, low-cost lunch or snack. Fresh baked white and sweet potatoes with a variety of toppings, about $2.50.

Fruit and Vegetable Wagon. Usually on the square behind the Columbia Harbour House and the Liberty Square Wagon. Various fruits and vegetables from a "farmer's market" wagon.

Attractively-presented fruits and vegetables for alternative snacks and additions to meals. The selection includes apples, peaches, grapes, star fruit and even pickles, squash and potatoes.

FANTASYLAND

Pinocchio Village Haus. Next to It's A Small World under the Skyway. Turkey burgers, turkey hot dogs, chicken, salads, pasta. Lunch and dinner, $4.

A large dining hall in a Disneyfied Tudor style. Several small rooms, including a favored location overlooking the It's A Small World ride. The pasta salad is filling and tasty. You can also select turkey burgers and hot dogs to avoid beef and pork. The Monstro Dog is a quarter pound turkey hot dog. Burgers and hot dogs served with fries or fruit. Cake, fruit and french fries also available.

As at many Disney fast food restaurants, the service lines move slowly at peak time as a single cashier serves two lines of customers. Come early or late to avoid wasting time.

Gurgi's Munchies and Crunchies. Across from 20,000 Leagues Under the Sea, near the Mad Tea Party ride. Sandwiches, children's meals, $2.75-$4.

Outdoor dining in front of a Tudor-style building. Festive atmosphere with brightly colored umbrella tables. Childrens' offerings include activity boxes. Grilled cheese sandwiches sell for about $3; chicken nuggets under $4. Ice cream and sundaes are available next door at The Round Table. The limited adult menu includes ham and cheese sandwich or chicken filet sandwich, each about $4.

The Round Table. Next to Gurgi's, and sharing outdoor seating with the sandwich shop. Ice cream and soft drinks, $1.50-$2.75. Soft serve ice cream for about $1.50; brownie sundae, $2.75.

 **King Stefan's Banquet Hall.** Upstairs in Cinderella Castle. Prime rib, fish, chicken, beef, salads. Lunch ($7-$14) and dinner ($21-$25). Reservations recommended.

If you enter the castle from the Fantasyland side, the restaurant is on the outside left. Lines for lunch begin early because seating is limited. Among the more expensive restaurants in the Magic Kingdom, the restaurant is a favorite of some children, especially little girls who dream of meeting Cinderella herself. Reservations are accepted at the door on the day you wish to dine; guests at Disney hotels can make telephone reservations up to two days ahead of time.

You enter the restaurant through a "great hall" entrance on the ground floor. This interesting room is complete with torch lanterns and swords on the wall. The slate floor and high, exposed beam ceiling enhance the "castle" feeling of the restaurant. You'll move upstairs via an interesting, winding stairway or in an elevator. Take the stairs if they're not a problem.

Upstairs the restaurant is well lit and carries a dark, wood atmosphere. A sunken polygon dining area is in the center of the room, with raised dining around the outside. The house specialty is prime cut roast beef, but the broiled chicken and shrimp and scallops brochette also are worthy of consideration.

Troubadour Tavern. Next to Peter Pan's Flight and across from It's A Small World. Soft drinks and snacks, $1-$2. Coffee and hot chocolate under $1 and a 20 oz. souvenir soft drink cup for about $2. Counter service; no seating.

TOMORROWLAND

Tomorrowland Terrace. Between the Carousel of Progress and "American Journeys." Soup, fruit salad, barbecued pork, grilled chicken, cold sandwiches. Lunch and dinner. $2-$4. Child's Peanut Butter and Jelly, $1. For something different, try the chef or seafood salad for about $5. Chicken noodle soup is about $2.

Tomorrowland Terrace seems stuck in the late 1960s, when plastic was chic and palettes all seemed to be drawn from day glo selections. This restaurant has a very large, spacious feel with lots of seating. A few outdoor tables are available, you'll probably want to enjoy the air conditioning on hot days.

KEY

= FAST FOOD

= PUB

= FULL-SERVICE RESTAURANT

KEY

| = **Fast Food**

Y = **Pub**

▲ = **Full-Service Restaurant**

|| **Plaza Pavilion.** In the walkway between Main Street and Tomorrowland. Pizza, sandwiches, salads, $3-$5. Covered outdoor dining in a pleasant setting for about 650 people. There are three dining areas, one overlooking a portion of the central lagoon and offering an excellent view of the Cinderella Castle. The area offers cool shade and ample seating away from the main service area and transient crowds.

Try the Italian Hoagie at about $4.25, or the chicken parmesan sandwich for a dollar more. Deep dish pizza is available by the slice for about $3.25 to $4.75. Fix up your ice cream with the brownie sundae ($2.75) or an ice cream float for about $2.30.

|| **Lunching Pad.** Near Starjets and across the broad plaza from Space Mountain. Juice, snacks, frozen yogurt, $1-$3. Mostly "natural" refreshments, such as an apple juice float made with yogurt at about $2.60. Offers a handful of outdoor tables and few within.

|| **Space Bar.** At the Star Jet elevator in the middle of Tomorrowland. Disney's Handwiches, snacks, and drinks, $2.75-$3.50. Step up to the bar for sandwiches in a "Jetson" atmosphere of purple and pink plastic. Round outdoor tables are sheltered by a saucer-shaped pavilion. Seats about 100 persons.

The Vegetable Handwich, for example, contains three kinds of cabbage, tomatoes, lettuce and Italian dressing in a cracked wheat bun. It's good for you, but "We sell more hot dogs," confided one of the servers at the Space Bar.

Magic Kingdom Attractions

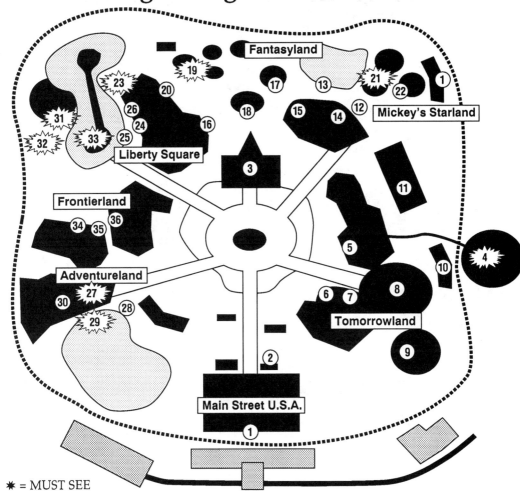

✳ = MUST SEE

1. Walt Disney World Railroad
2. Main Street Cinema
3. Cinderella Castle
✳4. Space Mountain
5. Mission to Mars
6. Circlevision 360
   "American Journeys"
7. Dreamflight
8. StarJets
9. Carousel of Progress
10. Skyway
11. Grand Prix Raceway
12. Mad Tea Party
13. 20,000 Leagues Under the Sea
14. Mr. Toad's Wild Ride
15. Snow White's Adventure
16. Magic Journeys
17. Dumbo, the Flying Elephant
18. Cinderella's Golden Carrousel

✳19. It's a Small World
20. Peter Pan's Flight
✳21. Mickey's Hollywood Theater, etc.
22. Grandma Duck's Farm
✳23. The Haunted Mansion
24. The Hall of Presidents
25. Liberty Square Riverboat
26. Mike Fink Keelboats
✳27. Pirates of the Caribbean
28. Swiss Family Treehouse
✳29. Jungle Cruise
30. Tropical Serenade
✳31. Big Thunder Mountain Railroad
✳32. Splash Mountain
✳33. Tom Sawyer Island
34. Country Bear Vacation Hoedown
35. Frontierland Shootin' Arcade
36. Diamond Horseshoe Jamboree

Magic Kingdom Restaurants

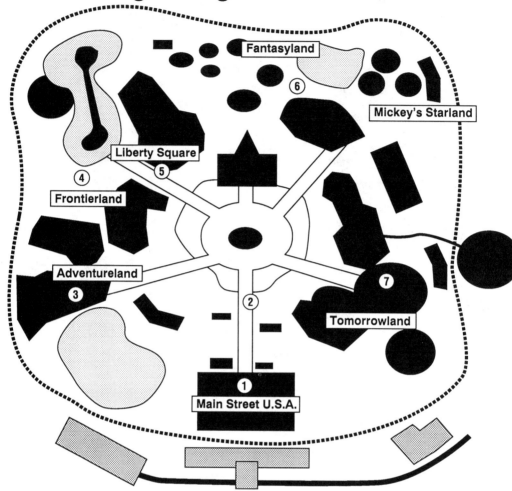

1 Main Street Wagons
Main Street Bake Shop
Plaza Ice Cream Parlor

2 The Crystal Palace
Tony's Town Square Restaurant
The Plaza Restaurant

3 Adventureland Veranda
Sunshine Tree Terrace
El Pirata & El Perico
The Oasis
Aloha Isle
Egg Roll Wagon

4 Pecos Bill Cafe & Mile Long Bar
Westward Ho
Turkey Leg Wagon

5 Columbia Harbour House
Sleepy Hollow
Liberty Tree Tavern
Liberty Square Wagon
Fruit & Vegetable Wagon

6 Pinocchio Village Haus
Gurgi's Munchies & Crunchies
The Round Table
King Stefan's Banquet Hall
Troubadour Tavern

7 Tomorrowland Terrace
Plaza Pavilion
Lunching Pad
Space Bar

CHAPTER 7
Epcot Center

Walt Disney's original concept called for construction of a modern city from scratch: homes, offices, farms and factories. It was intended as a showcase for new ideas and technologies from American industry and educational institutions.

Disney called his dream the Experimental Prototype Community of Tomorrow, which is the almost-forgotten name behind the acronym, Epcot.

Disney lived long enough to set the broad outlines for Epcot; at The Walt Disney Story in the Magic Kingdom you can see an old film of him pointing to a model of the city. But just as the model looks nothing like the theme park that exists today, Epcot is quite different from the prototype community he first planned.

The second theme park at Walt Disney World is like a permanent World's Fair. Roughly half the park is given over to imaginative pavilions that explore the frontiers of science: communication, energy, human life, transportation, technology, creativity, agriculture and the seas. And then spread around the "world lagoon" are exhibits, films and a handful of rides that share some of the cultures of the globe: from Canada, the United Kingdom, France, Morocco, Japan, America, Italy, Germany, China, Norway and Mexico.

Although it is most likely the lure of Mickey and Minnie's Magic Kingdom that brings most visitors to Walt Disney World, many adults and quite a few children will tell you that the memory they bring home from Florida comes from Epcot: Figment at Journey into Imagination or the fam-

Facts and figures.
EPCOT, at 260 acres, is more than twice the size of the Magic Kingdom. The World Showcase Lagoon is about 40 acres in size; the promenade that circles it and leads to the national showcases is 1.2 miles in length. Initial construction costs were about $1.3 billion, one of the largest private construction jobs ever completed, in 1982.

MUST-SEES

WOW

Spaceship Earth
(Future World)

Universe of Energy
(Future World)

Wonders of Life: Body Wars
(Future World.)

Wonders of Life: Cranium Command
(Future World)

Horizons
(Future World)

World of Motion
(Future World)

Journey Into Imagination
(Future World)

The Land: Listen to the Land
(Future World)

El Rio del Tiempo
(Mexico)

Maelstrom
(Norway)

Wonders of China
(People's Republic of China)

The American Adventure
(United States)

THE
POWER TRIP

The key to getting the most out of a visit to Epcot is to adopt a contrarian's view of the park. Most visitors saunter into the park in mid-morning and join the crowds at the pavilions of Future World before beginning a slow–and crowded–circle of the World Showcase section in a clockwise direction. Another important bit of information is the fact that Spaceship Earth and the surrounding Earth Station and Communicore buildings open 30 to 60 minutes before the rest of Epcot. Therefore, do the following:

Get there early. Walk onto the empty **Spaceship Earth** ride when the turnstiles open. Go downstairs to Earth Station and make reservations for an evening dinner, if desired, at one of the World Showcase restaurants.

When the gates to the rest of Epcot open, walk through Future World without joining any of the growing lines and head for the World Showcase. Bear to the right and circle the lagoon in a counterclockwise direction. The World Showcase is all-but deserted in the early morning, and you will be going against the natural inclination of most visitors.

After you come out of the World Showcase, tour the pavilions of Future World, this time moving in a clockwise direction-starting at Journey Into Imagination and heading toward the front of the park and Spaceship Earth. Double back at the golf ball and visit Energy, Life, Horizons and Motion to complete your tour.

With luck, you will complete the tour of Epcot at nightfall and can enjoy a leisurely dinner before coming out to the lagoon for a view of the spectacular Illuminations show.

Here's a by-the-numbers power trip, pavilion-by-pavilion. 1: **Spaceship Earth**; 2: **Canada**; 3: **United Kingdom**; 4: **France**; 5: **Morocco**; 6: **Japan**; 7: **United States**; 8: **Italy**; 9: **Germany**; 10: **China**; 11: **Norway**; 12: **Mexico**; 13: **Journey Into Imagination**; 14: **The Land**; 15: **The Living Seas**; 16: **Universe of Energy**; 17: **Wonders of Life**; 18: **Horizons**, and 19: **World of Motion**.

AN ALTERNATE PLAN

Epcot is unique among the three parks at Walt Disney World in that it has two entrances–the main door, which leads directly to the Spaceship Earth, and a second, less-used gate at the World Showcase, between the pavilions of the United Kingdom and France. Trams or little ferry boats run between the International Gateway here and the Swan, Dolphin, Beach Club and Yacht Club resorts.

If you enter here, you'll save 30 minutes in the morning stroll from the main entrance to the World Lagoon. We'd suggest you immediately head around the World Showcase to France, Morocco and so on, moving on to Future World after the Mexican pavilion.

ily of the future at Horizons or the troll at Norway or the film view of the Great Wall at China.

Spend the time at Epcot and talk about the things you learn there; that may be the greatest legacy of Disney.

FUTURE WORLD
SPACESHIP EARTH

WOW **Spaceship Earth.** The huge geodesic sphere that is the symbol of Epcot–referred to by most visitors as the "golf-ball"-is 180 feet (18 stories) high, and 160 feet in diameter. It weighs almost 16 million pounds including 1,750 tons of steel. The building is not a dome, since it is completely spherical, and it is not a perfect ball in shape.

As impressive as the shell is, the real excitement of Spaceship Earth can be found on the ride within, which is sponsored by communications giant AT&T. (Each of the major exhibits at Epcot's World of the Future is sponsored by a major American corporation. The commercialism is relatively low-key at each.)

The exhibit was designed by an interesting collaboration that included science fiction author Ray Bradbury, the Smithsonian Institution and newsman Walter Cronkite, who narrates the show. You'll board "time machine" chairs for a trip through the sphere that will take you back through history to the age of the Cro-Magnon man some 30,000 years ago to the present, along the way passing through the great ancient civilizations of Egypt, Phoenicia and Rome. The narration may be a bit beyond the comprehension of young children, but they'll still enjoy and learn from the sights.

You'll note some of the truly important developments of our time, including the development of written language and an alphabet, the first books, the development of the printing press and on to modern communications. Great cultural figures from Michelangelo (the painter, not the Ninja Turtle) at work in the Sistine Chapel to Howdy Doody and Ed Sullivan. At the very top of the ball is the most spectacular sight of all, a huge sky of stars and planets. Not all of the special effects of this ride are visual ones; Disney engineers created smell cannons that fill the air with odors including those of burning Rome.

Because of its position at the front of the park, lines for this ride are usually longest at the start of the day, although early arrivals can still expect to be able to walk right on. If the line builds up, though, we'd suggest coming back in the afternoon or on your way out of the park at the end of the day.

Tubular, dude. The Spaceship Earth sphere is built from four structural parts. The outer shell is strictly for decorative purposes, and is connected to an inner waterproof sphere by hundreds of small support columns. A column that runs up the center of the ball supports the internal ride, which circles around the column like a spiral staircase. And finally, a platform at the bottom of the sphere supports the inner structure and the ride itself.

Hard ride. As befits the unusual building, the time machines in this ride take an unusual route. You'll slowly spiral up, up and up around the sides of the ball until you reach the starfield at top; then your chair will turn around for a steep, backward descent to the base. Some riders might find the trip down a bit uncomfortable.

Smell-o-vision. It is not just your eyes and ears that are reporting your relocation to prehistoric times. Damp air and sulphur-like odors are blasted from hidden nozzles. (A complementary system of filters quickly removes the smells from the air so that they don't linger.)

Earth Station. In the base of the sphere is an interesting collection of communications devices, including the WorldKey Information Service. WorldKey features several dozen touch-screen video terminals at various locations in Epcot Center, is a prototype audio-video-text information system. It was developed by Walt Disney Productions and AT&T. The terminals offer up-to-the-minute information on Epcot attractions, showcases, restaurants, shops and services. You can also use the terminals to make reservations at most major Epcot Center restaurants, speaking with a host or hostess using a television camera and hands-free microphone.

Communicore East. An interesting collection of hands-on interactive activities for children and adults, perfect for a rainy day or a break from the heat of a Florida summer. **Computer Central** includes the **Compute-a-Coaster** game, an interactive computer-assisted design simulation of a roller coaster, and the **Energy Exchange,** an interactive simulation of the search for oil and gas, an outgrowth of the Exxon's Energy pavilion.

Also within is **Travelport,** a full-service American Express travel and financial services agency.

Communicore West. Past Spaceship Earth to the right is another collection of futuristic exhibits. At **FutureCom** you'll find a demonstration of communications technologies including computers, speech synthesis and laser beams. There's not much "gee whiz" for the sophisticated adult here, but kids may enjoy some of the hands-on exhibits, including **Expo Robotics.**

And Disney deserves credit for **Epcot Outreach,** an information and resource center for all visitors. Are you interested in some of the oil drilling technologies shown in the Energy movie? Want to know how Circlevision 360 films are made? Do you have a question about the history of Morocco? Ask one of the librarians here and they'll draw answers from computerized databases, books and documents. There's even a **Teacher's Center** where educators can obtain free copies of lesson plans about Future World topics and preview films, videos, computer software and other media resources.

UNIVERSE OF ENERGY

Universe of Energy. The most theatrically and technically dazzling exhibit at Epcot, it tells the story of the role of energy in our lives in a series of spectacular films and a trip back in time to the days of the dinosaurs that will leave you breathless with wonder and fills the minds of young children with questions and answers.

Before you begin your journey, you will gather in the preshow area to view an exciting and innovative film presentation. The "screen" is made up of 100 triangular elements with black, white and reflective surfaces. Five 35mm projectors are linked to a computer system that rotates the triangles among about one billion different combinations.

The magic starts the moment that your seats in a huge auditorium suddenly start moving–whole sections of rows break up into travelling cars that enter directly into the world of the dinosaurs. The huge beasts will droop their heads over your cars, hungrily eyeing your camera bags. Great leathery birds circle overhead. Pools of lava bubble all around and the heavy vegetation drips with humidity.

The 5-minute film in the Universe of Energy Theater which opens the show tells the story of the creation of fossil fuels. One of the most ambitious animated and live action films ever done, it is projected on a screen 22 feet high and 155 feet wide. The 35mm film moves horizontally, with each frame about six times larger than a standard movie image.

The second major movie is presented in the Universe of Energy Theater II, on a gigantic wraparound screen 30 feet high by 210 feet wide. A set of three 70 mm projectors operate at 30 frames per second–standard projection rate is 24 fps–to eliminate flickering images. The footage of the North Sea and Alaskan oil fields are stupendous (although there is not an Exxon Valdez anywhere to be seen) and the pictures of the blast off of the Space Shuttle are the next best thing to being there.

As marvelous as the films are, we'll still bet a set of mouse ears that it is the ride you tell your friends about when you return home.

This is, as we have noted, a not-to-be-missed show at Epcot. Lines begin to build in the morning and continue until late afternoon; it's best to visit the ride early or late in the day. In any case, the auditorium is quite large, swallowing about 600 visitors every 15 minutes.

The very best seats in the house are in the front row of the leftmost theater car; this section moves first and there are no other visitors in front of you to disturb the illusion of time travel. If you can't maneuver into that seat, try to

Alternate sources.
The traveling theater cars are driven by electrical motors that draw their power from batteries; the batteries are recharged by electromagnetic induction without direct contact.

On the roof is a solar energy system made up of 80,000 photovoltaic cells, the largest private solar power system in the world. Each four-inch cell can generate about one watt of DC power on a sunny day. The 70,000 watts of DC power are fed through an inverter and converted to AC and used to help power the Traveling Theatres within. The equivalent power could be used to supply all of the energy needs of 15 single-family homes.

get into the front row of the two other sections.

WONDERS OF LIFE

A world of its own, under one roof you will find two of Epcot's best attractions, plus a healthful Fitness Fairground for children of all ages and a set of entertaining and informative films and presentations on subjects from exercise to reproduction.

WOW **Body Wars.** Strap on your seat belts and prepare for blastoff on a journey to Inner Space. Body Wars is a fantastic simulator ride that takes you on a repair expedition inside a human body–a training mission to remove a splinter from within.

The simulation cabin bounces and twists through the veins and arteries of the human body, ending up at the brain where your vehicle will recharge its batteries with a bang.

Amazingly, for a vehicle that doesn't really go anywhere, this ride carries as many health warnings as a roller coaster. No pregnant women or persons with back or heart ailments are allowed aboard, and children under seven must be accompanied by an adult. Those less than three years of age cannot ride. If you're the type who gets queasy on an elevator–and you know who you are-you might want to pass this one by.

WOW **Cranium Command.** One of the wildest and most offbeat shows anywhere in Walt Disney World, this is a combination AudioAnimatronics and film journey into one of the most unstable places on earth. (Your screaming leader, Gen. Knowledge, will inform you that you have been assigned to pilot the most unstable craft in the fleet–the mind of a 12-year-old boy.)

This is a presentation that has something for everyone, from corny jokes and a food fight for the kids to smart one-liners and comic performances from well-known comedians including George Wendt (Norm from "Cheers") as superintendent of the stomach, Bobcat Goldthwait in a typecast role as an hysterical adrenaline gland, and Charles Grodin as the smug, all-knowing Right Brain. All this to teach about the benefits of stress management!

It's a very clever show, and rarely more than a 15-minute wait; don't pass it by.

Fitness Fairgrounds. The various exhibits in the center of the dome can occupy visitors for hours, and are a great place to get out of the sun or rain. Our only warning

Super helix. The huge sculpture at the entrance to the Wonders of Life pavilion is a 72-foot-tall representation of a DNA molecule, the basic building block of life.

Back to the future? The Body Wars story is a spinoff of the classic science fiction movie, "Fantastic Voyage," which included Raquel Welch in a body suit.

about this place is that it is quite easy to misplace young children in the busy aisles.

"Goofy About Health." You wouldn't ordinarily include our old friend Goofy on a list of contenders for the Olympic team, but this very entertaining film presentation teaches about the value of exercise and health habits as it entertains.

AnaComical Players. A lively and pun-filled tour of the human body, presented by a clever improvisational theater group.

"The Making of Me." Okay, parents: here's an opportunity to teach your children some of the facts of life in an entertaining 14-minute film starring comedian Martin Short. He begins with a visit to the birth of his mom and dad and follows them right through his own conception (lovemaking is described as a private moment between lovers, with just enough detail to guarantee your kids will come up with their own questions.) There is spectacular footage of the beginnings of life and childbirth. Lines for this show–presented in a tiny theater–can begin to stretch to as much as an hour at the most crowded parts of the day; go early or late. Highly recommended.

Coach's Corner. Step up to the batting tee, the tennis net or the fairway for a quick sports lesson. Your swing will be videotaped and you'll receive a quick taped comment from one of sport's greatest players. It's all in good fun, although some adults seem to take their moment of stardom very seriously.

Wondercycles. A very high-tech set of exercise bicycles which present videodisc images that are keyed to your pedaling speed. You can "visit" Disneyland, a winding mountain road or a big city bike path.

Sensory Funhouse. A set of interesting demonstrations of human senses, including sight, sound and touch.

Met Lifestyle Revue. A computer will ask you all sorts of personal questions, and then offer a personalized set of lifestyle suggestions.

The best way to tour Wonders of Life is to keep an eye on the waiting lines for Body Wars and Cranium Command and dive in when they seem reasonable. There is plenty to occupy visitors between trips to those attractions.

Everything new is old someday. It's amusing to contrast the entertaining Horizons show with the very dated Carousel of Progress at the Magic Kingdom's Tomorrow-land, which was originally produced for General Electric's pavilion at the 1964-1965 New York World's Fair.

Cybernetic cats. There's a great deal of attention to detail in the family scenes; we're fond of the pussycat robot chasing mechanical fish in a pond outside the home of the future.

Neon sign. The "speed tunnel" which makes you feel that your vehicle is moving rapidly makes unusual use of liquid neon, illuminated in segments as it moves through tubes. The blue sheet lightning from the airport of the future is generated by a pair of helium-cadmium lasers.

HORIZONS

Horizons. Epcot has been called a permanent World's Fair exhibit, and the Horizons show fits that definition to a futuristic T. You'll climb into a four-seat vehicle for a beautifully crafted glimpse at a vision of the future that includes the Omega Centauri space colony, the Sea Castle underwater city and the robotic farm station Mesa Verde.

The ride also casts a bemused eye backward at some of the predictions of old, including Jules Verne's novels and other futuristic writings of the past century.

Horizons includes a spectacular journey into space as your ride car travels deep into a huge hemispherical screen; talk about a front row seat! You'll also progress into a DNA molecule and swim with the fishes.

You'll visit a world of tomorrow in which scientist-farmers manage farms in the desert, cities beneath the sea and space colonies. The last segment of the ride allows the four passengers in your vehicle to "vote" on a destination for a quick exploration trip just for your car.

Lines for this excellent attraction are usually quite manageable, so long as you don't become caught in the throng when the nearby Universe of Energy theater lets out. If the doors to that 600-seat theater show have just opened, come back between shows and save yourself much of the wait.

WORLD OF MOTION

World of Motion. Another World's Fair-type exhibit, it traces the history of transportation from the invention of the wheel (check out the square failures that came first) to modern time. Along the way you'll see some marvelous antiques and reproductions and more than 140 Audio-Animatronic figures in 24 different scenes. Check out the robo-cop on a motorcycle hiding behind the billboard. And pay close attention to the sternwheeler; is that paddle wheel going backwards?

After the 15-minute ride, you'll enter into the **TransCenter**, where sponsor General Motors has an interesting display of new automobile and transportation technologies including weird-shaped aerodynamic vehicles. Oh, and there is the single most overt bit of commercialism at Epcot: a showroom of (surprise!) GM cars.

There is rarely much of a line at this exhibit because the nearby Horizons and Energy pavilions tend to soak up and even out the flow of visitors in the area. Therefore, one "contrary" way to visit this part of Epcot is to go to Motion first, then either Horizons or Energy, depending on waiting lines there.

JOURNEY INTO IMAGINATION

WOW **Journey into Imagination.** This attraction includes some of the most unusual special effects at Epcot and is a clear favorite among youngsters. The wonderment starts outside the doors: stop for a while at the fountains to the left of the entranceway and watch jets of water arc majestically from tube to tube.

The ride within introduces you to Dreamfinder and his pet purple dragon Figment (as in "of imagination".) They'll take you along on an expedition to collect colors, sounds, shapes and stories with which to create new ideas. The opening segment of the ride puts your vehicle on the outside track of a large rotating room—there are several Dreamfinders and Figments in pie-wedge shaped stages that move with a group of viewers for a while.

The Magic Journeys segment of the 13-minute ride presents some of the highest-resolution and most astounding 3-D images ever created. Disney technicians developed a 65mm 3-D camera capable of shooting as many as 75 frames per second—three times the speed of a conventional camera—for use in creating slowmotion displays. The 3-D system consists of a pair of linked cameras—one that shoots through a partially silvered beamsplitter mirror and the other that shoots a right angle to the mirror. Some other images were entirely created on a computer, a glimpse at the future of 3-D imaging.

As we've noted, this ride is a treat for the kids; some adults might find it a bit too sweet. Lines can build up to an hour or so by midday; visit early or late.

Image Works. When the ride is over, don't pass up the chance to climb the stairs or ride the glass-tube elevator to the Image Works area upstairs. Here you'll find some of the most interesting "hands on" experiences at Epcot.

You can conduct an Electronic Philharmonic by waving your hands through light beams. Youngsters can step into a special effects movie in Dreamfinder's School of Drama, where computers merge foreground, background and live-action video images. Banks of computers allow visitors to change their own appearance on video screens. At the Rainbow Corridor, visitors are assigned one of five colors by a computer and then tracked by infrared detectors as they walk or run through the tube.

Back door. You don't have to line up to take the Journey into Imagination ride to visit the Image Works. Just walk to the left of the waiting area for the ride and head for the stairs or elevator.

In fact, for some younger children, Image Works is one of the high points of Epcot, worth an hour or so of indoor exploration, especially valuable on a rainy or overly warm day.

Magic Eye Theater: Captain EO. Whether you worship Michael Jackson as the "King of Pop", or consider him one very strange dude, you can't help but marvel at the fantastic 17minute movie put together by director Francis Ford Coppola ("The Godfather," "Apocalypse Now" and other films.)

It's a loud, flashy rock 'n roll science fiction opera that combines two Jackson songs ("We Are Here to Change the World," and "Another Part of Me") with spectacular 3-D effects and laser beams.

You'll be issued a pair of plastic glasses at the door. How real are the 3-D scenes? Take a look around when Hooter the owl flies out over the audience: everyone in every corner of the theater is reaching out to touch him.

Lines ebb and flow at the theater, reached from an entrance inside the doors of the Journey Into Imagination to the left of the loading area for the theme ride. Waits rarely reach more than 20 minutes.

THE LAND

Everyone has to eat, and The Land is a tasty collection of informative exhibits about food and our environment. The building, in part a gigantic greenhouse, also includes a popular food court restaurant.

WOW **Listen to The Land.** A boat ride through the past and future of agriculture. Your guide (no, he or she is not an Audio Animatronic robot, although "Dan", our guide on one quiet day, was so bored he could have passed for a cyborg) leads you through a rain forest, desert and plain–traditional sources of food–and then into some amazing experiments with hydroponic farms, cultivated seafood farms of shrimp and fish and a desert made to bloom with crops through high-tech irrigation.

Among the advanced techniques you will see are "intercropping" of different plants to make the best use of soil and nutrients–coconut, cacao and sweet potatoes in one example; growing plants vertically in hydroponic (soilless) containers which make them easier to feed and inspect for pests and an experiment in growing plants in simulated lunar soil, based on analysis of the real thing brought back from the moon by American astronauts.

A fish farming "aquacell" grows crops of fish selected

Gomez, mon amour. The evil Supreme Leader in "Captain EO" is played by Academy Award winner Angelica Huston, who may be better known to youngsters as Morticia in the recent "Addams Family" movie.

Farm stand. The simulated tropical and desert farms of The Land create vegetables for some of the restaurants in the pavilion.

Wide world. The Land is one of the largest attractions at Walt Disney World. It covers some six acres and is as big as the entire Tomorrowland area in the Magic Kingdom. Stop and take a look at the huge mosaic at the entrance: some 3,000 square feet in size, it is made of 150,000 separate pieces of marble, granite, slate, smalto (colored glass or enamel), Venetian glass, mirror, ceramic, pebbles and gold in 131 colors.

for their ability to thrive in a crowded environment. Fish under development on one trip included Sunshine Bass, Tilapia and the strange-looking Paddlefish, which is cultivated for its caviar.

Among the most educational of all the exhibits at Epcot, it is also a gentle place for a 15-minute break. Preschoolers may be bored, but anyone else will be sure to find something to learn. Lines build by midday to as much as an hour in length; come early or late.

Kitchen Kabaret. If you need a break from the seriousness of some parts of Epcot, step into the Kitchen Kabaret for some seriously silly entertainment.

This is an Audio Animatronics show, sort of an edible version of the Country Bear Vacation Hoedown at the Magic Kingdom. Your stars include that well-known comedy team Hamm and Eggz, the Boogie Woogy Bak'ry Boys and assorted wise-cracking fruits and vegetables such as Mr. Broccoli and Mairzy Oats. There are four acts to this play, each devoted to one of the main food groups. Youngsters will be enthralled; older visitors may enjoy the awful puns.

Lines are rarely more than one show length (about 15 minutes), and so this is a good place to chill out at midday while other attractions are crowded.

Harvest Theater: Symbiosis. A marvelous, sweeping 70mm movie that tells of our failures and successes with the environment. Filming took place in some 30 nations around the globe. The very young will likely snooze.

Lines are rare for this 20-minute show, except at midday.

Inside glimpse. If you hunger to learn even more about agriculture of the future, make reservations for the free 45minute behind-the-scenes **Harvest Tour.** Sign up at the Guided Tour Waiting Area, on the lower level of The Land, all the way to the right of the food court near Broccoli and Co. Tours begin every half hour from 9:30 a.m. to 4:30 p.m.

THE LIVING SEAS

An ambitious but ultimately unsatisfying bust. If you or your children are truly interested in learning about the watery two-thirds of our planet, you would be much better off visiting Sea World or a big-city aquarium.

But, as long as you are in Epcot, check out some of the exhibits and interactive areas. Take a look at some of the early diving gear in the waiting area. When you enter the auditorium for a short film, lag back a bit and get a seat along the left side so that you will be first in line to enter the "hydrolators."

Caribbean Coral Reef Ride. The idea was great–take visitors on a tour within a huge saltwater aquarium filled with strange and wonderful marine life including sharks,

Don't read this. We don't want to spoil the illusion here. So, if you don't want to know an inside tip about the hydrolators, stop reading this sidebar right here. Okay? You've been warned. The hydrolators don't really dive down beneath the sea; the floor moves a few inches to simulate movement and bubbles move up the sides of elevator. Then you walk out the door on the other side of the wall.

stingrays, parrot fish and more. But the trip takes just three minutes and the set-up to the ride–the trip deep down below the sea in elevator-like "hydrolators" is hokey–and there's no chance to stop and study. Check out the phony "Dept. of Pelagic Safety" certificate in the hydrolator.

Sea Base Alpha. A series of sometimes interesting exhibits about underwater technologies and sea life. Spend a few moments studying the wave tank to understand the physics of breakers at the beach. Youngsters will enjoy climbing into the diving suits, and adults can grab a good picture when they poke their heads into the breathing bubbles.

Lines tend to build through the day at The Living Seas, so if you insist on visiting the exhibit, go early or late.

EATING YOUR WAY THROUGH EPCOT & FUTURE WORLD

🍴 **Stargate Restaurant.** *Communicore East.* Omelettes, burgers, salads, and snacks, $1-$5.50. Breakfast, Lunch, Dinner.

A large fast food restaurant with a few unusual offerings including a Spanish omelette-like concoction called Stellar Scramble, made from eggs, ham, onions, cheese, green peppers and more. The "Morning Star" is a less complicated omelet that includes cheese and Canadian bacon. Each is about $4.

More standard fare includes pizza, burgers and salads. The "Grand Solarburger" is a fancy name for a large cheeseburger with french fries, $5.25. A chicken breast sandwich is $4.

Lemon pie ($1.50) and apple pie ($2) are available daily, along with a "pie of the month."

🍴 **Sunrise Terrace Restaurant.** *Communicore West,* opposite Stargate Restaurant. Vaguely Italian, including pizza, pasta, salads, and snacks, $2-$6. Children's menu, $3-$4. Lunch, Dinner.

The very futuristic decor is colored in purple, black and white. The dining area is large, with high ceilings and open rooms. The large round tables seat 5 or 6 easily.

The pasta here is about as fresh as you could hope for; you can watch it being made in the glass enclosed booth alongside the serving lines. Select "Pasta and Pizza," or "Pasta, Pasta, Pasta" for pasta samples, $4.25. Lasagna is $5.25 and deep dish pizza by the slice, $3.25. For the light appetite, choose the small chef's salad, $2, or the antipasto salad with meats for $5.

KEY

🍴 = FAST FOOD

🍷 = PUB

🏠 = FULL-SERVICE RESTAURANT

🍴 **Pure & Simple.** *Wonders of Life,* across from the AnaComical Players' stage. Waffles and fruit, salads, sandwiches, frozen yogurt and sundaes. "Guilt free goodies," $1.50-$5.

Well named for its small offerings of frozen yogurt and shakes, muffins and other healthy fare, presented in an attractive cafe-like setting. Seating is at colorful blue metal tables and chairs, like something out of the Jetsons.

ODYSSEY COMPLEX

🍴 **Odyssey Restaurant.** *Between Future World and the World Showcase near the Mexico pavilion.* Burgers, hot dogs, fried chicken, and snacks, $3.50-$5. Lunch, Dinner.

This very large restaurant offers familiar burger and fried chicken fare; a modest salad bar offers toppings for burgers and hot dogs. A char-broiled chicken sandwich is $5; a quarter-pound hot dog is $4.25. The "OrbitBurger" is a lean beef hamburger for $4.25. Desserts include key lime pie ($2), Toll House pie ($2.25), or peanut butter cookies ($1.10).

The dining area is a large, spacious room with plenty of windows, a high ceiling, and interesting mirrors. Large round tables seat five or six easily. Even if you don't decide to eat here, you may want to use this restaurant as a cut through to Mexico from Future World.

THE LAND

🍴 **Farmers Market.** The Farmer's Market is a series of different food shops located downstairs in *The Land* pavilion. The food court is dedicated to healthy meals and snacks, $1.25-$7. Breakfast, Lunch, Dinner. A most interesting concept: fast *good* food.

This downstairs location offers an interesting view of the pavilion's four-story ceiling that includes three large balloons that move up and down over a central fountain. Seating is available in this center section around the fountain.

Stands include the **Barbecue Store,** offering beef and chicken sandwiches ($4.50-$5) or chicken and ribs ($6-$7); the **Picnic Fare** with cheeses, sausages and fruit; the **Bakery,** a fine place for breakfast bagels, rolls and muffins and luncheon breads, cakes and cookies; the **Cheese Shoppe,** offering quiche, pasta, vegetable lasagna and . . . cheese, and the **Potato Store,** selling baked potatoes with stuffing including cheese, bacon and beef ($2-$3.25). Dessert counters include the **Beverage House** ($1.25-$2.50) and the **Ice**

KEY

🍴 = FAST FOOD

🍸 = PUB

🏠 = FULL-SERVICE RESTAURANT

Mickey goes futuristic. Check out the schedule for the Disney character shows that are presented on a small stage at the back of the Odyssey Restaurant, facing the lagoon. They're a nice treat for younger visitors who keep looking back over their shoulders toward the Magic Kingdom.

Food pile. While you're chowing down on your turkey burger, consider the fact that the site of the Odyssey Restaurant was originally a 6-acre sinkhole, with mud and quicksand as deep as 130 feet. Engineers brought in huge amounts of sand, and then drove hollow piles as long as 280 feet. The piles were filled with cement and then used to support the slab for the building.

Hold the grease. One of the best things about eating at The Farmers Market in The Land is that everyone in your party can eat something different, shopping at the various stands and meeting at a table in the court. Just don't promise your kids a hot dog, a greasy burger or fries when you arrive to eat; you'll have to get those elsewhere.

Fast food? The speed of rotation of the Land Grille Room is adjusted to about one revolution per meal. The lunchtime speed is slightly quicker (about 448 feet per hour); dinnertime slows the turntable down to about 422 feet per hour. Either way, you're not likely to suffer from jet lag.

Glassy-eyed. The best seats in the tank, err . . . restaurant called The Coral Sea are eight tables along the glass wall. Other tables are as much as 20 feet from the fish. However, the restaurant is arranged in three terraces that give all guests a relatively good view of the aquarium wall.

Cream Stand ($1.50-$2.75). Select a double chocolate brownie ($1.25), giant cookies ($1.50), or apple pie ($2).

For younger appetites, choose "Mickey's Children's Meal," with peanut butter and jelly sandwich, potato chips, cookie and a surprise, for $2.75.

The Land Grille Room. Upstairs in *The Land* pavilion. Lobster, shrimp, steak, ribs and sandwiches. Lunch, $8.50-$20; Dinner, $16-$26. Lunch and dinner children's offerings, $3-$5.50. Breakfast, $5-$14.

One of the most attractive and interesting full-service restaurants in the Future World section of Epcot, the entire room revolves around a portion of the "Listen to the Land" boat tour down below. Unfortunately, the food is a bit overpriced and by most reports a bit overrated; in other words, come for the view. A selection of lunch salads is offered for $2.50-$8.50; soup and salads included with dinner. Lunch entrees include stir fry shrimp, salmon, chicken, fish or beef. Dinner includes larger portions of the same, with the addition of prime rib, lobster and spare ribs.

Reservations are suggested for lunch and dinner; parties holding confirmed reservation tickets will be permitted to enter directly into The Land pavilion within a half hour of reservation time, bypassing any lines on crowded days.

THE LIVING SEAS

Coral Reef Restaurant. In the lower level of *The Living Seas* exhibit, to the right of the main entrance. Fish, shellfish, beef, chicken, and salads. Lunch, $14.50-$36; Dinner, $19-$38.50. Children's lunch and dinner menu, $3.25-4.50. Beer, mixed drinks, and a full wine list. Reservations are necessary.

Enter under a large, curved entrance that resembles a giant clam to a pleasant waiting area decorated with macrame fish.

This place gives a new meaning to the title, Seafood Restaurant. We kept seeing diners nervously eying the passing sharks in the coral reef behind the huge windows alongside the tables; we suspect they worried they were going to *be* the seafood.

Anyhow, there is a fine selection of fish and shellfish; there are also some beef and chicken selections. Choose from 11 lunchtime appetizers from $3-$11, among the most interesting, the "Seas Sampler (barbecue shrimp, Oysters Rockefeller, baked clams), $9.50. A chilled Rockefeller Salad includes fried oysters and spinach, $10, and entrees include smoked grouper ($14.50) or pan-seared swordfish ($18.50). Children can choose from four smaller portions, including fettuccine with tomato and meat sauce ($4) and fried chicken strips ($4.75).

The dinner appetizer selection is the same as for lunch. For an entree, consider the mixed seafood grill (tuna, salmon, shrimp), for $22.50, or "Woodsman" chicken ($17.50), beef tenderloin ($24), and oriental seafood ($22).

Six dessert items are available for lunch and dinner, including key lime pie ($3) and fresh strawberries in a white chocolate shell with Grand Marnier sauce ($5.50).

KEY

🍴 = FAST FOOD

🍸 = PUB

🎪 = FULL-SERVICE RESTAURANT

WORLD SHOWCASE
MEXICO

The pavilion is set within a striking pre-Colombian style pyramid, festooned with giant serpent heads and sculptures of Toltec warriors. Inside is a magical wonderland of a happy Mexican village. You'll enter into the colorful **Plaza de Los Amigos** village plaza, filled with carts selling handcrafted sombreros of varying sizes, toys, sandals and other objects–sold at prices that are relative bargains within Walt Disney World. On a terrace near the "river," a mariachi band lets loose with its almost-impossibly happy sound.

And down by the water, there's a charming Mexican cantina. The food is good, not great, but in our opinion the **San Angel Inn and Restaurant** is one of the most spectacular settings for dinner within the park, a magical indoor setting.

El Rio del Tiempo. A charming, happy journey to Mexico–sort of a south-of-the-border version of the Magic Kingdom's "It's A Small World." This boat ride, though, is sure to appeal to children of all ages. There's a touch of Mexico's majestic past as a regional power, a greeting from a Mayan high priest, a humorous acknowledgement of the country's present day as a tourist mecca (enjoy the salespeople who scuttle from screen to screen to try to sell their wares and a dazzling indoor fireworks salute as dozens of animated dolls dance around you.)

The Mexican pavilion can become quite crowded at midday; we suggest a visit before 11 a.m. or after dinner.

NORWAY

The Land of the Midnight Sun has constructed one of the more interesting exhibits at Epcot. You'll enter on cobblestone

Art of Mexico (Reign of Glory). Take a few moments on your way into or out of the pavilion to look at the small but spectacular collection of ancient Mexican art.

Northern exposure. The San Angel Inn within the Mexico pavilion is run by the same company that operates the well-known restaurant of the same name in Mexico City.

Cold fire. The indoor fireworks of **El Rio del Tiempo (The River of Time)** are produced with cool fiber optics.

streets of a simulated ancient village; take special note of the wood-stave church modeled after one built in 1250 A.D. There's also an interesting—and very expensive—set of stores offering clothing, crafts and toys.

WOW **Maelstrom.** A dramatic and entertaining look at Norway from Viking times through modern days on a storm-tossed oil platform in the North Sea. You'll board Viking longboats like those used by Erik the Red 1,000 years ago and set sail into a world of fjords, forests and the occasional troll. Some very young visitors may be momentarily scared by the "monsters"; all riders are likely to be thrilled by the indoor lightning storm in the North Sea.

You'll know you are in trouble near the end of the short four-minute ride when one of the trolls will get angry: "I cast a spell: back, back, over the falls." Sure enough, your boat will appear to travel over a cliff to land in the World Lagoon of Epcot, before reversing direction for a gentle plunge down a waterfall.

The Maelstrom ride can become quite crowded at midday; visit early or late.

CHINA

One of the most successful of all of the Epcot pavilions at transporting the visitor to a foreign land. The building is a small-scale but beautifully replicated version of Beijing's Temple of Heaven. On busy days, look for dragon dancers and acrobats performing outside near the replica of the Zhao Yang Men (Gate of the Golden Sun).

WOW **Wonders of China.** Simply breathtaking and not to be missed. A Circle-Vision 360 tour of China guaranteed to open your eyes to the beauty and vastness of this still scarcely known nation. We've all seen pictures of the Great Wall, although never so spectacularly as presented here. And recently, we've been granted views of the fabulous Forbidden City of Beijing, but what a thrill to be able to look back over your shoulder at the gate through which you came. But then, there is more: the incredible Shilin Stone Forest, the Gobi Desert, the Grand Canal, tropical palms and snow-capped mountains.

Lines for this 19-minute film build during the day, but rarely add up to more than about half an hour; come early or late to avoid them altogether. The only drawback to this presentation is the fact that the theater has no seats. There are rows of rails to lean upon—sitting on the rails is frowned upon–and small children and short adults may have a hard time seeing the screen without a lift. To make things even worse, no strollers are allowed within.

House of Whispering Willows. An impressive exhibit of ancient Chinese artifacts in the hallway as you leave the theater.

Yang Feng Shangdian Shopping Gallery. Just like it sounds, an indoor shopping mall of Chinese merchandise, including silk clothing, embroidered items and crafts. A huge collection, it includes some of the more interesting foreign items at Epcot, including silk robes, wooden toys, jewelry and prints. You can also have your name written in Chinese characters on a scroll, t-shirt or sweatshirt at a booth just outside.

GERMANY

Wunderbar! A visit to a make-believe German village complete with a beer garden, Teddy Bear toy shop, wine cellar and a pastry shop of your dreams.

Biergarten. A lively full-service restaurant and beer garden, almost as loud and fun as a hall at the Oktoberfest in Munich–especially as the night goes on. Next door is the **Weinkeller,** which stocks several hundred varieties of German wines as well as a selection of beer mugs, wine glasses and other drinking items.

Der Bücherwurm. A bookworm's delight, filled with books from and about Germany.

Der Teddybär. You've been warned: this is a children-parent-grandparent trap full of fabulous toys, dolls and stuffed animals.

Die Weihnachte Ecke. It's Christmas every day in this shop full of ornaments, decorations and gifts.

Glas Und Porzellan. An outlet of Goebel, a large glass and porcelain maker best known as the maker of Hummel figurines.

Süssigkeiten. We're uncertain whether to recommend you visit this shop on an empty or a full stomach. Let's put it this way: a full stomach will save you a lot of money. The cookies, candies and pretzels are unlike anything you will find this side of Germany, and worth a trip from anywhere.

Volkskunst. A wondrous crafts bazaar of carved dolls, cuckoo clocks, clothing and more.

Big thirst. Germans are serious about their beer; if you ever had any doubts, check out the mugs available for sale at the **Weinkeller.** One of them is big enough for a couple of gallons of brew if you're prone to severe thirst.

Real gold, fake marble. The detailed replica of the angel on top of the campanile (bell tower) in the recreated Venice is covered with real gold leaf. The marble stones for the buildings, though, have no marble in them: they are a modern synthetic.

ITALY

Like China, one of the more successful pavilions in terms of giving the visitor a feeling of walking the streets of a foreign land. Spend some time to study the various architectural styles. Out front is a 105-foot-tall campanile or bell tower, a version of one of the landmarks of St. Mark's Square in Venice and the replica of the square itself is beautifully constructed; all that is missing are the pigeons, which explains why this version of St. Mark's is so Disney-clean.

Down at the edge of the World Lagoon is a gondola mooring. And around the square is a collection of delicious and attractive stores. Outside the square, look for the lively and irreverent performances of Il Commedia di Bologna.

Delizie Italiane. An open-air market with sweet delicacies of all description.

La Bottega Italiana. A stunning collection of fine leather goods, clothing and accessories.

La Gemma Elegante. Elegant gems, gold and less expensive trinkets.

Il Bel Cristallo. Fine crystalware including Venetian glass and porcelain figurines.

THE AMERICAN ADVENTURE

Grumpy and Dopey were absent that day. In the auditorium of The American Adventure, the 12 statues flanking the stage are said to represent the "Spirits of America." On the right, from the back of the hall to the front, you can see Adventure, Self-Reliance, Knowledge, Pioneering, Heritage and Freedom. On the left, from back to front, are Discovery, Compassion, Independence, Tomorrow, Innovation and Individualism. The 44 flags in the Hall of Flags represent the banners that have flown over the Colonial, Revolutionary and independent United States.

WOW **The American Adventure.**

In our early visits to Epcot the United States pavilion was one we passed by as the day got long. It's located at the very back of the park, and besides, we're Americans, so why should be interested in something called "The American Adventure"?

Boy, were we ever wrong! The exhibit here is the ultimate in Disney Audio Animatronics, a rip-roaring flag-waving show on a larger scale than almost anything else at Walt Disney World or anywhere else. The unlikely co-stars of the production are author Mark Twain and statesman and inventor Ben Franklin. Never mind that Twain wasn't born until 45 years after Franklin died; such things don't matter when figures from history are brought back as robots.

The 29-minute show starts with the Pilgrims landing at Plymouth Rock, moves on to scenes including the Boston Tea Party and Gen. George Washington's winter at Valley Forge. There's an eclectic collection of well-known and lesser-known figures of American history and culture, including–to Disney's credit–women, native Americans and blacks. The audience will meet characters such as Teddy Roosevelt, Alexander Graham Bell, Susan B. Anthony, Charles Lindbergh, Frederick Douglass, Chief Joseph and Martin Luther King Jr. On the cultural side are representations of Lucille Ball, Muhammed Ali, Marilyn Monroe, John Wayne and even Walt Disney himself. And don't overlook the imposing Georgian building itself and the various paintings and statues in the hallways.

Lines at The American Adventure can build at midday, but except on the busiest days are rarely larger than the seats in the large auditorium. The best seats are in the first few rows nearest the stage.

American Gardens Theatre. Check at WorldKey or at the United States pavilion for any scheduled folk dance and musical shows at the amphitheater along the World Lagoon.

JAPAN
A typically understated but elegant Japanese setting, featuring a reproduction of an Eighth-Century pagoda from the Horyuji Temple. Each of the five levels of the pagoda symbolize one of the five basic elements: earth, water, fire, wind and sky. Amateur gardeners will marvel at the detail in the rock gardens and ponds.

Bijutsu-kan Gallery. A small museum of Japanese arts, culture and craft. The exhibition is changed from time to time, making it worth a repeat peek if you've seen it before.

Mitsukoshi Department Store. The furthest west branch of a large Japanese department store, offering a selection of clothing, dolls, toys and trinkets. The food section includes some unusual items such as fried sweet potatoes, shrimp flavored chips and tomato crackers. Gardeners may want to bring home a grow-it-yourself bonsai kit.

MOROCCO
Step through the Bab Boujoulad gate to a beautifully detailed replica of the Koutoubia Minaret in Marrakesh and a world of fezzes, veils and belly dancers. Bab Boujoulad is the main gate to the ancient city of Fez, known as the Medina. It was founded in the year 786 by the Idrissids.

Gallery of Arts and History. A museum of arts, crafts and culture, with a changing display. Nearby is a branch of the **Moroccan National Tourist Office** with information for visitors who would like to make a journey to the real thing.

Deep meaning. Among the special effects employed in The American Adventure is multiplane cinematography, first developed by Disney technicians to add the illusion of depth to animated films including "Snow White" and "Pinocchio."

Made in America. Most of the plants and trees of the Japanese garden are native to the Southern U.S., but were selected because they were similar in appearance to those in Japan.

Veiled threat. Belly dancing first came to America in 1893 at the Chicago World's Fair when a Syrian dancer who called herself Little Egypt scandalized viewers with what later came to be named the "hootchy-kootchy." Belly dancing is believed to have originated in Persia (now Iran) and is still popular throughout the Middle East.

Within the courtyard is a collection of fascinating shops, including **Casablanca Carpets** for hand-made Berber and Rabat rugs; **Tangier Traders** for leather goods, woven belts and fezzes; **Medina Arts** for crafts, and **Jewels of the Sahara,** selling silver, gold, beaded and precious and semi-precious jewel items.

FRANCE

Vive la France. France lives in a small scale reproduction of a section of the streets of Paris, complete with an ele-gant theater, shops and a bakery and sweet shop of your dreams. There's even a one-tenth scale Eiffel Tower atop the pavilion. It's for appearance only, though–there is no top-level observation tower as there is in the real thing.

Spend a few moments to look at the architectural styles, which include mansard roofs and iron work harking from France's Belle Epoque (Beautiful Time) in the late 19th century.

"Impressions de France." Enter into the Palais du Cinema for a lovely 18-minute film that hits all of the highlights of France–from Paris to Versailles to Mont St. Michel to Cannes, and lots of lesser-known but equally beautiful settings, accompanied by lovely and familiar music by Jacques Offenbach, Eric Satie, Camille Saint-Saëns and others. The large screens extend 200 degrees around the theater, which has the added advantage of seats for all viewers.

Lines build at midday; visit early or late on crowded days.

Plume et Palette. One of the most high-tone of all shops in Epcot, with its entranceway modeled after one of the more famous decorative entranceways to the Paris Metro subway. The interior of the store and the showcases com-pete with the lovely gifts and artworks for sale here.

La Signature. Get a whiff of the perfumes and a peek at the clothing.

For the gourmand, there is **La Maison du Vin,** which like its name suggests, is a Gallic House of Wines. You can also purchase tastes of finer bottles for about $2 to $4. **Tour Pout Le Gourmet** is everything for the gourmet, including cooking utensils, herbs, spices and specialty foods. And send your sweet tooth to **Galerie des Halles,** a bakery and candy store in a building that is modeled after the famous Les Halles market of Paris.

UNITED KINGDOM

Merry Olde England (and the rest of the United Kingdom)

is represented at Epcot by a selection of attractive shops and a first class pub with a nice selection of British beers; it may be one of the few places in Florida where you can get a decent kidney pie.

The Toy Soldier. Playthings for men and boys, women and girls of all ages. The shop's exterior is modeled after an ancient Scottish manor.

Lords and Ladies. More toys, of a slightly nobler fashion: chess sets, dart boards, beer mugs, stamps and coins and more, inside a hall where the Knights of the Round Table would have felt at home.

Pringle of Scotland. Lay down your chips for beautiful knit sweaters and other articles of clothing.

The Queen's Table. Her Highness may be the only one among us with the available cash to do some serious shopping here, but it's fun to poke (carefully) among the fabulous Royal Doulton china, figurines and Toby mugs.

The Magic of Wales. A gift shop of small items and souvenirs from Wales; prices are most reasonable among U.K. emporia.

The Tea Caddy. Here you'll find considerably more kinds of leaves in bags and cans than you're likely to find at the corner grocery.

CANADA

The vast range of experiences of Canada is reflected in the landmarks of the pavilion. At front is a native Totem pole, out back is a scaled-down Canadian Rocky Mountain and between is a reproduction of the stone and tine Château Laurier in Ottawa.

O Canada! Another breathtaking Circle Vision 360 movie that brings you up close and personal with bobcats, wolves, bears and other creatures of the wild, with human glories like the Cathédral de Notre Dame, on the ski slopes of the Rockies and onto the ice of a hockey game in a scene so real you'll wish you had pads on. Did we mention getting caught in the middle of the rodeo ring in the Calgary Stampede or the breathtaking camera ride down the toboggan slide at Quebec City?

The waiting area for the film is a cave-like mountain lodge from the Canadian Rockies. Be advised that you'll have to stand for this 18-minute movie; it's worth it.

Northwest Mercantile. A modern-day version of a fron-

Disney reality. Look for typical attention to detail in the construction of the buildings in the interesting streets of the United Kingdom. Never mind that the thatched roofs are made from plastic fibers (for fire protection) or the smoke stains applied by artists with paint brushes; you probably didn't notice that until we pointed it out.

Transplants. The gardens of the Canada pavilion are based on the famed Butchart Gardens of Victoria, British Columbia in western Canada.

tier trading post. You'll trade dollars (credit cards accepted, too) for sheepskins, lumberjack shirts, maple syrup and Indian artifacts and crafts.

La Boutique des Provinces. Canadian products from its French regions.

EATING YOUR WAY THROUGH THE WORLD SHOWCASE

MEXICO

🏠 **San Angel Inn.** Traditional Mexican dining. Lunch, $11.50-$15. Dinner, $12-$26. Children's menu, $4-$5. Reservations are suggested.

This restaurant is located inside a simulated Aztec pyramid in the center of the Mexican exhibit.

Probably our favorite location for a restaurant at Epcot. Diners sit on a terrace overlooking the passing boats on the River of Time, under a make-believe starlit sky. It feels about as real as anyplace north of Mexico City. Live percussion music and a mariachi band add to the atmosphere and the enjoyment. Look beyond the River of Time to view pyramids, a volcano and a campfire.

The food is above-average Mexican fare. Lunchtime offerings include the interesting and traditional Mole Poblano (chicken and spices with a chocolate-based sauce), $11.50, or a combination platter (beef taco, enchilada, quesadilla and avocado dip), $10.50. For dinner consider the baked California lobster ($26) or Camarones Enchiladas (Shrimp sauteed with pepper) for $22.50. Notice that the traditional Mole Poblano is offered at dinner for $15.50. If you want to try this interesting meal, try a late lunch and save $5 per plate.

Lunch or dinner children's offerings include soft tortilla with chicken or beef, fried chicken or grilled beef taco. Traditional Mexican desserts include flan ($3) or capirotada (bread pudding) for $4. Alone or with dessert, try Mexican coffee with Kahlua, tequila and cream ($5).

Dos Equis and Tecate beers ($3.50), margaritas ($3.50) and a full wine list also are available.

🍴 **Cantina de San Angel.** Tacos, salads and burritos, $3.50-$5.50.

This outdoor cantina is located opposite the Aztec pyramid, beside the lagoon. Get a quick Mexican fix at this attractive outdoor cafe: tortillas, tostados and sweet churros (fried dough dipped in powdered sugar and cinnamon.)

Night light. The outdoor Cantina de San Angel, outside of the Mexico pavilion along the lagoon, is an interesting place to view the nightly Illuminations show over a cold beer or soft drink. Tables will fill up early.

KEY

🍴 = FAST FOOD

🍸 = PUB

🏠 = FULL-SERVICE RESTAURANT

Small, round, wooden tables seat four under colorful umbrellas during the day and under high, soft-light lanterns at night. Your meal is accompanied by Mexican music in a setting that includes native flowers on a tiled patio inside a stucco wall.

The Platos Mexicanos include corn or flour tortillas filled with chicken or beef ($3.50-$5.50). Side dishes include refried beans or chips and salsa.

For dessert, select Flan ($2) or Churros ($1.50). Drinks include frozen margaritas ($3), or Mexican beer ($3.50).

NORWAY

KEY

⦗Ⱡ⦘= FAST FOOD

⦗Y⦘= PUB

⛰ = FULL-SERVICE RESTAURANT

⛰ **Restaurant Akershus.** Buffet with hot and cold meat, cheese, pasta, and dessert. Lunch, $11 adult or $5 children; Dinner, $17 adult or $8 children. Reservations are available, and necessary on busy days.

This restaurant is located inside a replica of the famous castle of Akershus in the Oslo harbor on the right side of the Epcot Norway exhibit.

Visitors are offered a version of a Royal Norwegian Buffet *koldbord,* or "cold table" with more than 30 items. You'll find more types of herring than you ever imagined possible, along with hot and cold smoked salmon, turkey or mackerel. You can also find meat balls, scrambled eggs, lamb with cabbage, mashed rutabaga, hot smoked pork with honey mustard sauce, and more. Be sure to take advantage of the offers of the waiters and waitresses for guided tours of the koldbord.

Early meals. Oslo, the capital and major port of Norway, lies at the head of the Oslo Fjord. The earliest settlement was on the Akershus Peninsula, where a royal fortress was built about 1300. The building still stands, used for state banquets.

Desserts, wine, beer and soft drinks are a la carte; free refills are offered on soft drinks.

Akershus is an interesting excursion for the adventurous, although most children we know will find the offerings a bit strange and unappealing. Even some adults will consider the buffet to be an unending selection of appetizers with no main course.

The white stone walls and tile floors offer a pleasant, cool atmosphere for lunch or dinner. The "rustic elegance" of high ceilings and exposed wooden beams are enhanced by the appetizing odor of cabbage and vinegar.

⦗Ⱡ⦘ **Kringla Bakeri og Kafé.** Open faced sandwiches, pastries, cakes, $3-$4.

This interesting Kafé is located on the left side of the Norwegian exhibit, behind the replica of the church.

What else would you expect from a Kringla Bakeri than

fresh kringles? All right: a kringle is a candied pretzel. Also available are vaflers, which are waffles covered with powdered sugar and jam and other interesting sweets. Sample the wonderfully-white rice cream pudding ($1.75) or chocolate ball, like a 3-inch truffle ($3.20).

Open faced sandwiches are very well presented for a medium to small serving. Offerings include tongue, beef, smoked salmon ($5), mackerel ($3) and ham. A delightful herring platter is $4.

Chairs and tables are available outside, between Norway's Ancient church and the shops at the pavilion.

CHINA

¶¶ Lotus Blossom Cafe. Stir fry, eggrolls, sweet and sour chicken, soup and more, $2-$5.50. Lunch, Dinner.

This is a quality fast food restaurant located near the entrance to the China exhibit beside the Nine Dragons Restaurant. It offers covered outdoor dining in a cafe or patio setting. The dining area is tastefully decorated; the food is better than most fast food operations.

For the most variety for your money, try the combination platter for a sample of stir-fried beef with vegetables, egg roll and fried rice ($5.50). For a lighter meal, sample a bowl of soup for under $2.

Chinese beer ($3.50), tea and soft drinks are available.

🏯 Nine Dragons Restaurant. Varied traditional Chinese cuisine in Mandarin, Cantonese, Kiangche, and Szechuan style, plus appetizers, $4-$17.50. Lunch and dinner. Children's menu offers three items from $5-$5.50. Lunch, dinner. Reservations required.

This is a palace-like, oriental setting located near the entrance of the China exhibit, on the left side as you enter. Look up as you walk into the waiting area to see an interesting golden dragon hanging from the ceiling. An ancient robe hangs on the back wall of the waiting area.

As fancy as it is, the selection of food is no better than many average Chinese restaurants, and a lot less impressive than gourmet eateries. It features Mandarin pork ribs ($12), stir-fried garden vegetables ($8.50) or lobster tail ($17.50), or braised and deep-fried treasure duck ($12).

Children can select sweet and sour pork ($5.50), shrimp, or pork fried rice ($5) at both lunch and dinner settings.

The dinner menu is very similar to the lunchtime offerings, but the cost is generally $2 more per plate.

Goes great with chili dogs. For an unusual treat, try the red bean ice cream offered as a dessert at the Nine Dragons restaurant in China.

KEY

¶¶ = Fast Food

Y = Pub

🏯 = Full-
Service
Restaurant

Chinese beer ($3.50) as well as specialty drinks and Chinese cordials also are available.

GERMANY

🏠 **Biergarten.** Traditional German fare of potatoes, pork and bratwurst, $9-$11. Lunch and dinner. Children's menu, $3.50-$6. Reservations suggested on busy days.

Located at the rear of the German exhibit off the Sommerfest courtyard, the Biergarten offers a loud and raucous atmosphere that gets louder as the evening wears on.

Once inside you'll feel like you are in a German beer hall at night. You'll dine at long tables, served by waiters and waitresses in alpine dress. The setting also includes simulated small-town shops and a stage for the nightly music performances.

The food includes typical German fare, including all of the better wurst: bratwurst, bierwurst, jaegerwurst, bauernwurst and more. There are potato dumplings, sauerkraut and much more.

For a truly traditional treat, try kartoffelpuffer mit Apfelmus (potato pancakes with apple sauce) as a side dish ($3). Both dinner and lunch entrees range from $9 to $11 and include interesting chicken, pork and "wurst" offerings.

Wash it all down with a huge 33-ounce stein of beer (up to $7.50) or German wine and sit back and enjoy the floor show of oompah music and other lively tunes. All in all, a lot of fun.

🏠 **Sommerfest.** Bratwurst und strüdel und Black Forest Cake und beer, $1.50-$3.60. Lunch, dinner, snacks.

Sommerfest offers German fast food treats served at an attractive outdoor cafe located at the right rear of the German exhibit outside the Biergarten. You won't have any trouble finding this interesting and different establishment; follow the sharp odor of Wurst and sauerkraut.

Select a German beer to accompany one of the sandwich offerings. Ask for sauerkraut and all the fixings with your bratwurst sandwich and still pay only about $4.

ITALY

🏠 **L'Originale Alfredo di Roma Ristorante.** Veal, chicken, pasta and seafood entrees plus appetizers and dessert in an Italian atmosphere. Lunch entrees, $11-22.50; dinner entrees, $12.50-$24.50. Children's lunch and dinner entrees, $4-$5. Reservations are required.

Enter by crossing the stone-paved square, beside the huge Neptune fountain and walled patio. The pink, stucco exte-

One million bottles of beer on the wall . . . The famous Oktoberfest is celebrated in Munich, Germany every October. Germany has the highest per capita beer consumption in the world, about 40 gallons per person per year.

KEY

🍴 = FAST FOOD

🍸 = PUB

🏠 = FULL-SERVICE RESTAURANT

Originally elsewhere. L'Originale Alfredo di Roma Ristorante is not the original, Alfredo's, actually: the real thing is in Rome, and is credited with the invention of the creamy pasta dish Fettucine Alfredo (noodles in butter and Parmesan cheese).

KEY

| = Fast Food

Y = Pub

= Full-
Service
Restaurant

Not invented here.
What could be more American than hamburgers, hot dogs and chili? Well, actually, there are some doubts as to the lineage of hamburgers (as in Hamburg, Germany), hot dogs (a sausage, like those made in Frankfurt, Germany, but placed on a roll) and chili (influenced by Mexico well before Texas was a state.)

---

rior, complete with columns, stone benches, and lanterns, provide an appropriate atmosphere.

A semi-formal decor with interesting wallpaper and upholstered seating greet you to the cool interior and pleasantly lively atmosphere. Check out the numerous photographs on the wall of the waiting area; you'll see many familiar personalities being served pasta.

The menu features a wide selection of freshly made pasta (including spaghetti, rigatoni, ziti, lasagna and more) with various delectable sauces. Also available are eight veal dishes (about $18 for lunch, $22 for dinner), sausage, eggplant, chicken ($15 for lunch, $17 for dinner) and beef dishes.

House wines available by the glass ($3.50) or by the liter ($12.50).

THE AMERICAN ADVENTURE

| **Liberty Inn.** Burgers, sandwiches, chili, and salads, $2-$6. Lunch and dinner. Child's menu, $3.50-$4. Indoor and outdoor seating with traditional stateside fare.

There's nothing here to startle a youngster, or for that matter, to educate the palette of an adult, but the food is acceptable and typical of what many American families eat most of the time.

The outdoor patio is a very pleasant, tree-shaded affair that includes umbrella tables and colorful landscaping. The inside dining room is very spacious and has large window walls to maintain a bright, light atmosphere, even late in the day.

Lunch and dinner offerings are essentially the same, with a few more options for dinner. For example, you can select a chicken breast sandwich served with french fries or fresh fruit for about $5 lunch or dinner. At dinner, you can also choose a roasted half chicken with french fries and cole slaw for about $6. The evening offerings also include jambalaya, a sort of southern stew that includes pork, shrimp, crawfish, chicken, sausage, vegetables and rice ($5.50). "Colonial" chicken salad ($5) and a variety of "Yankee Doodle" desserts round out the offerings.

For the children there is fried chicken ($3.50) or hot dogs ($3.75). Another lower-price option is the bowl of chili ($2).

JAPAN

Teppanyaki Dining Room. Table-prepared Japanese entrees of beef, chicken and seafood. Lunch entrees, $8.50-

$13.75. Lunch for two, $21-36. Dinner entrees, $13.50-$23. Dinner for two, $35.50-$54 and children's dinner offerings, about $8. Reservations are usually necessary.

Find this interesting restaurant on the second floor of the building on the right of the Japanese exhibit, above the Mitsukoshi Department Store.

An entertaining and tasty break from the hubbub of Epcot. Groups of diners are assembled around a hot table, facing a chef equipped with a set of sharp knives; he carries salt and pepper shakers in holsters. Depending on the luck of the draw, your chef may be a multilingual comic, playing games with the chicken, shrimp and beef as he slices and stir fries the food. Teppanyaki fare is fresh and simple, featuring vegetables and meat over rice.

The dining experience is definitely not for someone who wants a quiet, leisurely and private time. But children–and adults who enjoy a floor show with their meal–are certain to have fun.

For lunch, choose Yasai salad (mixed greens with ginger dressing) for $2.25, or soup for $2. A variety of grilled appetizers also is available from $4.50-$6. Lunch entrees are served with grilled fresh vegetables and steamed rice: chicken ($8.25), shrimp ($9.50), sirloin ($12), and lobster, shrimp or scallops ($13.50).

Dinner entrees are the same as for lunch, but the prices are higher and the portions slightly larger.

Before and during your meal, sample exotic alcoholic and non-alcoholic drinks for $1.50-$10.50. For example, the Sakura at $5 includes light rum, white Curaçao, strawberries and lemon juice.

Note that there are several Teppanyaki-style Japanese restaurants outside of Epcot, generally offering better prices and smaller crowds.

🏯 Tempura Kiku. Batter-fried meat and vegetables. Lunch, $8.50-$10.50 for adults and $5 for children; Dinner, $13.50-$19.50 for adults and $7 for children.

Tempura Kiku is located upstairs at the right side of the Japanese pavilion, next to the Matsu No Ma Lounge. Exotic drinks from the lounge are available at the restaurant.

Reservations are not accepted; waits are rarely long.

🍴 🍸 Matsu No Ma Lounge. Exotic drinks, sushi and more, $1.50-$7.

The lounge is located upstairs at the right side of the pavilion.

Future tech. Disney planners were hard at work on the designs for a major expansion of the **Japan** pavilion. The attraction, to be situated on the lagoon in World Showcase, is expected to include **Mount Fuji,** a thrill ride like Space Mountain and Disneyland's Matterhorn. Visitors will zoom through the *inside* of the mountain. Also featured will be a replica of the flashy neon Tokyo shopping district, the Ginza. An opening date has not been announced.

At one time, Disney had planned a pavilion for the Soviet Union. There is no word on a possible Russian replacement for that attraction with the end of the former Soviet government. Other possible Epcot attractions include **Switzerland** and a **Journeys in Space** pavilion for Epcot Future World.

KEY

🍴 = FAST FOOD

🍸 = PUB

🏯 = FULL-SERVICE RESTAURANT

Here you can sample Sake (warm rice wine) for $3.40 to $6.50, try other wines ($3-$3.75), or sip Japanese beer ($3.40). Exotic mixed drinks cost about $5.

Non-alcoholic drinks range from $2 to $3 and include Ichigo (strawberries, pineapple juice, lemon) and Mikan (Mandarin orange and pineapple juice with lemon).

Appetizers include tempura ($5), Kabuki beef or chicken ($4) and Sashimi ($7). Assorted Nigiri sushi also available ($7).

Yakitori House. Japanese fast food including beef, chicken, seafood and salads, $2.60-$8. Lunch, dinner, snacks.

Yakitori House is located in the rear left portion of the Japanese exhibit, behind the fountain, within the Japanese gardens in a replica of the 500-year-old Katsura Imperial Summer Palace in Kyoto.

Dine indoors or outside, but—weather permitting—the rock walled-patio with fragrant landscaping is a pleasant getaway for lunch or dinner. Imitation paper lanterns give the evening meal a pleasant glow.

The restaurant offers Japanese fast food, serving yakitori (skewered chicken basted with soy sauce and sesame), teriyaki chicken and beef and guydon (a beef stew served over rice).

The Shogun Combo offers a good selection of foods, including steamed rice and beef teriyaki for $5. An excellent seafood salad is filling yet light ($5.50); soups are suitable as meals or accompaniment, $1.80.

Plum wine or Japanese beer, $3.50.

MOROCCO

Restaurant Marrakesh. Traditional Moroccan food. Lunch entrees, $10-$13. Dinner entrees, $14-$19. Children's lunch and dinner selections, $4-$5.

Sign in at the podium at the front of the Morocco exhibit, then wind your way through the Fez gate to the back of the Medina to find the Marrakesh amid the narrow streets and quaint shops.

A most unusual setting, with waiters in ankle-length *djellaba* robes, strolling musicians and belly dancers provides an interesting and entertaining backdrop for a delightful meal. Even if you have to wait in the lobby briefly for your table, you'll be entertained by the music, native costumes and decor.

Once inside, the dining area with raised, segmented dining rooms that overlook a central entertainment area adds interest to your meal.

Among the traditional delicacies you can sample for lunch are Meshoui (lamb roast in natural juices with rice, almonds, raisins and saffron) at $13, couscous (rolled semolina) steamed with a variety of garden vegetables ($10), chicken ($12), or lamb ($13). You might also consider ordering one of the sampler plates with small portions of various offerings for yourself or to share with someone. The "Emir" brochette sampler with chicken and shish kabob is $13, for example.

The dinner menu is similar, but with more variety and larger portions. Try the Tangier sampler ($19) for a selection of items, including specialties marinated in spices including ginger, cumin, paprika, garlic with olives and pickled lemon. An interesting and tasty grouper dinner is $17.

Children and the less adventurous may find the menu too strange. Reservations are available, but not required.

FRANCE

🏛 **Chefs de France.** Traditional French cuisine. Lunch, $8-$14.50. Dinner, $9-$21. Children's lunch and dinner menu, $4-$5. Reservations are required.

Chefs de France is located on the ground floor of the large building at the left of the entrance to the France exhibit, to the right of the Au Petit Cafe outdoor dining area.

C'est merveilleux! Right here in Epcot, just across the way from umpteen hot dog and pizza stands, is a restaurant nearly as fine as any in France.

Enter this intriguing restaurant under the red awning off of the stone-paved street of the France exhibit. The building is of classic French architecture with stone and a metal roof. Inside is an elegant French dining room complete with fresh tablecloths, paintings, chandeliers; table service in elegant continental style with a bustling, active atmosphere. Pleasant and helpful personnel speak French (English, if you insist) and are ready and willing to help you make selections.

To the right of the main dining room is a pleasant, glassed sun room that provides bright, sunny dining in a dark green and wood tone motif.

Lunch and dinner meals include ten or more salads and appetizers and about as many entrees. All of this comes at only a slightly high premium, compared to other Epcot

KEY

🍴 = FAST FOOD

🍸 = PUB

🏛 = FULL-SERVICE RESTAURANT

Recipe for success. The chefs of France who are behind the restaurant of the same name are Paul Bocuse and Roger Vergé, operators of two of the country's finest restaurants, and Gaston LeNôtre, considered a national treasure for his pastries and desserts.

table-service restaurants. At lunch, for example, a chicken breast and gruyere appetizer is $10 (a little high), but the traditional onion soup is $4. Entrees range from $8 (crepe with mushrooms, ham and gruyere) to $14.50 (sauteed strip steak with Bordelaise sauce and french fries). A vegetarian plate is $9.

The dinner menu is only a bit more costly. A snapper filet with spinach in a baked pastry shell (nice!) is $20, for example, and chicken with pearl onions and wine sauce is $14.

As you might expect, desserts are worth drooling over, with at least a dozen selections from $3 to $6. The ultimate crème caramel (baked French custard with caramel sauce), for example, is $4.

Beer ($3.50) and wine ($3.50 by the glass or $8.50 for the carafe) also are available.

Bistro de Paris. Traditional French cuisine in a light, quiet setting. Entrees $20-$24. Children's menu, $4. Reservations are available, and necessary on busy days.

Upstairs over the Chefs de France, this bistro is entered through a rear door at the back of the building. A bistro is an intimate little cafe or pub, and that's what the designers of the Bistro de Paris had in mind in this lighter and (usually) quieter version of Chefs de Paris. The same master chefs designed the menu, which includes a variety of appetizers, soups, entrees and desserts.

A salad of duck liver pate, for example, makes an elegant (though costly) appetizer at $14, while the Gratin d'escargots de Bourgogne (casserole of snails in herbal butter) is $7.50. The cream of lobster soup ($4.50) is a tasty beginning, or select a mixed green salad with true Roquefort dressing and walnuts at $7.50.

Four meat and poultry entrees are offered. The sauteed breast of duck with cherries and red wine sauce is $20; rack of lamb with vegetables for two is $48.

At least ten dessert items are available, from fruit and sherbet with raspberry sauce ($6) to vanilla creme in a puff pastry shell and topped with caramel sauce ($4).

Au Petit Café. French cafe fare from soup to quiche, $4-$14.50. Children's offerings, about $4. Lunch, dinner, snacks.

This is a Parisian-style sidewalk cafe located to the left of Chefs de France. You'll find it through the smell of fresh flowers coming from the many hanging baskets that adorn the posts that support the awning over the patio.

The World Showcase is not quite the Champs-Elysées, but the little sidewalk cafe here with its formal black-jacketed waiters gives a nice taste of the time-honored people-watching stations on the streets of Paris.

The menu ranges from the traditional onion soup with cheese ($4) to sauteed strip steak and Bordelaise sauce with french fries ($14.50). In between are such familiar items as quiche lorraine and salads (about $7.50).

Fruit sorbets, ice cream, pastry shells filled with light cream and chocolate sauce, and ice cream souffle with Grand Marnier sauce ($3-$5) round out the menu.

No reservations are accepted, and lines can become quite long on busy days.

Boulangerie Patisserie. French pastries and fresh croissants, $2.25-$3.50. Breakfast, snacks.

This quaint bakery shop is across the narrow French street from the bistro.

A wonderful place to grab breakfast or a sweet snack any time of the day. The bakery is managed by the Chefs of France, which is as tasty a recommendation as can be found at Epcot.

Any of the assorted tarts, apple turnovers, quiche lorraine and chocolate treats is good. Dark, flavorful coffee makes a good accompaniment for the sweet treats.

UNITED KINGDOM

Rose & Crown Pub and Dining Room. English pub fare in a pleasant atmosphere, entrees $7.50-$10. Children's menu, $4. Lunch, dinner, snacks. Traditional afternoon tea at 4:00 p.m. Reservations for the dining room are recommended, and necessary on busy days; no reservations are accepted for the pub.

Located across the street from the main portion of the United Kingdom exhibit, the Rose & Crown is an interesting British dining experience. Very ordinary pub food in England seems very exotic in Orlando. You order steak-and-kidney pie ($10), lamb and barley soup ($2.50), chicken and leeks ($10) or real fish and chips ($4). The dinner menu expands to include mixed grills of pork, beef and veal kidney. A selection of sweets, such as traditional sherry trifle, available for $4-$6.

There is a decent selection of beers and ales, including

KEY

= FAST FOOD

= PUB

= FULL-SERVICE RESTAURANT

Warm comfort. Tea dates back several thousand years to ancient China and Tibet. It was introduced into England in the 1600s and soon thereafter into the American colonies by British merchants in the East India Company. The classic English Breakfast Tea is a Chinese black tea called Keemun. The popular Earl Grey tea is a black tea flavored with bergamot or lavender oil.

Bass from England, Tennent's from Scotland and Guinness Stout and Harp Ale.

The decor is appropriately rough and dark, with elements of both city and country drinking establishments in the United Kingdom. Frosted and etched glass adds an elegant interest to this beautiful setting.

The pub, which can become quite crowded, offers appetizersized portions of the dinner menu along with beers and mixed drinks. Notice the curved, dark wood benches, the patterned plaster over the curved, wooden bar and brass rail.

CANADA

🔺 **Le Cellier.** Pork pie, rib roast, salads and sandwiches. Lunch entrees, $7.50-$12. Dinner entrees, $8.50-$12. Children's menu for lunch and dinner, $4-$6.

Le Cellier is located toward the front of the Canada exhibit, but entered via the formal gardens to the right of the main walkway. The "Victoria Gardens" were inspired by the Butchart Gardens of British Columbia and serve as a "reminder and a reflection of horticulture as a work of art and a labor of love," according to a plaque at the entrance.

The only cafeteria in the World Showcase, this restaurant modeled after a wine cellar in a castle and located downstairs in the Canada pavilion. The atmosphere is pleasant with stone walls, high ceilings and lots of wood.

What exactly is Canadian food? Well, it includes specialties like Tourtière, a pork and potato pie from Quebec for $7; fresh salmon ($12), prime rib ($9) or a fruit and cheese plate ($8). Desserts include maple syrup pie and trifles–cake, strawberries, whipped cream and custard, soaked in sherry ($2-$5).

Though a cafeteria in design, Le Cellier's prices are not much different from those of a sitdown restaurant. No reservations are required, though, which can be a life saver on a busy day. Most crowded during prime lunch hours, from about 11:30 a.m. until 2 p.m.

KEY

🍴 = FAST FOOD

🍸 = PUB

🔺 = FULL-SERVICE RESTAURANT

They always get their horse. The Royal Canadian Mounted Police, also known as the RCMP and best known as the Mounties, are Canada's federal police force. It augments provincial and municipal police in much of the country and is the only police force in remote Yukon Territories and the Northwest Territories. It still has some members of the force on horseback.

Epcot / Future World
Attractions & Restaurants

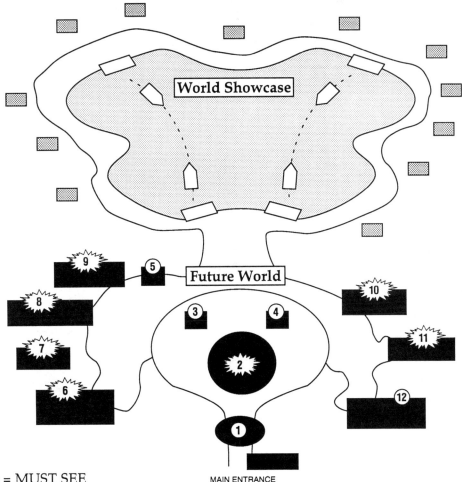

✳ = MUST SEE

1 Entrance Plaza
✳2 Spaceship Earth
3 East Communicore
  Stargate Restaurant
4 West Communicore
  Sunrise Terrace Restaurant
5 Odyssey Restaurant
✳6 Universe of Energy
✳7 Wonders of Life
  Pure & Simple

✳8 Horizons
✳9 World of Motion
✳10 Journey into Imagination
✳11 The Land
  Farmers Market
  The Land Grille Room
12 The Living Seas
  Coral Reef Restaurant

Epcot / World Showcase
Attractions & Restaurants

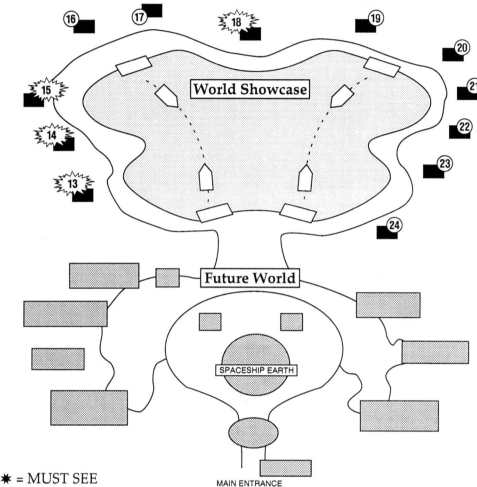

✳ = MUST SEE

✳ **13** Mexico
San Angel Inn
Cantina de San Angel

✳ **14** Norway
Restaurant Akershus
Kringla Bakeri og Kafé

✳ **15** China
Lotus Blossom Cafe
Nine Dragons Restaurant

16 Germany
Biergarten
Sommerfest

17 Italy
L'Originale Alfredo
di Roma Ristorante

✳ **18** The American Adventure
Liberty Inn

19 Japan
Teppanyaki Dining Room
Tempura Kiku
Matsu No Ma Lounge
Yakitori House

20 Morocco
Restaurant Marrakesh

21 France
Chefs de France
Bistro de Paris
Au Petit Café
Boulangerie Patisserie

22 International Gateway

23 United Kingdom
Rose & Crown Pub & Dining Room

24 Canada
Le Cellier

CHAPTER 8
Disney-MGM Studios

Let's go to the movies: The Disney-MGM Studios Theme Park is Disney's newest major American park, opened in 1989. Its tone sits somewhere between the silly fun of the Magic Kingdom and the entertaining education of Epcot Center.

While the Magic Kingdom draws most of its classic themes from great fairy tales and works of fiction, the Disney-MGM Studios Theme Park allows guests to step into some of the greatest–or at least the most popular–movies of the 20th Century. Disney also pushes pretty hard for its current hits, including "Beauty and the Beast," "The Little Mermaid" and "Who Framed Roger Rabbit."

How does Disney-MGM Studios compare to Universal Studios Florida? In our judgment, the Disney operation–like everything within Walt Disney World–offers a more polished and better planned experience than almost anywhere else we know. Universal Studios is larger and has several rides and attractions that are considerably wilder and more entertaining that anything that Disney offers. If you have the time, we suggest you visit both Disney-MGM and Universal; if you are on a very tight schedule and must choose between the two parks, we'd suggest Disney-MGM if you are with young children and Universal for older parties.

The overall theme of Disney-MGM Studios seems to be: "Nothing is what it appears to be." This will be apparent from the moment you spot the park's distinctive Earffel Tower (a set of mouse ears atop a 130-foot-tall water

Coming soon! The future of Disney-MGM Studios includes some major expansion based on film hits old and new.

Announced and under construction is the "Twilight Zone Tower of Terror," a high-speed thrill ride that is scheduled to open sometime in 1994. Also due is Sunset Blvd., a new road of (just what you needed) shops and restaurants.

New projects under consideration include "Toontown Transit," a simulation of a wacky trolley ride through Roger Rabbit's home town, and "Baby Herman's Runaway Buggy Ride," based on the Roger Rabbit short, "Tummy Trouble." Disney Imagineers are working on a new stop for the Backstage Tour, the "Journey to the Center of the Earth," featuring rivers of flaming lava and all sorts of strange creatures.

THE
POWER TRIP

Arrive early. This tour allows time for a quick fast food lunch and a more leisurely dinner.

Head up Hollywood Boulevard and turn left at the first corner along Echo Lake. Note the Hollywood & Vine and 50's Prime Time Cafe as possible dinner stops; you may want to make a reservation as you go by.

The goal is **Star Tours,** your first ride of the day. (Pass by the Indiana Jones Epic Stunt Spectacular–it'll wait.) After the show, make a sharp left turn and head for **Jim Henson's Muppet*vision 3D**, a treat for all ages. While you're in the area, check out Mama Melrose's Ristorante Italiano, another interesting food stop, or the Sci-Fi Dine-in Theater Restaurant, a must-see eatery; make reservations early if you are so inclined.

The next stop is **The Great Movie Ride** at the top of Hollywood Boulevard. (Along the way, you have passed by the Monster Sound Show and Superstar Television.)

Continue moving in a counterclockwise direction through the archway to the studio section of the park. If you are traveling with young children, join the line for **The Voyage of the Little Mermaid** stage show; free adults are hereby granted a pass. The next stop is the **Backstage Studio Tour.**

It should be time for lunch now; the Soundstage Restaurant is in the studio area and is as good a fast food stop as any other.

Go next to **The Magic of Disney Animation** tour; don't let youngsters talk you out of this visit–they'll enjoy the Peter Pan movie in the preshow and you'll want to see the artists at work.

At this point, you have visited all of the attractions with the largest lines. Backtrack or continue in a counterclockwise direction to see shows like the **Indiana Jones Epic Stunt Spectacular** (consult the daily schedule for show times), **Superstar Television** and **The Monster Sound Show.** Youngsters will want to see the **Honey I Shrunk the Kids Movie Set Adventure** and one of the outdoor stage shows including **Teenage Mutant Ninja Turtles** and **Beauty and the Beast.**

In season, the spectacular **Sorcery in the Sky** fireworks show is presented over the lake at dusk.

tower) to your first view of the very realistic New York street scenes or see some of the inside magic of the studio production tours.

Be sure to find time to stroll Hollywood Boulevard near the entranceway–we suggest coming back to this area at midday when lines are longest at the attractions. The boulevard is a constant street theater. Pretty girls may be approached by "producers" handing out their business cards. Would-be actresses looking for work will give you the eye; vain stars will expect you to swoon at their feet. Actors perform skits and gags from old silent films. The street actors stay in character all of the time they are "on"; for fun, try asking one of them for directions, or some personal questions about their careers.

ATTRACTIONS

WOW **The Great Movie Ride.** The interior of the Chinese Theater is a bittersweet reminder of how full of marvel were the grand theaters of the early years of movies and how ordinary are our local quadraplex mall theaters. In the lobby you'll find what may be the world's most expensive shoes: Dorothy's ruby slippers from the 1939 MGM classic "The Wizard of Oz."

Your first stop is a waiting area in a theater that is continually showing original trailers from some of the most beloved movies of all time, including "Singing in the Rain," "Fantasia," "Footlight Parade" with Jimmy Cagney, Joan Blondell and Ruby Keeler, and a stark preview of "Alien." You'll go within all of those movies and more in the ride to come.

Your moving auditorium will be presided over by a host or hostess who will narrate the tour. The excitement begins soon, when your leader will be hijacked (depending on which set of seats you are in) by a 1920s gangster or a Wild West desperado). Don't worry, though: the good guys will prevail later on in the ride.

In addition to the West and old Chicago, you will visit a recreation of the "By a Waterfall" scene (with more than 60 Audio-Animatronic dancers) from Busby Berkeley's "Footlight Parade." You will also travel into and through the Nostromo spaceship, home of the Alien; an extended "Raiders of the Lost Ark" set, including wriggling robotic snakes; the jungle world of Tarzan; Mickey Mouse's Fantasia, and finally a short drive down the Yellow Brick Road of Oz.

Fly it again, Sam. According to the Hollywood mythmakers, the Lockheed Electra 12A on display in the "Casablanca" set was actually used in the real movie, a happy accident.

The heart of darkness. The space ship that is invaded by a murderous alien–the most chilling scene of the Great Movie Ride–was named "Nostromo." That name comes from a 1904 book by the English novelist Joseph Conrad who spent much of his early life as a seaman on a succession of freighters.

Going my way? The Great Movie Ride brings to MGM-Epcot the same "moving theater" cars first introduced at the Energy pavilion at Epcot.

The last stop on the ride is a high-tech theater that will surround you with the sound and images of a well-done short film with some of the best-known scenes of all time. See how many stars and films you can recognize as they fly by.

The lines for this attraction build at midday. If the lines extend outside of the building, we'd suggest you come back at another time; there is still a lengthy queue within the theater.

Behind the screens. The trick behind the Super Star Television show is the use of "color key" technology allowing electronic insertion of images or backgrounds. Some of the old television scenes have had elements "matted" out.

The same technology is used at Universal Studios in the Screen Test Home Video Adventure attraction, where visitors can pay to place themselves into the action on a videotape.

WOW SuperStar Television. Casting for the show goes on in the waiting area about 15 minutes before show time; if you want to be picked, the best position is down front. If you want to avoid your moment of fame, hang back and try to blend into the wallpaper–which may or may not work when the "casting director" comes down off the stage and walks among the audience. There will be calls for couples young and old, singles of both sexes and even youngsters.

The 30-minute show moves quickly from one setup to another, with the cast members sharing electronic space with some of television's old and new stars: reading the news with Dave Garroway on the original Today Show in 1955, on the set of the Howdy Doody Show, a guest appearance as a singing group on The Ed Sullivan Show, a cameo appearance on "Gilligan's Island" and more. One lucky woman will get to appear in one of the most famous scenes of the "I Love Lucy" show–the candy factory scene. Some of the couples will trade cracks with Woody from "Cheers," and others will make appearances on "The Golden Girls," the "Tonight Show," and "Late Night with David Letterman." Finally, some lucky kid (of whatever age) will get to hit a game-winning homerun in a televised baseball game.

Sounds like . . . The Foley Stage is named after the acknowledged creator of the Hollywood sound-effects stage, Jack Foley. The same sort of devices were used in adding sounds to live radio dramas of the 1930s and 1940s.

The work of the audio engineer is called "sweetening," and includes the use of sound filters, the addition of echo and the inclusion of sound effects.

The Monster Sound Show. An odd name for a funny show; don't let the title scare away youngsters. This is an entertaining introduction to the use of sound effects in film. The audience will view a short film starring Chevy Chase and Martin Short (a short-Short?) that takes place inside a pretend haunted house, complete with the sounds of thunder, rain and all sorts of things that go bump in the night. Next, a group of recruits from the audience operate some of the tools of the "Foley" stage as the now-silent film scrolls by on the overhead screen. And finally, the often-miscued new version is projected once more.

Don't pass by the interactive discovery areas at the end of the show, either.

Indiana Jones® Stunt Spectacular! A huge covered outdoor theater, but it still fills up within ten or fifteen minutes of afternoon showtimes, even earlier on busier days. It's a good place to park at the busiest, hot times of the day. The best seats are in the center of the theater; they are filled first and it is from this section that the "casting director" usually selects a dozen or so "extras" to participate. All must be over the age of 18; there's a ringer among them–see if you can spot him or her. The extras don't have an awful lot to do.

The stunt show starts with a real bang as a double for Indiana Jones rocks and rolls across the huge stage; most of the later actions rely less on mechanisms and more on the skills of the stunt actors. It's a world of Nazis, Arab swordsmen, fiery explosions and bad jokes.

WOW **Star Tours – The Ultimate Star Wars® Thrill Ride.** "Whenever your plans call for intergalactic travel," say the travel posters, please consider flying Star Tours to the vacation moon of Endor.

Disney builds the atmosphere and excitement beautifully, from the moment you walk beneath the huge space machine outside, continuing as you walk through the indoor waiting area that simulates a gritty space garage. Our favorite flaky robots, R2D2 and C3PO are the mechanics.

When your time comes, you will enter into a 40-passenger simulator cabin and meet your pilot, Captain Rex. The doors will be closed and your seat belts tightly cinched before he informs you that this is his first trip. Too late–you're off. You'll make an uneasy takeoff and then blast (accidentally) into and then through a frozen meteor, stumble into an active intergalactic battle zone and finally make a wild landing at your goal, the vacation moon of Endor.

This is quite a wild ride, at about the same level of twisting, turning and dips as the Body Wars show at Wonders of Life in Epcot Center. It's a short ride, but a bit rough for the very young; pregnant women and others with health problems are advised to sit this one out.

After the ride, note the travel posters for other Star Tour destinations, including lovely Hoth and Tatoine.

Voyage of the Little Mermaid. A stage show that features some of the songs from the hit movie opened at the

Hidden lines. Most of the queue for Star Tours is inside the building; if visitors are lined up outside the building onto the plaza you've got about a 45-minute wait; if the line extends outside and into the covered space "forest", you might want to plan your expedition to Endor for later in the day.

The **Voyage of the Little Mermaid** includes snippets from the movie, more than 100 puppets, live performers and audio-animatronic robots.

Beauty and the Beast. Another new live action show, presented outdoors at the Theater of the Stars. Check the daily entertainment schedule for times.

WOW **The Magic of Disney Animation.** Disney cartoons are, after all, the foundation upon which all of Walt Disney World, Disneyland and the Disney empire was built. And, this tour offers an extraordinary glimpse at the history and process of animation.

The Disney-MGM Studios is a satellite operation of the main studio in Burbank; 75 artists work in Florida. Their first full work was "Roller Coaster Rabbit," a short that ran with the "Dick Tracy" feature film.

The tour opens with an exhibit of old and new animation cels, featuring the megahit "Beauty and the Beast" and new projects like "Aladdin," as well as drawings from the archives. Check out the Oscar statue.

Next is an entertaining short movie starring one of the all-time odd couples: former newsman Walter Cronkite and present wild man Robin Williams in "Back to Never Land."

The best part of the tour comes last, when visitors are let loose in a glass-walled hallway where they can literally look over the shoulders of animators and technicians in the studios below. We found it hard to tear ourselves away from watching the detailed work.

The self-guided tour can take about 30 minutes; lines build at midday, so a morning or late-in-the-day visit is best.

The gift shop after the tour offers actual painted cels from Disney movies–beautiful but quite pricey for objects that once were thrown out as trash. Some of the cels sell for several thousand dollars.

WOW **Honey I Shrunk the Kids Movie Set Adventure.** A most inventive playground based on the hit movie about a mad inventor whose shrinking ray accidentally reduces his children and a few friends. Play areas include giant cereal loops, ants, spiders, a huge roll of film and a leaky garden hose. It's a great place for youngsters to burn off some energy; be advised, though, that it is quite easy to lose a child in the playground. The best strategy is to station an adult by the single exit from the park, rather than chasing through the various adventures.

Short subject. A lot of effort went into the animation of the Cronkite-Williams film, as well into striking a balance between tall Walter and diminutive Robin–we suspect there was a soap box somewhere, as well as some creative camera angles employed.

Half the trouble. The Honey I Shrunk the Kids play area is next to the Studio Catering Co.; the restaurant is nothing special, but its location allows a family to have lunch while kids burn off energy at play.

Teenage Mutant Ninja Turtles® Think on this: human actors dressed as cartoon figures of turtles who think they are human. These guys take to the stage in the New York backlot for a singing performance; afterwards Leonardo, Raphael, Michelangelo and Donatello will stick around for a while to press the scales with their fans. Consult the daily entertainment schedule for times.

Jim Henson's Muppet*Vision 3D®. We have to admit that we passed by this attraction the first few times we brought our kids to the studios–Bert and Ernie and Kermit The Frog seemed a bit too silly, even for an eight-year-old. Were we ever wrong!

The fun begins the minute you enter into the theater, which is designed as "Muppet World Headquarters." Pause just inside the entranceway to read the office directory on the wall. Listings include the "Institute of Heckling and Browbeating–Statler and Waldorf, Curmudgeons in Chief"; the "Sartorial Accumulation Division," run by Miss Piggy, of course; and the "Academy of Amphibian Science," under the tutelage of Kermit The Frog. The security desk at the door advises that the guard will be back in five minutes, but the key is under the mat.

But the real fun is within the beautiful 584-seat theater, which is decidedly more opulent than your neighborhood quintupleplex. There's a robotic all-penguin orchestra in the pit and a private box at the front for Waldorf and Statler. The film includes some marvelous 3-D special effects as well as flashing lights, a bubblemaker, smell-o-vision and a special surprise from the skies as well as a live actor and a cannon.

Don't pass this extraordinary multimedia show by.

Backstage Studio Tour. The Disney-MGM Studios is a working movie lot, and the 25-minute backstage shuttle tour is a great way to see some of the real–and not-so-real elements of moviemaking.

The large trams run continuously and lines are generally short in the morning and late in the day. Remember this: the left side of the cars (the first person into each row) is the wet side, no matter what the guide says at first.

As you pull out of the tram station, you will pass by the **Car Pool,** which includes some of the vehicles used in movies. In recent years the lot has included a futuristic vehicle from "Blade Runner" and an assortment of gangster cars from

Road show. The preshow area for Muppet*vision includes a wonderfully goofy collection of packing cases with equipment for the Muppet Labs (Tongue Inflators, Gorilla Detectors and Anvil Repair Kits) and roadshow suitcases for the Muppet band, "Dr. Teeth and the Electric Mayhem" including Paisley Bell Bottoms, Nehru Jackets, Beatle Boots and Love Beads.

Two pants, one jacket. Tailors at the costume shop make as many as 12,000 costumes a year. Disney claims the world's largest working wardrobe with more than 2.5 million items available. Among articles on display is a hot red dress from "Pretty Woman" and Michael Jackson's "Captain EO" suit.

"The Untouchables" and "Dick Tracy." The trams next pass through the **Costuming** shops.

Carpenters and designers at the **Scenic Shop** construct just about anything and everything for the movies; you'll also glimpse the huge stock of lighting fixtures for filmmaking.

The backlot of Disney-MGM Studios includes a **Residential Street** with some familiar sights–you may recognize the suburban homes from "Golden Girls," "Empty Nest" and other television and movie settings. These are empty shells, of course, and are used for exterior shots; interior filming is performed within soundstages in California or elsewhere.

At the end of the street you'll make a right turn past the **Boneyard**, home of some of the larger props from former productions. Look for the trolley from Toontown in "Who Framed Roger Rabbit" and the UFO from "Flight of the Navigator", among other props.

And finally, it is on to a demonstration of large-scale special effects in the area known as **Catastrophe Canyon**, which simulates a working oil field in a narrow desert canyon. We won't spoil the fun except to point out that the "set" includes hydraulic shaker tables, a series of tanks storing 70,000 gallons of water and flames and explosions and ...

Fill 'er up. The oil field at Catastrophe Canyon bears the markings of Mohave Oil, a fictitious company that is also represented at the old-timey Oscar's Super Service Station on Hollywood Boulevard.

Lines build by midday; come early or late in the day to avoid a long wait.

Inside the Magic: Special Effects and Production Tour. Ever wonder how they can recreate a fierce naval battle without hiring–and sinking–an entire navy? How did they get those kids to ride on a bee in "Honey I Shrunk the Kids"? You'll learn the answer to these and other questions in the special effects tour, a one-hour (no bathroom break) walking tour.

Water Effects Tank. This pool, home of the "Miss Fortune" tugboat and other miniature or partial boat sets, demonstrates how technicians use fans, explosions and a 400 gallon splash tank to recreate a raging storm and a battle at sea. Two volunteers from the audience will get to play captains courageous.

Special Effects Workshop and Shooting Stage. A technician will demonstrate how miniatures and matte paintings are combined in thousands of hours of work to produce extraordinary special effects for films like "Dick Tracy" and "Cocoon." Two lucky kids from the tour will get to demonstrate a wild bee ride–all of the action is in the computer-controlled camera, not the bee.

Soundstages I, II and III. Depending on production schedules, you may get to see sets, rehearsals or even scenes in production at one of the soundstages; no photography is permitted in this section of the tour. In 1991, some of the scenes from "Honey I Blew Up the Baby" were made in Orlando. The stages are often used for Disney Channel television productions. Next you will see a cute film starring Bette Midler, called "The Lottery," that demonstrates the use of special effects and post-production editing. The two-and-a-half minute short required the efforts of a crew of 100 and five days of shooting at the Orlando studios.

Post Production Editing and Audio. Some of the tricks of the editors and "Foley Artist" sound technicians are demonstrated.

The Walt Disney Theater. Finally, you'll enter a small theater for previews of coming Disney and MGM films, introduced by company president Michael Eisner.

EATING YOUR WAY THROUGH DISNEY-MGM STUDIOS

🍴 **Disney-MGM Studios Commissary.** *Behind SuperStar Television.* A fast-food cafeteria offering basic fare including burgers, large hot dogs, chicken breast sandwiches and stir-fry chicken, with prices ranging from about $4 to $5. Children are offered hot dogs, chicken strips and more for about $4.

🏛 **The Hollywood Brown Derby.** *At the end of Hollywood Boulevard, near the entrance to the Studios.* A replica of the famous Hollywood landmark, featuring an art deco and rococo interior with drawings of the stars on the walls. Lunch includes the famous Cobb Salad introduced at the original Brown Derby, as well as filet of dolphin, corned beef and cabbage and pasta and seafood, with prices from $9 to $16. Dinner entrees include baked grouper, filet mignon and sauteed medallions of veal, with prices ranging from about $15 to $24. Also offered are appetizers including snails, fried camembert and pasta with wild mushrooms.

The child's menu includes pasta, burgers, fried fish, chicken and pizza for about $4.

Time pieces. Watch carefully when Disney honcho Michael Eisner sits down in the theater next to his company's symbol. Eisner wears a Mickey Mouse watch; the corporate mouse wears an Eisner timepiece.

Stetson steaks. The Brown Derby was the "in" restaurant and night spot of Hollywood in 1930s. Owner Bob Cobb reportedly told his friends that food was all that matters–in fact, he said, his menu would be so good that people would eat out of a hat. So he built his restaurant in the shape of a derby.

KEY

¶¶ = FAST FOOD

Y = PUB

▲ = FULL-SERVICE RESTAURANT

Movie souvenirs. If you are a movie fan, Sid Cahuenga's One-of-a-Kind shop near the entrance gate at Crossroads of the World offers the most reasonably priced collection of souvenirs you can find anywhere at Disney-MGM. There are large color posters from many classic movies from Disney, MGM and other studios (we found "Bambi," "Sleeping Beauty," and "Pinocchio" for $15 each.) Also available are small lobby cards for about $3 and even original press kits for major motion pictures.

Tip board. Look for the bulletin board at the end of Hollywood Boulevard. Attendants use walkie-talkies to keep the listings of show times and waiting times for rides current.

▲ Hollywood & Vine. *At Hollywood and Vine, on the main gate side of Echo Lake.* An oldstyle cafeteria with a hot table and an art deco interior. Offerings include the Serenade of Life–a shrimp, chicken and fruit salad; Backlot Ribs, and Cahuenga Chicken, for about $9 to $11. The child's menu includes chicken, fried fish, tenderloin tips and peanut butter and jelly sandwiches, from $3 to $6.

¶¶ Starring Rolls. *At the right side of the Brown Derby.* A small bakery almost hidden along the right side of the Brown Derby. A good place to stop for a quick breakfast, or anytime during the day for dessert. Offerings include bagels, small loaves of bread, croissants, pastries, donuts, muffins and cheesecake, with prices from about $2 to $4.

▲ 50's Prime Time Cafe. *Along Echo Lake, near the Indiana Jones Stunt Spectacular!* Step right into a kitchen of the 1950s; Mom will greet you at the door, and your waitress will stand by to make sure you clear your plate. Luncheon appetizer offerings include Mom's Chili over angel hair pasta for about $4, Dad's Bachelor Chili for about $2.50, and fried zucchini for about $3. Entrees include magnificent meatloaf, chicken pot pie, Granny's Pot Roast and the All-American Burger, for about $8 to $15.

Dinner offerings include Auntie's Roasted Lamb and a charbroiled T-Bone steak, with prices ranging from about $13 to $23.

Book a reservation early in the day to assure a seat.

¶¶ Min and Bill's Dockside Diner. *On Echo Lake, near SuperStar Television.* Belly up to the hatchway in the "S.S. Down the Hatch," moored at a dock on the studio pond. Snack offerings include nachos with cheese, fruit cup, danish, soft yogurt and ice cream sodas, with prices from about $2 to $3.

¶¶ Dinosaur Gertie's Ice Cream of Extinction. *Across from the Indiana Jones Stunt Spectacular!* Cold treats from within the belly of a dino, or so it appears. Some of the same frozen items can be purchased from wagons around the park.

¶¶ Backlot Express. *In the Studio Shops between Star Tours and Indiana Jones Stunt Spectacular!* An interesting setting for a burger and hot dog fast foodery, set among the props of the Studio Shops. Offerings include charbroiled chicken with flour tortillas, burgers, hot dogs, chili and chef's salad, with prices ranging from $4 to $7. Make good use of the condiment bar, which includes 24 toppings.

¶¶ Soundstage Restaurant. *Within the Studios area, across from the Voyage of the Little Mermaid.* A cavernous fast food eatery offering four distinct types of fare. The building includes "sets" from "Beauty and the Beast"; from time to time, a "beauty" will appear on the stairs to read stories to youngsters, while her "beast" watches. All of the restaurants offer a children's Peanut Butter and Jelly meal for about $1.50.

> **Sandwiches, Soup and Salads** offers exactly what its name promises. Its Northern Bean Soup is available served within a hollowed-out sourdough bread bowl for about $2.50; a combination sandwich goes for about $6.

> **Bar-B-Que** offers a barbecue beef, chicken or pork sandwich for $4 to $5; a smoked turkey leg is sold for about $4.

> **Pizza and Pasta** sells individual deep dish pizzas, linguine with a variety of sauces and a pasta and vegetable salad, each for about $4.

> **The Catwalk Bar** up above the Soundstage Restaurant offers bar fare including peel-your-own shrimp for $8 and nachos with red bean salsa for about $2, along with a nice selection of beers and California wines.

¶¶ Studio Catering Co. *Off the streets of New York, next to the "Honey I Shrunk the Kids" playground.* It's an outdoor fast food restaurant under a corrugated tin roof. Just outside is an ice cream and sundae bar.

▲ Mama Melrose's Ristorante Italiano. *In the streets of New York near the Muppet*vision theater and Star Tours attractions.* A new and very attractive eatery. Much more than your basic pizzeria, you'll enjoy the wood-fired pizza oven smell as you enter.

"Tutta La Pasta Che Puoi Mangiare" (All the pasta you care to eat) costs about $9; grilled tenderloin of beef goes for $14, while a special Quattro Formaggi (Four Cheese–brie, romano, mozzarella and gorgonzola) individual pizza goes for about $8. Other offerings include fresh fish, vegetable lasagna and chicken Marsala. The child's menu includes spaghetti, pizza, burgers, hot dogs and chicken strips, for about $4 to $6.

There are 292 seats available, but things can become quite hectic between 1 and 3 p.m.

When is a set not a set? It's a bit of a stretch to call the decorations at the restaurant "sets." As an animated movie, "Beauty and the Beast" was entirely based on drawings and had no actual sets.

KEY

¶¶ = FAST FOOD

Y = PUB

▲ = FULL-SERVICE RESTAURANT

Fishy statue. Note the statue between the Studio Catering Co. and the Special Effects Tour. It's the actual mermaid fountain from the 1984 film, "Splash."

 **Sci Fi Diner.** *Behind Monster Sound and across from Star Tours.* Ya gotta see this place–it's a must-see eatery, among the most unusual settings of any restaurant anywhere. Each group of diners sits in their own little convertible, facing a large drive-in movie screen showing weird and wonderful science fiction movies of the 1950s and 1960s. Reservations are essential.

Luncheon offerings include: Journey to the Center of the Pasta, Attack of the Killer Club Sandwich, Return of the Killer Club Sandwich, Revenge of the Killer Club Sandwich and Beach Party Panic (filet of fish, of course), with prices ranging from about $8 to $12. At dinner, look for some of the same dishes, plus Red Planet (linguine and tomato sauce) and Saucer Sightings (a ribeye steak), priced from about $10 to $17.

The child's menu includes grilled cheese sandwiches, chicken strips, burgers and spaghetti, priced from $3.50 to $5.

On the cover of Rolling Stone. The Cover Story shop offers visitors the chance to be on the cover of one of more than a dozen well-known national magazines. After you choose the ego trip of your dreams, a costumer will help you into appropriate garb and help you pose for the cover. Most color covers cost about $17.

KEY

🍴 = FAST FOOD

🍸 = PUB

🏠 = FULL-
     SERVICE
     RESTAURANT

Disney-MGM Studios Attractions

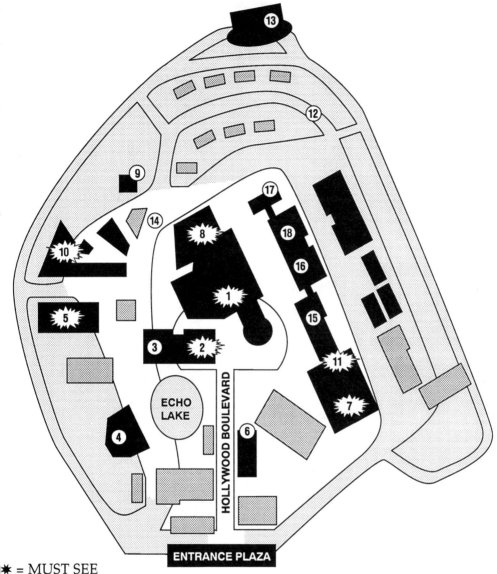

✸ = MUST SEE

✸1 The Great Movie Ride
✸2 SuperStar Television
3 The Monster Sound Show
4 Indiana Jones
Epic Stunt Spectacular!
✸5 Stars Tours
6 Theater of the Stars
✸7 The Magic of Disney Animation
✸8 Honey I Shrunk the Kids
Movie Set Adventure
9 Teenage Mutant Ninja Turtles®

✸10 Jim Henson's
Muppet★Vision 3D®
✸11 Backstage Studio Tour
12 Residential Street
13 Catastrophe Canyon
14 New York Street
15 The Voyage of The Little Mermaid
16 Special Effects Tour
17 Water Effects Tank
18 Soundstages I, II and III

Disney-MGM Studios Restaurants

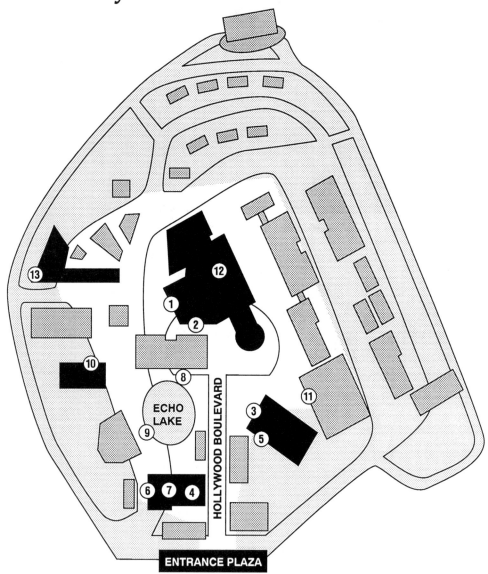

1 Sci-Fi Dine-In Theater Restaurant
2 Disney-MGM Studio
   Commissary
3 The Hollywood Brown Derby
4 Hollywood & Vine
5 Starring Rolls
6 50's Prime Time Cafe
7 Tune In Lounge
8 Min and Bill's Dockside Diner
9 Dinosaur Gertie's
   Ice Cream of Extinction

10 Backlot Express
11 Soundstage Restaurant
   The Catwalk Bar
12 Studio Catering Co.
13 Mama Melrose's
   Ristorante Italiano

CHAPTER 9
Typhoon Lagoon, River Country, Discovery Island, & Pleasure Island

TYPHOON LAGOON

Disney has taken what has become the ordinary water park and made it extraordinary. Once again, it is a matter of setting.

First of all, there is the story: according to Disney legend, this was once a beautiful tropical resort until a rogue typhoon roared through. What was left standing was knocked down by an earthquake. Oh, and then there was a volcano. (Sounds like a lovely place to vacation.) But the villagers refused to give up, and they rebuilt their paradise in and among the destruction.

The fabulous water slides are built into realistic miniature mountains, the huge wave pool has a sandy beach and the river rafting ride passes through jungle canopies, a rain forest and caves. There is hardly any sign of the artificial nature of the park–the water that cascades down the mountainside emerges from rivers and creeks without a pipe in sight.

Mount Mayday is one of the tallest peaks in Florida, even if it is a Disney-created simulation. It rises some 90 feet into the air, and is topped by the wreckage of the shrimp boat, "Miss Tilly." The smokestack on the boat erupts in a plume of water every once in a while, adding to the cascades all around.

The namesake central pool is **Typhoon Lagoon**, which is almost three acres in size. Every 90 seconds, you can catch the world's largest man-made waves, as high as six feet tall. Two sheltered pools, **Whitecap Cover** and **Blustery Bay**, serve the less adventurous.

Slip, sliding away. According to local myth, more than a few women have lost their bikini tops on the old Kowabunga. Always willing to please, Disney has built a little viewing stand at the bottom. We spent part of our afternoon there–strictly for research purposes–but the only lost articles we observed were sunglasses.

(We'd strongly recommend wearing an eyeglass strap or carrying your glasses in your folded hands when you ride one of the slides. You should also use plenty of suntan lotion.)

Pay tubes. Disney provides innertubes for all of the slides as part of the basic admission. You can, though, rent your own slightly larger tube for $5 for a single or $10 for a double; the advantage of renting your own is that you can skip the waiting lines at the bottom of slides where plungers wait for available free tubes. You'll still have to wait your turn in any line at the top; we'd only recommend this added expense on the busiest of days.

Up before down. As enjoyable as Typhoon Lagoon is, be aware that there is quite a bit of climbing involved in using the slides. And the serious water park fan might also want to explore the areas outside of Disney, such as Wet 'n Wild on International Drive.

Night slide. Consider ducking out of the Magic Kingdom or Epcot some hot summer afternoon for a cooling dip as they sun goes down. River Country is open until 8 p.m. during summertime, and ticket booths have in past years offered lower-cost tickets after 3 p.m.

Hang on to your bathing suit as you drop 51 feet, at speeds of up to 30 miles per hour, down the 214-foot-long **Humunga Kowabunga** water slide. Do we actually pay good money and wait on line for the privilege of falling this far, this fast? The moment of truth will come when you reach the top; try not to stop and consider the folly of it all. Just lay down on your back, cross your ankles and fold your arms over your chest. And then come back another time and try the slide with your eyes open.

Or, try the nearby **Storm Slides.** The trio of body slides, **Rudder Buster, Jib Jammer** and **Stern Burner** crash through waterfalls, caves and geysers. Each of the slides is somewhat different–on a busy day you'll have to take the slide assigned to you by the lifeguard at the top of the stairs. Our favorite is the center slide, which passes through an unexpected dark tunnel midway down the hill. Top speed on the slides is about 20 mph.

Mayday Falls and **Keelhall Falls** send you down a slide on a large innertube on a tour through caves, waterfalls and more. Mayday is the taller and longer ride, at about 460 feet in length. Keelhall is shorter, about 400 feet, but includes sharper twists and turns.

Entire families can go for a relatively tame white water adventure at **Gangplank Falls.** Your circular boat will work its way down the mountain in and among waterfalls and obstacles. Don't say the wrong thing to the person who loads your raft at the top of the slide–with the flick of a wrist, he or she can send your raft under the waterfall at the loading zone.For the youngest swimmers, **Ketchakiddee Creek** features water slides, boats, squirting animals and other toys for children only.

And finally, you can take a tour on the lazily flowing **Castaway Creek** that circles the park for almost half a mile; it takes about 30 minutes to circle completely around. If the traffic gets too thick or if the float is *too* lazy, you can get out and walk in the three-foot-deep creek or even leave and cross the park to your starting place.

Perhaps the most unusual attraction at the park is the **Shark Reef,** where guests get to strap on a snorkel (provided) and float through an artificial coral reef in and among small nurse and bonnethead sharks, and thousands of other colorful little fishies. We're assured that these are peaceful creatures. In fact, naturalists worry more about visitors damaging the fish with their suntan lotions and other pollutants; you'll have to take a shower first.

Admission to the park is about $20 for adults. Lockers and changing rooms are available near the entranceway and at Typhoon Tilly's, a fast food restaurant. You can also rent towels.

RIVER COUNTRY AND DISCOVERY ISLAND

River Country is Disney's version of Huck Finn's swimmin' hole. Get there on a short boat ride from the Magic Kingdom across Bay Lake.

Bay Cove at the heart of **River Country**, includes rope swings, a ship's boom and other interesting ways to fly out over and into the water below. Bay Cove is actually a part of Bay Lake, which is itself connected to Seven Seas Lagoon at the Magic Kingdom.

The heated swimming pool includes two water slides that end about seven feet above the water; the rest of the way down is up to you. Also at the park are a pair of corkscrew flume rides at **Whoop 'N' Holler Hollow.**

The park can become quite crowded in summer, and the gates are sometimes shut before noon; they'll reopen in late afternoon, and the park stays open late in season. Admission to River Country is about $10 for children 3-9 and $13 for adults; a combination ticket that also includes admission to Discovery Island is about $12/$16.

Discovery Island is Disney's private 11-acre zoological park, stocked with a fascinating collection of wild animals, both native to Florida and from far away. The island is a serious preserve that is home to hundreds of birds (including free-running peacocks and trained and untrained macaws, cockatoos and other parrots). You'll also fund Caribbean Flamingos, huge Galapagos tortoises and brown pelicans.

Boats for Discovery Island leave from River Country, Disney's Fort Wilderness Resort and Campground, Disney's Contemporary Resort, Disney's Polynesian Resort, Disney's Grand Floridian Beach Resort, or from the Magic Kingdom. Tickets for the park are about $5 for children and $9 for adults; combination tickets with River Country are described above.

PLEASURE ISLAND

Merriweather Adam Pleasure, also known as "MAD Pleasure" or the "Grand Funmeister," disappeared in 1941 on a circumnavigation expedition of the antarctic. By 1955 his beloved home island was in disrepair; the coup de grace was administered by a rogue hurricane.

Whoa! It's you against gravity as you plunge down the flumes at River Country and Typhoon Lagoon. You can somewhat control your speed, though, by the way you lie down.

FASTEST: Lie on your back with your hands over your head. Arch your back so that only your shoulders and heels touch the track.

FAST: Lie on your back with your hands crossed on your chest and your ankles crossed.

SLOW: Sit up.

SLOWEST: Walk back down the stairs.

Man-made discovery. Discovery island was completely invented by Disney, with tons of earth and stone brought in to create the land. At first the Disney concept was a recreation of "Treasure Island," complete with a sunken pirate ship just offshore. The ship is still there, but the theme is more natural.

Kids on tour. Youngsters between the ages of 8 and 14 can take a four-hour guided tour of Discovery Island in the summer months (most of June, July and August). The Discover Island Kidventure costs about $25. Call (407) 824-3784 for information and reservations.

The six-acre island languished in ruins until it was rediscovered by Disney archaeologists, who painstakingly rebuilt the town. And if you believe that story, perhaps you'd like to join the "Pleasure Island Histerical Society," whose plaques dot the landmarks of the island, which is located next to Disney Village.

There is no cover charge or age restriction to visit Pleasure Island during the day, or at anytime to enter the restaurants. The shops open at 10 a.m. The ticket gates go up at 7 p.m., charging $11.95; after 7 p.m., visitors under the age of 18 must be accompanied by a parent.

It's New Year's Eve every night of the year at the nightly New Year's Eve Street Party. The celebration begins at 11:47 p.m. and includes music, dancers, confetti and fireworks. In 1994, the celebration changes to a **Mardi Gras** party.

Mannequins Dance Palace. A contemporary club with a rotating dance floor and a high-tech (recorded) sound, light and dance show presented several times each night.

XZFR Rock & Roll Beach Club. A wild and somewhat frenetic club featuring classic rock and Top 40 dance hits from live bands and DJs. Somewhat quieter locations can be found among the billiard tables on the upper floors. The name of the club, by the way, is pronounced "zephyr," as in west wind.

Neon Armadillo Music Saloon. Live country-western music and southwestern food. Opens about 7 p.m., with first show at 8 p.m.

CAGE. An underground music and video dance club with almost 200 video monitors; for guests over 21. When Pleasure Island first opened in 1989, this space was called Videopolis East and was aimed at younger visitors.

The Adventurers Club. Five strange rooms filled with strange actors and you, their guests. Stick around and see what happens. The Adventurers Club is one of the most entertaining "performance spaces" you'll find at Walt Disney World. According to the cover story, this is the place where Mr. Pleasure stored all of the strange items he brought back from his journeys; it's enough fun just to cruise among them. You'll likely meet the curator, the maid and other oddball friends of Pleasure who will share their stories. At least once an hour, visitors are invited to enter into the library for an oddball show.

The Comedy Warehouse. Several shows each night; the club is small and seats are often filled well before showtime.

Propeller Heads. You'll also find a small video arcade that offers some of the hottest new games.

EATING YOUR WAY THROUGH
PLEASURE ISLAND

The major restaurants on Pleasure Island are located outside the turnstiles between Pleasure Island and Disney Village and can be visited without purchasing a ticket.

The **Empress Lily** paddleboat includes three restaurants and a lounge.

 **Steerman's Quarters.** (Dinner, 5:30-10 pm.) "Disney's Traditional Steak House." Prime ribs $20 to $22; 20-ounce Porterhouse Steak $26.

 **Empress Room.** (Dinner, 6:30-9:30 pm.) The fanciest and priciest restaurant at Pleasure Island, featuring French and French-sounding steak, seafood and poultry dishes. Here are some examples: shrimp and sea scallops with Roe, over black and white linguine with saffron, $28; sauteed medallions of beef tenderloin with Shrimp on a sauce of Cabernet Sauvignon and tomato hollandaise, $34; roasted breast of African pheasant with natural juices and truffles, served with three-grain pilaf, $31.

 **Fisherman's Deck.** (Lunch, noon-2 p.m. and Dinner, 5:30 p.m.-10 p.m.) Simpler fare. Luncheon entrees include sandwiches, burgers and salads from $6 to $8; trout at $10. For dinner, the menu includes lobster at market price, Seafood primavera at $18 and beef filet and shrimp for $23.

 **Portobello Yacht Club.** A first-class northern Italian eatery, with offerings ranging from thin-crust pizza cooked in a wood-fired oven ($7 to $8) to steak, chicken and fish dishes. Lunch salads include Insalata Caesar at $5, Insalata Caesar di pollo (Caesar salad with chicken, at $7) and Insalata di Pollo (salad with chicken at $8). A sample of lunch entrees include panino di vitello, veal flank steak charcoal grilled and sliced open faced over sourdough toast with wild mushrooms in rosemary sauce, for $9; angel hair pasta with smoked chicken, sun-dried tomatoes, olive oil, garlic and pesto, for $8. The same salads and pizzas are available at dinner as appetizers, plus entrees ranging in price from $13 to $16 for pasta and $17 to $23 for steak and chicken. A child's menu is also available.

KEY

〵| = FAST FOOD

 Y = PUB

 = FULL-SERVICE RESTAURANT

Hill Street Diner. Cheese steaks, personal pizzas, hot ham and cheese. $3 to $4.

Fireworks Factory. A brick-wall warehouse setting, piled with boxes. Lunch offerings include meatloaf, $7, BBQ trio (beef, pork, chicken) $10; burgers $7-$8, sandwiches $6 to $9, salads $3.50 to $10. For dinner, you can order catfish $15, crabcakes $16, chicken, ribs, meatloaf $13-$18. Steaks $17-24.

DISNEY'S VILLAGE MARKETPLACE

When the going gets tough, the tough go shopping, and the Village Marketplace is one of Disney's most interesting collection of shops.

Of course, there are lots of shops selling t-shirts, sweatshirts and hats with pictures of Mickey or Minnie, but perhaps the single largest collection is at **Mickey's Character Shop.** For the sporting fan, **Team Mickey** offers Disney paraphernalia for fans and players.

It's Christmas all the time at the **Christmas Chalet.** Other shops for children of all ages include **You and Me Kid.**

Board Stiff offers a bodacious selection of surfing apparel and equipment. **Conched Out** includes tropical mementos and dumb souvenirs.

Eurospain sells an interesting collection of handcrafted Spanish crafts.

DISNEY VILLAGE RESTAURANTS

The **Empress Lily**, with its three eateries, the **Empress Room**, the **Fisherman's Deck** and **Steerman's Quarters** is described above under Pleasure Island.

Chef Mickey's Village Restaurant. Breakfast, lunch and dinner. A pretty setting along the lake, featuring Disney music and settings. Chef Mickey himself will stroll among the tables at dinnertime. Breakfast goes for $2-$7; luncheon offerings include soup, salad, sandwiches and entrees from $6-$10, and the dinner menu offers pork chops, steak and seafood from $10-$18. The children's menu includes burgers, pasta, fish $3.50-$6.50.

Cap'n Jack's Oyster Bar. Lunch, dinner. Pretty setting on a little shack built into the village lake. Chowder, shellfish, crab cakes $3.50-$10. Child's menu features pasta, $4.

KEY

¶{ = Fast Food

Y = Pub

 = Full-
　　　Service
　　　Restaurant

 **Minnie Mia's Italian Eatery.** Lunch, dinner. Pizza $11-$13.50, $2-$2.50 per slice; pasta $5, subs $4-$5. Beer and wine.

 **Lakeside Terrace.** Lunch, dinner. A large fast-food restaurant with tables across from the lake. Burgers, hot dogs, fried fish, barbecued chicken $2.50-$5.

A MOVIE THEATER, TOO

And in your spare time, if you'd like to catch a flick, there is the **AMC Pleasure Island 10 Theatres.** Not just Disney movies, either.

KEY

= FAST FOOD

= PUB

= FULL-
SERVICE
RESTAURANT

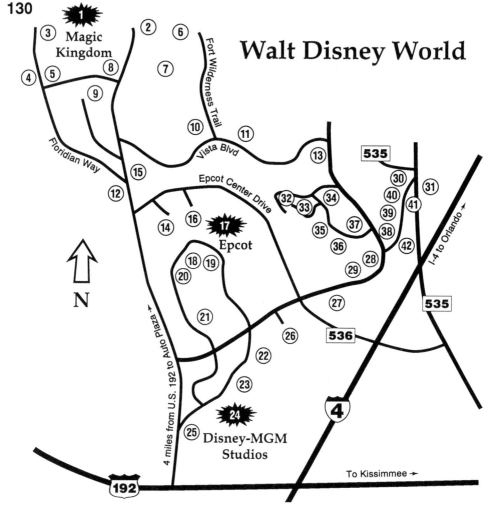

Walt Disney World

1 Magic Kingdom
2 Disney's Contemporary Resort
3 Disney's Grand Floridian Beach Resort
4 The Disney Inn
5 Disney's Polynesian Resort
6 Discovery Island
7 River Country
8 Transportation & Ticket Center
9 Parking
10 Disney's Fort Wilderness Resort
   and Campground
11 River Country & Pioneer Hall Parking
12 Car Care Center
13 Kinder-Care
14 Epcot Center Auto Plaza
15 Main Entrance Auto Plaza
16 Parking
17 Epcot Center
18 Disney's Yacht Club Resort
19 Disney's Beach Club Resort
20 Walt Disney World Dolphin
21 Walt Disney World Swan
22 Auto Plaza

23 Parking
24 Disney-MGM Studios Theme Park
25 Auto Plaza
26 Disney's Caribbean Beach Resort
27 Typhoon Lagoon
28 Disney Village Marketplace
29 Pleasure Island
30 Buena Vista Walk-In Medical Center
31 Crossroads
32 Treehouse Villas
33 Fairway Villas
34 Walt Disney World Conference Center
   and Club Lake Villas
35 Lake Buena Vista Club
36 Vacation Villas
37 Reception Center
38 Buena Vista Palace
39 Grosvenor Resort
40 Travelodge Hotel
41 Guest Quarters Resorts
41 Hotel Royal Plaza
42 Howard Johnson Resort Hotel
42 The Hilton

CHAPTER 10
Golfing, Tennis, Swimming and Horseback Riding with Mickey

Depending upon your point of view, Walt Disney World is either three theme parks surrounded by 99 holes of golf, or a country club so huge it includes three theme parks.

Either way, it's one version of golfing heaven. It's a way for mom or dad or even junior to come to Walt Disney World without having to spend all their time in the company of a bunch of cartoon mice.

But wait, perhaps you prefer tennis, horseback riding, swimming, fishing, biking . . . just about any popular form of recreation can be found within the park boundaries.

GOLF COURSES

There are five championship-level 18-hole golf courses within the World, plus a 9-hole practice course. Two of the courses are good enough to be stops on the PGA Tour.

Magnolia. At the Disney Inn. Named for the more than 1,500 magnolias on the course, this course plays to 6,642 yards from the middle tees and is the setting for the final round of the Walt Disney World/Oldsmobile Golf Classic. There's water on 10 of the 18 holes.

Palm. Considered one of the most difficult courses, included among *Golf Digest's* "Top 25 Resort Courses." It plays to a relatively short 6,461 yards from the middle tees but water and sand seems to be almost everywhere. The 18th hole has been rated as the fourth toughest hole on the PGA Tour.

Lake Buena Vista. A wide open and heavily wooded course

More, you say? In addition to the Walt Disney World courses, there are 18 other municipal, public and semi-private golf courses in and around the Disney area in Orange County.

Cypress Creek Country Club. Orlando. Semi-private 18 holes. (407) 351-2187.

Dubsdread Golf Course. Orlando. Municipal 18 holes. (407) 246-2551.

Eastwood Golf & Country Club. Orlando. Semi-private 18 holes. (407) 281-4653.

Grand Cypress Resort. Orlando. Resort 45 holes. (407) 239-4700.

The Greens. Orlando. Public 18 holes. (407) 351-9778.

Hunter's Creek Golf Club. Orlando. Public 18 holes. (407) 240-4653.

International Golf Club. Orlando. Resort 18 holes. (407) 239-6909.

Lone Palm Par 3. Orlando. Public 9 holes. (407) 275-7273.

Marriott's Orlando World Center. Orlando. Resort 18 holes. (407) 239-4200.

Meadow Woods Golf Club. Orlando. Semi-private 18 holes. (407) 850-5600.

MetroWest Country Club. Orlando. Semi-private 18 holes. (407) 299-1099.

Orange Lake Country Club. Kissimmee. Semi-private. (407) 239-1050.

Rosemont Golf & Country Club. Orlando. Semi-private. (407) 298-1230.

Ventura Country Club. Orlando. Semi-private 18 holes. (407) 277-2640.

Wedgefield Golf & Country Club. Orlando. Semi-private 18 holes. (407) 568-2116.

Winter Park Municipal. Winter Park. Municipal 9 holes. (407) 623-3339.

Winter Pines Golf Club. Winter Park. Public 18 holes. (407) 671-3172.

Zellwood Station Country Club. Zellwood. Semi-private 18 holes. (407) 886-3303.

that reaches to 6,655 yards, extending from the Disney Village Clubhouse.

Disney's new **Bonnet Creek Club** opened at the start of 1992, with two more championship par 72 courses:

Osprey Ridge. Designed by acclaimed golf course architect Tom Fazio, it includes a circulating 18-hole routing with holes that play in every direction. The course extends 6,705 yards from the middle tees, including some remote tropical settings. Some of the tees, greens and viewing areas are as much as 25 feet above grade; much of the earth was moved from the excavation at nearby Eagle Pines. The namesake "ridge" plays an important role in the course: you'll climb the ridge for the tee for Hole 3, the green for Hole 12 is built into its side, and the green for Hole 16 is atop it.

Eagle Pines. Eight of designer Pete Dye's courses are included in *Golf Magazine's* top fifty. Unlike the high mounds and ridges of Osprey Ridge, this new course offers a low profile although many balls will end up in the surrounding pines. Eagle Pines plays 6,224 yards from the middle tees, and is considered a bit more forgiving than the other courses. Dye included a lip on the edge of fairways along water hazards to reduce the number of wet balls.

Executive Course. At the Disney Inn. A nine-hole, 2,913-yard par-36 course with small rolling greens and elevated tees. It's no pushover, though, with some of the most difficult greens at Walt Disney World. No golf carts are allowed.

Fees, including a required cart, were about $75 at Magnolia, Palm and Lake Buena Vista and about $85 at Osprey Ridge and Eagle Pines. Twilight rates, beginning at 3 p.m., were about half the full charge.

The Walt Disney World Golf Studio includes small group instruction, videotaping and custom coursework. Studio sessions are offered several times a day at the Magnolia driving range. Call (407) 824-2270 for reservations.

Private lessons are available at the Disney Inn and the Village Clubhouse. Rates were about $25 per half hour with an assistant, or $45 with one of the pros. Call 824-2270 for the Disney Inn or 828-3741 for the Clubhouse.

Clubs, balls and shoes are available for rent at the pro shop.

Each October, the PGA Tour comes to Orlando for the

Walt Disney World/Oldsmobile Golf Classic, which therefore is a good time to come to watch but not to play. If you've got the scratch, though, you can pay about $5,000 for a one-year membership in the Classic Club. Each member gets to play with one of the pros in the tournament for three of the four days of the contest. For details, call (407) 828-2255.

Nearly 400 other tournaments of all types take place each year. For information and reservations, call the Walt Disney World Master Starter at (407) 824-2270.

TENNIS

There were, at last count, 15 lighted courts within Walt Disney World at various resorts. The largest tennis facility is at the Contemporary hotel, including backboards and an automatic ball server for practice. Other courts can be found at the Disney Inn, the Yacht Club, Beach Club and the Swan and Dolphin resorts. A pair of clay courts can be found at the Grand Floridian.

Courts can be reserved no more than 24 hours in advance, with fees from $10 to $12 per hour at the Contemporary, Grand Floridian, Swan and Dolphin. Tennis is free at the Disney Inn, the Village Clubhouse, Fort Wilderness, Yacht Club or Beach Club. Call the resorts for reservations; racquets and balls can be rented or purchased at some of the resorts.

A tennis clinic is offered at the Contemporary resort. The course includes video recordings of your game.

MARINAS

Walt Disney World offers the country's largest fleet of pleasure boats, a larger collection than many navies of the world. There are three major areas: the Seven Seas Lagoon, which sits between the Magic Kingdom and the Ticket and Transportation Center and surrounded by the monorail; Bay Lake, the largest body of water, which includes Discovery Island, and the Buena Vista Lagoon, a 35-acre body of water that fronts on Pleasure Island and Disney Village.

Marinas are located at the **Contemporary Resort, Fort Wilderness, Polynesian Resort, Grand Floridian, Caribbean Beach, Yacht Club** and **Beach Club.** There is also a boat rental station at the **Disney Village,** where a variety of boats are available for rental to day visitors as well as guests at Disney resorts. Guests at some of the Disney resorts can purchase a pass that includes unlimited use of boats during their stay. In the summer, waiting lines for boats can be quite lengthy at midday.

Water, water everywhere. Not to drink, but to swim in, boat on and waterski and parasail over. In addition to the offerings within Walt Disney World, there are numerous places for aquatic recreation in the Orlando area.

Turkey Lake Park offers sand beaches, swimming pool and nature trails. For general information, call (407) 299-5594. You can reach **Turkey lake Park Boat Rentals** at (407) 677-5554.

You can rent a houseboat for cruising on the St. John's River through **Houseboat Vacations, Inc.** at (800) 262-3454 or from **Hontoon Landing Marina** at (800) 458-2474 or (800) 248-2474.

Ski Holidays offers parasail thrill rides, jet ski rentals and waterski charters on a private 400-acre lake adjoining Walt Disney World. Contact them at (407) 239-4444.

Experienced divers can explore the Atlantic or Gulf Coasts or inland springs with equipment rented from **The Dive Station.** Call them at (407) 843-3483.

No mice. Fort Wilderness offers a small petting farm behind Pioneer Hall. Animals include sheep, goats, chickens and a friendly Brahma bull. Youngsters can also hop aboard a pony.

Water Sprites. Small and low-powered, they're still zippy enough to be a lot of fun. They rent by the half hour, for about $11; children under 12 are not allowed to drive. Available at Contemporary, Polynesian, Grand Floridian, Fort Wilderness and Disney Village.

Water Skiing. A powerboat with driver and equipment is available at Fort Wilderness, Polynesian, Grand Floridian and Contemporary marinas. The rate is about $65 per hour.

Slow Boats. Pontoon Flote Boats putter around, very slowly, from Disney Village and most of the resort marinas. Rentals cost about $35 per hour. Also available are Canopy Boats, 16-foot V-hulls with an outboard. They can be rented at Disney Village and Port Orleans, for about the same hourly rate.

Sailboats. Wind-powered vessels, from little two-seat Sunfish and speedy Hobie Cat catamarans to heavier six-seater Capris are offered at Contemporary, Polynesian, Grand Floridian, Fort Wilderness, Yacht Club and Beach Club marinas. Prices range from about $10 to $15 per hour.

People-Power. One-person Pedal Boats, for about $8 an hour, are available at most marinas. Canoes for canal paddling can be rented at the Fort Wilderness Bike Barn for about $4 per hour, or $9 for the day.

FISHING

Although Bay Lake is well-stocked with bass, fishing opportunities are extremely limited within Walt Disney World.

Guests at Fort Wilderness can fish from the shore or on any of the canals. Twice a day an escorted fishing expedition leaves the Fort Wilderness marina; the price is about $110 for two hours, and $25 each additional hour for a party of up to five persons and includes all gear.

SWIMMING

Guests at Disney resorts are surrounded by water, with swimming encouraged almost everywhere. There are more than five miles of white sand beach along the shores of Bay Lake and Seven Seas Lagoon. Both waterways were engineered by Disney; the sand was mined from beneath the lake muck during construction.

Beaches can be found at Contemporary, Grand Floridian, Caribbean Beach, Fort Wilderness, Polynesian, Yacht Club and Beach Club resorts.

All of the hotels within Walt Disney World offer swimming pools, some more exotic than others. For example, water slides can be found at the Polynesian and Caribbean Beach resorts.

Use of these pools is restricted to guests at Disney resorts, although we have never seen a swimmer "carded" for a guest pass. Day guests looking for cooling water are encouraged to visit River Country or Typhoon Lagoon.

HORSEBACK RIDING

Trail rides for resort guests as well as day visitors depart from the Fort Wilderness campground several times a day. Riders must be at least 9 years old; the horses are very gentle and experience is not required of riders. The trail rides cost about $15. Call (407) 824-2832 to make reservations, no more than five days in advance.

Giddy-up. Instruction and horseback trail riding is also available at the **Grand Cypress Equestrian Center** in Orlando.
(407) 239-4608.

BIKING

More than eight miles of bicycle paths can be found at Fort Wilderness and at the Disney Village resort; other places to bike include some of the spread-out resorts like Caribbean Beach. In an unusual departure for Disney entertainment, use of the paths is free–that is, if you bring your own bike.

Rental bikes can be engaged at the Bike Barn at Fort Wilderness, the Villa Center at Disney Village or the marina at Caribbean Beach. Rates are about $3 per hour or $7 per day; tandems ("bicycles built for two") can be rented at the Bike Barn.

Ice skating? Indoors, of course, at the **Dowdy Pavilion Bowling & Ice Rink** in Orlando, at (407) 352-2695, or the **Orlando Ice Skating Palace**, reachable at (407) 299-5440.

HEALTH CLUBS

Olympiad Health Club at Contemporary Resort includes Nautilus gym equipment, sauna and individual whirlpools. Open to resort guests and day visitors for $5 fee, $10 including whirlpool baths. Open daytime hours, closed Sunday. Call (407) 824-3410 for appointments and information.

Other clubs, open to guests only and each charging a daily or vacation-long fee, include **St. John's Health Spa** at the Grand Floridian, **The Magic Mirror** at the Disney Inn, the **Ship Shape Health Club** at the Yacht Club and Beach Club, **The Body by Jake** club at the Dolphin.

CHAPTER 11
Learning Adventures at Walt Disney

Feeling bad about taking your kids out of school for a vacation at Walt Disney World? How about giving them a little homework, Mickey-style?

Disney offers a range of educational seminars for youngsters *and adults.* You might want to discuss some of the options with your children's teachers.

Wonders of Walt Disney World. A learning adventure for ages 10 to 15. A six-hour backstage exploration of one of the Walt Disney World theme parks; participants receive a special book, classroom materials and follow-up activities, as well as lunch at a park restaurant. Call (407) 354-1855 for information and reservations. 1993 prices were $75 per program; a ticket to one of the theme parks is not included or required during the tour period.

Exploring Nature. Includes a visit to The Living Seas at Epcot Center; Discovery Island, home to many exotic birds and endangered animals; a hunt for alligators and other wildlife in Disney's off-limits 7,500-acre conservation area and more. Offered Tuesdays and Thursdays.

Art Magic. Meet with a Disney animator; study landscape, architecture and costuming and explore set design and special effects. Offered Mondays, Wednesdays and Fridays.

Show Biz Magic. Go behind the scenes and meet many of the Disney performers and stage crew. Offered Mondays, Tuesdays, Wednesdays and Thursdays.

Should you take your kids out of school? In the best of all worlds, probably not. There are enough interruptions in the normal school year as it is. However, if work and school vacation times do not coincide, or if you are taking our advice seriously and trying to avoid crowds, there are ways to work with your schools.

We'd suggest you meet with your childrens' teachers to determine if there are particular times when an absence of a few days (wrapped around or including a weekend or minor holiday) will not make a big impact on schoolwork. Consult your school calendar in search of local holidays or "workshop" half-days.

Florida Homework
See if you can coordinate a special assignment for your children. If there is an upcoming unit on Mexico, for example, perhaps they could be assigned to produce a special report with research performed at Epcot Center's Mexican pavilion.

Disney Learning Adventures for Adults. An in-depth exploration of some of the wonders of Epcot Center for visitors over the age of 16. Call (407) 345-5860 for schedules, information and reservations. 1992 prices were $20 per program; a ticket to Epcot Center is also required.

Hidden Treasures of World Showcase. A 4-hour walking tour to explore the art, architecture, costumes, customs and culture of the nations of Epcot.

Gardens of the World. Explore the green side of the World Showcase in a $3^{1/2}$-hour walking tour led by a Disney horticultural expert. Disney offers other special programs through advance reservation. These include:

The Disney Approach to People Management. A three-day seminar for upper-level managers.

The Disney Approach to Quality Service. A three day seminar for managers and supervisors in customer service.

Communicating, Disney Style: Adding 'Magic' to the Classroom. A three-day seminar on applying Disney's communication techniques to the classroom.

Marketing the Good News: Building Positive Images for your School. A three-day seminar applying Disney marketing strategies to educators seeking to build positive images and school pride among students, staff and the community.

Finally, Disney offers behind-the-scenes half-day tours of Walt Disney World and the Walt Disney World Nursery in programs designed exclusively for adult groups of 15 or more who are staying within the Walt Disney World Resort. Call (407) 363-6666 for information on these seminars.

Universal Studios Florida

CHAPTER 12
Universal Studios

It was 78 years ago that movie legend Carl Laemmle began to allow visitors–at 25 cents a head–to come to his studios to watch silent movies being made.

The tours at Universal Pictures Manufacturing Company in Hollywood were stopped when sound was added to film, but in 1964 the renamed Universal Studios reopened its doors to visitors.

Universal's Hollywood lot became the third most-popular tourist attraction in the nation; visitors board trams that take them in and around the historic backlot and soundstages of Universal City, and along the way into some very special attractions based on some of the movie company's greatest hits.

In 1990, Universal moved east to Florida with the opening of its gigantic Orlando studios. Here are a few things to understand about Universal Studios Florida:

 * It is a working studio, producing motion pictures, television shows and commercials;

 * The 444-acre site is the newest major theme park in Florida, including some of the most spectacular and state-of-the-art rides and attractions anywhere in the world, well beyond those of Disney and,

* The designers abandoned the Hollywood model of a single ride made up of a dozen or so elements in favor of a very traditional Disney-like park with lots of walking and alas, lots of waiting on busy days. And the waits can be longer than those at any other area park.

Made in Florida. Films shot at the Orlando studios have included "Psycho IV–The Beginning"; Sylvester Stallone's "Oscar", and "Problem Child 2." Some visitors might be impressed to learn that the New Kids on the Block made a music video here. Other television projects include dozens of commercials and numerous Nickelodeon series.

THE
POWER TRIP

Lines at some of the more popular attractions can build to as much as 90 minutes on busy days; the Power Tour puts you on a fast track for the major magnets in the morning with a more leisurely pace for the rest of the day.

The new **Jaws** ride and the older **Back to the Future** simulator are the biggest draws at the park; head for one or the other attraction as soon as you arrive at the park—and the earlier the better. To go to either of the rides, make your first right turn on Rodeo Drive and keep walking toward the lagoon. Warning: In our judgment, many young visitors and some older ones may find both rides to be too wild; if you're not up to the journey, go instead to the **E.T. Adventure** as your first stop.

When you are through at Jaws or The Future, you can check out the lines at the ride you missed, or make plans to come back late in the day.

Continue around the lagoon in a counterclockwise direction to **Earthquake—The Big One** and ride the subway to San Francisco. Exit that ride and continue to **Kongfrontation.**

Now, head to the front of the park and **The Funtastic World of Hanna-Barbera,** where you will probably find a growing line. It's worth the wait for youngsters; adults may choose to pass it by, especially if they've been to the Future already.

Youngsters will certainly want to visit **Nickelodeon Studios.** We also recommend to adults **Alfred Hitchcock: The Art of Making Movies.**

You have now seen the major attractions of the park. Check the daily schedule for show times and then make a second tour to visit **The Gory, Gruesome & Grotesque Horror Make-up Show,** the **E.T. Adventure** if you missed it the first time around and if the lines are of a reasonable length, the **Animal Actors Stage,** the **Wild, Wild, Wild West Stunt Show, Ghostbusters** and the **"Murder, She Wrote" Mystery Theatre.**

The **Dynamite Nights Stunt Spectacular** is worth a peek; while it's on and drawing thousands to the sides of the lagoon it's also a time to duck into one of the major shows for a second ride or to catch one you've missed. Go back to Back to the Future or Jaws now.

Here's our bottom line: Universal Studios is worth a day out of the tour of any vacationer in Central Florida, but it also requires the most careful planning for the day of a visit and a schedule within the park.

The best times to come to Universal Studios are the same as for other area attractions. Arrive between September and November, between Thanksgiving and Christmas or in mid-January and you may be able to walk around like you own the place. Show up during Christmas break, Easter vacation or mid-summer and you'll meet what seems like the entire population of Manhattan or Boston or Cleveland in front of you in line. Universal Studios is open 365 days a year. It is located near the intersection of Interstate 4 and the Florida Turnpike in Orlando. The main entrance is about one-half mile north of I-4 at exit 30B–Kirkman Road (Highway 435).

Another entrance is located on Turkey Lake Road. Take I-4 to Sand Lake Exit 29. If you were heading west on I-4, make a right onto Sand Lake and another right onto Turkey Lake Road. If you were traveling east on I-4, make a left onto Sand Lake and a right onto Turkey Lake Road.

Admission prices in 1993 were about $36 with tax for visitors over the age of 10, $29 with tax for children from 3 to 9. Two-day and yearly passes are also available.

Universal Studios sells "VIP Tours" through its guest relations desk. For about $91 each, a group of as many as 15 people will have their own guide for the day with the privilege of breaking through any line in the park. For about $900, you can hire an "exclusive" tour with only the people you choose. Neither tour includes lunch. As expensive as the tours are, they might begin to make sense if you are forced to visit the park on a day when all of the major rides have 90-minute waits.

EXPO CENTER

WOW **Back To The Future®. . . The Ride.™**

Dive into the world of the record-breaking movie trilogy, "Back To The Future" in Universal's incredible simulator adventure. This is about as wild a ride as anything you'll find in Florida, with the possible exception of the real Space Shuttle. There is absolutely nothing like it at Walt Disney World.

It seems that weird Doc Brown is back home conducting new time travel experiments. He has created his newest

Upgrading your ticket. If you decide that you want to come back for a second day at Universal Studios, visit Guest Relations to upgrade your ticket to a two-day pass. You must do this on the day of purchase of the original ticket.

Respect for elders. Senior Citizens should stop by guest services to pick up a VIP sticker that entitles them to preferred seating at several of the shows, including the Wild, Wild, Wild West Stunt Show and the Animal Actors Stage.

From 2001 to the Future. The director of the Back to the Future ride-film was renowned movie special effects designer Douglas Trumbull, who created special effects for hits including "2001: A Space Odyssey," and "Close Encounters of the Third Kind." The four-minute 70mm movie portion of the ride took two years to make, and cost as much as a feature film. Elaborate hand-painted miniatures were created for the filming.

Don't say you weren't warned. Back to the Future is described as a "dynamically aggressive ride." Visitors suffering from maladies including dizziness, seizures, back or neck problems, claustrophobia, motion sickness, pregnancy and heart disorders are advised to sit this one out. The ride also won't work for persons of a certain size or shape who cannot fit into the seats and safety harness. We suspect you know who you are.

vehicle–an eight-passenger Time Vehicle that is faster and more energy efficient than anything before . . . or since. That's the good news. The bad news is that Biff Tannen has broken into the "Institute of Future Technology" and threatens to end the universe as we know it! It's up to you to jump into your own DeLorean and chase down Biff.

Surrounded by images and sound and buffeted by the realistic motion of your flight simulator, you will soar into Hill Valley in the year 2015, blast back to the Ice Age for a chilling highspeed encounter with canyons of sheer ice, explode into the Volcanic Era for a once-in-a-lifetime encounter with a Tyrannosaurus Rex and then through a volcano and over the edge of a molten lava fall.

This is a state-of-the-art attraction that combines a spectacular Omnimax film with simulator ride vehicles (bearing Florida license plates "OUTTATIME.") The 80-foot diameter domelike screens of the Omnimax theaters occupy all of the viewer's peripheral vision, making the screen seem to vanish and taking the viewer into the scene.

The "Institute of Future Technology" in the waiting area features actual props from the "Back to the Future" movie series, including hoverboards (futuristic skateboards without wheels) and the all-important flux capacitors for time travel.

There are actually two identical rides within the building, each with its own set of 12 eight-seater DeLorean cars and movie dome. Each area has cars on three levels with three cars at the top, five in the middle and four at the bottom.

Universal insiders say that the very best experience can be had by sitting in the front row of the center car on the second tier; dispatchers call it Car 6. This particular vehicle is in the absolute center of the movie dome and you cannot easily see any surrounding cars which might distract from the illusion.

At about the midway point of the waiting line visitors will be divided among three rampways, one to each level. If you can at all arrange to go through portal number two to the middle level, you have a one-in-five chance of ending up in magic Car 6.

When you enter into the holding room for the simulator, try to maneuver next to the door to get a seat in the front of the car. (Some visitors find the small waiting room a bit confining; you can ask the attendant to leave the door open if you feel it necessary. Trust us: a much more intense experience is coming.)

As you wait to board your simulator, pay attention to the little movie about time travel safety; we enjoyed watching crash dummies "Fender" and "Bender" at work. When you feel a rumble beneath your feet, you'll know the car is returning to its base.

The preshow film and the movie shown in the ride itself were made specially for the simulator. Doc Brown (Christopher Lloyd) and Biff Tannen (Thomas Wilson) took part in the movie, but Marty McFly (Michael J. Fox) is nowhere to be seen. According to rumors, Fox asked for too much money.

The DeLoreans themselves rise about eight feet out of their garages at the start of the movie. Once in the air, four actuators drive the car—three for vertical movement and one for fore-and-aft movement. Although it may feel as if your car is soaring and dropping hundreds of feet, the entire range of movement for the vehicle is about two feet.

To give the feeling of traveling through space, the cars are surrounded with a fog made from liquid nitrogen.

On a busy day, lines easily reach to 90 minutes or more. Remember that the crowd you see out on the plaza is only about half the backup—there are internal walkways and hallways within the building as well. Each ride takes about 4 1/2 minutes, with about 96 persons entering each of the two simulator theaters at a time. By the end of the day on a quiet day, there may be no line at all. But, it still takes 15 minutes or so to walk into the gate, up the stairs, into a waiting room for one of the simulators and into your seat.

Before or after you join the line, check out the large prop to the left of the building. The Jules Verne Train was used in the closing scene of Back to the Future III, when Doc Brown returns from 1885 in this steam engine adapted to become a time machine.

WOW **E.T. Adventure®** One of the best-loved motion pictures of all times is given life in this imaginative ride which begins where E.T. left off. You will share a bicycle with our favorite extra-terrestrial in a voyage across the moon to save E.T.'s home, a planet dying for lack of his healing touch.

As marvelous as the ride itself is, don't overlook the incredible fantasy world of the waiting area. It will start when you register at the door and are cast as an actor in the coming adventure; be sure to hold on to the special card you are given.

You're being watched. We took a backstage tour of Back to the Future, visiting the computer rooms and the security "tower" where operators monitor all 12 cars in each theater using see-in-the-dark video cameras. They are able to turn off individual cars if anything goes wrong or a rider becomes ill or faints.

Meeting spot. If you're planning to do a baby swap, ask for advice from one of the attendants on the proper place to wait. And, if you need to meet someone after the ride, pick a specific spot like the Jules Verne Train, since there are two exits from the building.

Look down, look up. The huge miniature city beneath your bicycle includes 3,340 tiny buildings, 250 ultra-compact cars and 1,000 street lights. The stars above include some 4,400 points of light. The music for the ride was written by Academy Award-winning composer John Williams, who was also responsible for the movie score.

The entrance line wends its way through a mysterious redwood forest populated with all sorts of human and other-worldly creatures. All around you, government agents search for E.T.

Finally, you are at your bicycle. Higher and higher you climb, until the city looks like a toy beneath you. Will you arrive home at the Green Planet in time? Director Steven Spielberg created a phantasmagorical cast of new characters for the adventure, including Botanicus, Tickli Moot Moot, Orbidon, Magdol, Horn-Flowers, Tympani Tremblies, Water Imps, Big Zoms, Gurgles, Squirtals and Churtles.

Well, yes: and the celebration begins as E.T.'s friend the Tickli Moot Moot laughs again, Orbidon sparkles and Magdol sings. Baby E.T.s will dance and play all around you, and E.T. will thank you . . . personally.

WOW Animal Actors Stage. And you think you've a right to be proud when Bowser rolls over the third time you ask? Wait until you see the professionals at work–they've pawed and clawed their way to the top of animal show business.

Mr. Ed, unmuzzled. We hope we're not going to shatter any heartfelt illusions, but we trust you realize that Mr. Ed does not really talk. His trainers fill his mouth with peanut butter before he goes on stage, which makes him want to move his jaws any time his bit is loosened.

Lassie (actually, one of many collies who have held that name over the years), Benji and even a horsing-around Mr. Ed take the stage in a corny but interesting exhibition of animals trained for the movies.

Most of Universal Studios Florida's dogs and cats were rescued from the pound before they went on to stardom. Benji has appeared in four movies–three bearing his name, plus "Oh Heavenly Dog" with Chevy Chase. He has twice been named the Animal Actor of the Year by the American Guild of Variety Artists.

The open-air stadium will accommodate 1,500 people for its 25-minute show; it is a good place to take an afternoon break when lines are longest at the most popular attractions.

HOLLYWOOD

WOW The Gory Gruesome & Grotesque Horror Make-up Show. It's all in the name: actually, they left out "gross."

Most everyone loves a good monster or horror movie. Here's your chance to learn about some of the secrets behind the special effects. For example, where else would you find out the recipe for gore: shrimp sauce, oatmeal and red dye.

Among the devices demonstrated in the lively 25 minute film and live show are the metamorphosis of the "American

Werewolf in London" and the teleportation scene from "The Fly," somewhat humorously re-enacted on stage.

One extra from the audience–usually a woman–gets her arm sliced open and suffers other simulated indignities. She is usually selected from one of the front rows.

Some children may find the GG&G show too gory, gruesome and grotesque: parents be warned.

There are 355 seats in the theater, and visitors are often turned away at midday; go early or late on busy days.

AT&T at the Movies. A somewhat interesting interactive electronic playground, a good place to duck in out of the rain or the sun and enjoy a few Epcot-like science and computer games. You can remake your face into an electronic puzzle and even place a call on what is claimed to be the world's largest working telephone.

SAN FRANCISCO/AMITY

Earthquake® – The Big One. Why in the world would any sane human being want to travel all the way to Orlando, fork over a not-small number of hard-earned bucks and then wait in a long line for the privilege of riding right into a devastating earthquake?

Well, it has to be because this ride is devastating fun. This spectacular attraction is based on the motion picture "Earthquake," which was the first movie in history to win an Academy Award for special effects.

Check out the photos along the walls of the preshow area. Universal researchers uncovered a treasure trove of photos from the family of a survivor of the 1906 San Francisco earthquake. Six visitors–usually three women, a man and two kids–are hired as extras and "grips" for a demonstration

Heavy effects. The special effects of this ride are among the most spectacular ever created for an amusement park. To begin with, the rocking and rolling of the simulated earthquake would actually register a whopping 8.3 on the Richter scale. The mega-tremor releases 65,000 gallons of (recycled) water every six minutes. The falling roadway slab weighs 45,000 pounds.

Perhaps most interesting is the fact that the tracks themselves are flat; all of the rocking and rolling takes place with lifters within the train itself.

Backstage at the earthquake. We took an exclusive tour into the control room and observed the computer controls for the sophisticated ride. You can see the room along the right side of the train in the catastrophe station; it's the operator who runs out with a megaphone at the end of each adventure.

High Tech. The Jaws ride employs space-age underwater technology never before used in an amusement attraction.

The seven-acre lagoon holds 5 million gallons of water and there are eight boats. Much of the New England memorabilia scattered about was found in Gloucester, Mass. and surrounding fishing towns.

The 32-foot shark is made of steel and fiberglass, with a latex skin; it's teeth are made of urethane. When it attacks—and you know it will, time and time again—it moves through the water at realistic shark speeds of 20 feet per second, with thrusts equal to the power of a 727 jet engine.

of movie special effects. The kids get to fulfill a child's fantasy: dropping (foam) boulders on a bunch of adults; the male extra is in for a surprise dive.

We'd suggest you move all the way across the rows in the demonstration area so that you can move quickly to the train for your choice of seats. When the demonstration is over, you will enter into a realistic recreation of a subway station in Oakland and board a train heading to Embarcadero Station in San Francisco.

The front of the 200-seat train is to your left; the best car for the ride is the second car from the front. The first row of each car has a somewhat blocked view; try to grab a seat in the middle.

The train pulls out of the station and under the bay. Very quickly, something goes very wrong. The train begins to shake violently; lights flicker and then the ceiling starts to collapse. The street above your head caves in, and a huge propane tanker truck crashes its way toward you. But that's only the beginning: another train bears down on you at high speed aiming for a head-on crash. And a huge tidal wave races your way.

Cut!

Amity Games. Down by the waterfront there's a movie set version of a boardwalk, complete with games of chance including **Short Shot** basketball, **Milk Can Menagerie, Hoop Toss, Shark-Banger** (a version of the familiar whack-amole game), **Muffin Tin** and **Dolphin Dash.**

Jaws® Just when you thought it was safe to go back to Florida, Universal Studios went and opened **Jaws,** a spectacular new ride that opened in the summer of 1993.

It's always the Fourth of July in the picturesque seaside resort of Amity. You can walk the boardwalk and try your hand at carnival games or stop for a seafood snack. And, of course, you are going to want to hop on board the Amity Harbor tour boat for a peaceful jaunt.

The cruise starts out innocently enough. The vicious little shark that had previously terrorized Amity hangs—dead—from a hook in the village. So what could possibly go wrong?

It starts with a quick glimpse of a dorsal fin that zips past and then under your boat. Then he comes back!

Your boat captain will attempt to save the day, firing rifle grenades in a desperate attempt to stop the attacker. Somehow he will steer the boat into the safety of a deserted boat house. Hah! Suddenly there's a loud crash on the side of the boathouse and the wall all but comes down with the force of Jaws breaking through.

Now it's a race for life as the boat is chased by the frenzied creature. This time the captain's shots hit a chemical tank along shore and the lagoon fills with burning fuel as he attempts to break for safety on a barge that carries the main power supply cable to Amity Island.

Once again the shark attacks, but this time he grabs hold of the main power cable: instant fish fry! At last you're safe.

By the way, you wouldn't think that Universal Studios would possibly allow much time to pass before it would unveil a new attraction based on the 1993 movie thriller *Jurassic Park,* would you?

Get real! And pretty real you will get when a major new ride opens at the park—sometime in 1996, according to the latest plans—based on the movie and the book by Michael Crichton.

Dynamite Nights Stunt Spectacular. A wild demonstration of explosive movie stunts, performed on the Lagoon. There's no waiting line for the show–just pull up a piece of the railing (check the daily schedule for show time). There's a story line for those who care about such things: something about a high-energy shootout with desperate drug dealers.

Wild, Wild, Wild West Stunt Show.® Guns blaze, cowboys brawl and dynamite creates instant urban renewal in Universal's recreation of a 19th Century western town. Hollywood stunt players demonstrate how they simulate the dangerous action.

The show, held in a 2,000-seat arena, is short and intense and suitable for children of all ages, although some of the explosions and gunfire are a bit loud. There's a little story about a rough and tough "Ma" and her gang of boys; the guys in the white hats win, but not before there's a terrific battle down in the corral, up on the roofs and even out on the ropes that hold the sign ("Square Dance and Hanging, Saturday Night") across Main Street.

PRODUCTION CENTRAL
"Murder, She Wrote"® **Mystery Theatre.** Solving a mur-

One-Day Ticket
Adults (10 and older):
$34 ($36.04 with tax)
Children (3 to 9):
$27 ($28.62 with tax)

Two-Day Ticket
Adults (10 and older):
$53 ($56.18 with tax)
Children (3 to 9):
$42 ($44.52 with tax)

Annual Celebrity Pass (Good for one year)
Adults (10 and older):
$85 ($90.10 with tax)
Children (3 to 9):
$67.50 ($71.55 with tax)

Parking: $4 for cars and $6 for recreational vehicles and trailers.

Information line:
407-363-8000.

How long is that line for Jaws? Well, if it is long enough that the thought of counting the people waiting ahead of you is scarier than the ride itself, then you may have a problem. Here is a formula to estimate the wait: There are eight boats, each capable of holding 48 visitors and the ride takes six minutes. Allowing two minutes to load and unload, that means each boat will carry about 336 passengers an hour. The eight boats, then, will move about 2,688 victims per hour across Amity Harbor.

der is easy; getting a script from paper to the screen is the really difficult part. Step into the world of the popular television series and become the Executive Producer. You'll watch as technicians race against time to complete the editing, scoring and special effects of the latest episode within budget and on time.

This is your chance to see if you've got what it takes to be a movie executive. Can you make essential decisions in split seconds? Can you direct the movie and the crew? You'll have to choose a murder weapon, the bad guy, the caper and even the guest star. You'll supervise the editing, select the takes and add sound and special effects. Six "volunteers" will be selected-usually from front rows–for the sound effects room. When all the work is over, you'll be able to view the final results on the big screen.

This attraction is a sometimes entertaining and sometimes silly lesson in the critical world of post production–the painstaking work that goes on in the editing rooms after the scenes have been shot. The real "Murder, She Wrote" series often goes from story development to broadcast in just 15 days.

Lines for this attraction can build at midday; unless you're a serious fan of the television series, we'd prefer waiting in line for the Hitchcock show or coming back later.

WOW Alfred Hitchcock: The Art of Making Movies. At a theme park that celebrates the art of moviemaking, this show is the most serious exploration of the role of the director and a very entertaining stop.

Hitchcock, the king of cinema chills, made more than 50 motion pictures in his career, along the way creating some of the most famous scenes on film. From the dizzying heights of "Vertigo" to the terrifying shower scene of "Psycho" to the relentless aerial attack of "The Birds," you will relive the terror–and learn the techniques behind Hitchcock's brilliance. The "filmstrip" that wends its way around the preshow area includes the names of all of his films.

One volunteer will be chosen from the waiting line to participate in a recreation of the shower scene. Sorry, girls, but the winner will almost always be a young man of average height, wearing tennis shoes. The reasons for the specifications will become apparent later.

Enter the 258-seat Tribute Theater for a giant screen film journey through many of Hitchcock's movie and television works, including a portion of the rarely seen 3-D

Hitchcock at Universal. Hitchcock made 10 movies with Universal, beginning in 1934 with "The Man Who Knew Too Much" and ending with "Family Plot" in 1976; Universal was also the company behind his television series.

Rapid cutting. The shower scene in Alfred Hitchcock's original "Psycho" is made up of 78 different shots, edited in rapid sequence to simulate the violence of the attack. However, the knife is never shown piercing the skin. Hitchcock chose to shoot the film in black and white to lessen the gore. The "blood" is actually chocolate syrup, since stage blood photographs as grey in a black and white print.

version of "Dial M for Murder." (The movie was filmed in 3-D but while in production the public fascination with 3-D seemed to have passed and the movie was released in a standard version.) You're also in for a surprise conclusion, courtesy of some of the flying fiends of "The Birds."

Next, it's on to the Psycho Sound Stage. Anthony Perkins, who created the role of creepy motel owner Norman Bates, is your filmed host for a reenactment of one of the most terrifying scenes ever filmed. You'll see the scene as an unimaginative director might have shot it, and then learn how the master did it. The presentation includes actors (including a pretty model in a body stocking for the shower), our volunteer, reproductions of the Psycho house and the Bates Motel set and clips from the movie.

Finally, you'll visit a fascinating interactive area where you can explore more of Hitchcock's technique. Actor James Stewart will be your guide in an exploration of the visual shocks of "Vertigo." John Forsythe will assist you in the reenactment of the murder on a carousel in "Strangers on a Train." And Norman Lloyd, who played the villain in "Saboteur" and later produced Hitchcock's television shows, will lead you up the gigantic torch of the Statue of Liberty, the climactic scene in that film.

Be sure to climb the stairs for a fascinating simulation of the famous apartment building scene in "Rear Window." You'll be able to peer through binoculars at a wall of windows, each showing a different scene—in one of them, a murder takes place.

Back downstairs, Shirley MacLaine narrates a presentation about Hitchcock's famous cameos—his brief appearances in each of his films. Note the mannequins of the director in the room; the master was only about 5'3" tall.

The first two acts, including the Psycho Sound Stage, may be too intense and frightening to youngsters. You might choose to go directly to the final, interactive area. You can also enter into the gift shop and the interactive area without waiting on line for the show itself.

The Funtastic World of Hanna-Barbera. Yabba-dabbadoo. Children won't need to be persuaded, but adults: don't pass this one by. This show combines a wide-screen cartoon with state-of-the-art simulators—it's a wild ride for children of all ages.

Each group of eight seats in the 96-seat auditorium is actu-

Check it out. In the Bates Motel replica at the end of the tour, notice that the key to room #1 is missing. Even more interesting is what you'll uncover if you move the painting to the left of the check-in desk!

Back door. You don't have to wait in the sometimes-lengthy lines to the ride in order to get to the nifty play area of Funtastic Adventures. Enter through the Hanna-Barbera Store. This is a good place to let the kids burn off some energy in the rain or at the end of the day.

ally a flight simulator without the cabin, offering an unusual glimpse at the technology–that is if you can take your eyes off the screen during the show. Remember the view when you ride the much wilder Back to the Future attraction, which uses similar technology.

The adventure begins with an introduction to Bill Hanna and Joe Barbera, the rarely seen artists who launched some of our best-loved *non-Disney* characters, including Yogi Bear, the Flintstones, the Jetsons, Scooby Doo and more. Their work has garnered eight Emmys and seven Oscars along the way.

There's a story to the adventure, if such things really matter: Bill and Joe have decided to make Elroy Jetson their star of the future. But along comes that diabolical dog Dastardly, who kidnaps Elroy. It's up to you, Yogi and Boo Boo to rescue him.

Yogi will lead the entire audience–seated in their simulators–to a giant spaceship for a blastoff into the stratosphere and then back down into Bedrock for a prehistoric tussle with Fred, Wilma, Barney, Pebbles, Bam-Bam and the entire Flintstones family. From there it is on to Scooby Doo's weird world and eventually the fantastic future of the Jetsons.

It's every bit as silly as it sounds, but an exhilarating ride all the while. Lean back for the best ride. By the way, the auditorium includes a row of seats down front that don't move; the elderly, the very young, pregnant women and those with back problems are advised to sit there.

The fun and learning doesn't stop after Elroy is rescued, either. An interactive play area allows you to play with sound effects, color your own cartoon cel with an electronic paintbox and even see yourself as a cartoon character shrunk in size to play in Pebbles' dollhouse.

The Boneyard. The storage place for some of the largest props from recent movies. In recent visits, we have seen the houseboat from "Cape Fear" and the Love Rock from "Problem Child 2."

Production Tour. Don't confuse this short tram ride with the tour/demonstration at Disney-MGM Studios or the lengthy tour that is the heart of the Universal Studios Hollywood theme park. This open-air tour takes you in and among the same sets you can walk through by yourself; you may pick up a few interesting details from the narrator's spiel. A quick jaunt into the studio area itself gives a great

Out of business. On the streets of San Francisco, note the impressive facade of Ferries & Cliff, which was one of the biggest department stores in that city at the turn of the century. It collapsed in the great earthquake of 1906 and was never rebuilt, except at Universal Studios.

Instant stardom. Who gets picked to be a contestant on a Nickelodeon show? Shy guys and gals need not apply. Casting directors look for kids with enthusiasm and a clear speaking voice.

Teens in training. Nickelodeon, which began in 1979, is owned by MTV Networks, which is itself owned by Viacom International.

Inside Slime. Try as we could, we were unable to obtain the secret recipe for Gak and Slime. We can tell you, though, that slime is the stuff that is poured over people while gak is dumped. And slime sorta tastes like applesauce while gak is a bit like butter-scotch pudding gone wrong.

view of blank walls and closed doors and a few glimpses at some of the production "shops" and storage areas.

Nickelodeon Studios.® If you have children, they'll already know the way to The Network for Kids. Just look for the 17-foot-tall Green Slime Geyser out front; it's the planet's only known source of the stuff.

Nickelodeon's television facilities are in production 10 hours a day, 365 days a year creating such favorites as "Double Dare," "Super Sloppy Double Dare," "Family Double Dare," "Welcome Freshmen," "Make the Grade," "Fifteen", "Clarissa Explains It All," "Hi Honey, I'm Home," and "Nick Arcade."

Children of all ages are invited to tour the production facilities and the two large sound stages for the cable television network. From glassed-in catwalks above the stages, you can watch episodes being rehearsed or taped as well as look in on control rooms, make-up rooms and the "kitchen" where slime, gak and other concoctions used in the various game shows are made.

At the end of each studio tour, kids and their families enter the Game Lab, where the youngsters can try out some of the stunts used on the shows. And at least one kid will get slimed!

If you or your kids are hoping to be in the audience for the taping of one of the game shows, stop by early in the day and see if they are handing out tickets. You can also call the Nickelodeon operator and ask to be connected to the "hotline" number to find out about tapings: (407) 363-3000. Most taping is done on weekdays, and schedules in 1992 included "Clarissa Explains It All," "Fifteen," "Nick Arcade" and "Get the Picture."

NEW YORK

Ghostbusters™ Show. The Temple of Gozer, site of the sensational special-effects climax of "Ghostbusters" and one of the largest sets ever created in Hollywood, has been recreated at Universal Studios Florida.

A huge transparent shield protects the audience of nearly 500 from the goings-on–and also serves as the medium to carry some of the special effects. The best seats in the house are at right side in the back, offering an unobstructed view of the StaPuft Marshmallow Man and other treats.

Spirits swirl, strange howls and rumbles spread through the room and dark clouds gather overhead. The Terror Dogs

Expensive stains. The New York streets are made of concrete; a mold was applied to make the roads appear to be constructed of cobblestones. All of the cracks in the road, bubble gum on the sidewalks and rust stains on the stone (styrofoam, actually) walls were applied by artists.

Ghostly magic. Ghostbusters features what Universal calls the largest single magic illusion ever created, requiring 2,300 computer cues, 11 tons of liquid nitrogen and a unique laser system generating both visible and non-visible light.

suddenly crackle with energy and beams of light strike th Temple doors. The vault of Gozer cracks open, and all hel seems to break loose as the she-devil takes the stage. You know the question, right? WHO YA GONNA CALL?

That's right, the Ghostbusters. Actors playing the role of Spengler, Venkman, Zeddemore and Stantz take the stage Gozer blasts our heroes with ectoplasmic power; they fight back with bursts from their neutronic wands. A Terror Dog comes to life. But the gooiest mess is yet to come when the Marshmallow Man emerges from his jar.

Screen Test Home Video Adventure. Here's your chance for an additional charge of about $30–to put yourself right on the screen with "Star Trek", "King Kong" and "E.T."

You can choose between a short Star Trek scene in which you will trade lines with stars William Shatner and Leonard Nimoy, or film a highly fictional version of "Your Day a Universal."

After selecting their screen test, guests enter one of seven production studios where they will take their cue from a director. The studios are painted a special shade of blue that can be blanked out by Universal's Ultimatte 6 system and computer-controlled cameras and video technology and replaced with fantastic scenes much like the way special effects are added to real movies.

It is an amazing process, and the final result will astound even the most technically sophisticated or jaded visitor. Most visitors choose the Star Trek scene, but we will always treasure our Day at Universal tape, especially the scene where *we* escaped from *within* the Earthquake set.

When you exit the adventure, you will take with you an 8- to 10-minute VHS videotape to show over and over again at home. Versions for European PAL, Secam and Hi-8 players are also available.

WOW **Kongfrontation.**® It's the big banana himself, and you are a helpless captive in New York's Roosevelt Island tram. In fact, you're so close you can smell the bananas on his breath.

The adventure begins as you walk through a beautifully constructed replica of a Manhattan subway station complete with advertising posters appropriately redecorated with graffiti. Up above are a series of television sets and as you move through the building watch for news bulletins about the wild escapades of the famous ape.

The Big Apple has been turned into a war zone, with wrecked cars, burst water mains and massive fires. As your 60-seat tram makes a turn, you arrive at the Queensboro Bridge to find the big guy hanging from the supports. Uprooting telephone poles as if they were toothpicks, he reaches for your tram . . . until a helicopter makes a brave attempt to distract him.

Phew! You're safe. But are you, really?

The Kongfrontation set is based on Manhattan's lower West Side in 1976, the setting for the remake of King Kong starring Jessica Lange and Jeff Bridges.

This is a "must-see" show, but be forewarned that lines can build by midday.

Beetlejuice ~~LIVE~~ DEAD in Concert. Here's your chance to thrash around to the deathly music of Beetlejuice, plus regular manifestations by the singing Ghostbusters, at this stage at the end of New York's 57th Street. Check the daily schedule.

The Blues Brothers in Chicago Bound. They may be headed for the Windy City, but you'll find these two stand-ins for those strange rhythm and bluesmen performing on a stoop in New York's Delancey Street. Check the daily schedule for their next appearance.

EATING YOUR WAY THROUGH UNIVERSAL STUDIOS

There are some interesting and varied choices for food at Universal Studios, including a variety of foreign and ethnic foods and a spectacular branch of the Hard Rock Cafe.

We include general price ranges in our listings and men-

Movies, anyone? The International Food Bazaar is the only place at Universal Studios where they actually show real movies; shorts and classics appear on television monitors above the tables.

KEY

[fork/knife icon] = FAST FOOD

[pub icon] = PUB

[restaurant icon] = FULL-
SERVICE
RESTAURANT

tion specific prices for some items. Even where we use specific prices, however, you should consider this an approximate amount. Pricing on food is subject to change.

Soft drinks at Universal Studios outlets sell for $1.40 to $1.65.

THE FRONT LOT

[fork/knife icon] **The Fudge Shoppe.** Just like the sign says—no more no less. The Fudge Shoppe is located beside the Studio Store across from the main Universal Exit. This is a good stop to get something special for the road, or for a quick sweet treat on your way into the grounds.

The bonus: you can watch fudge being made. A wide selection of types and flavors is offered.

[fork/knife icon] **Beverly Hills Boulangerie.** Gourmet-style sandwiches and pastries, $1-$6.

At the corner of Plaza of the Stars and Rodeo Drive, The Boulangerie offers an interesting selection of sandwiches, sweet treats and drinks.

You'll appreciate the attractive presentation of pastries and the intimate round tables and metal chairs; a pleasant setting for a quick quality treat.

For a special sandwich, try the smoked turkey with avocado and sprouts ($6). Regular smoked turkey, ham and swiss and roast beef sandwiches also are available for $5.50-$6.

Sweets include macadamia chip cookie ($1.25), flavored croissant ($2), hazelnut eclair ($2.50) or key lime pie ($3) among many other tasty selections.

To quench that thirst, select from a variety of beers, including Kronenbourg ($3.25), wine ($3.25) and domestic ($3.25) or imported ($8) champagne.

EXPO CENTER

[fork/knife icon] **International Food Bazaar.** Gyros, bratwurst, burgers, pizza and more, $2-$6.

In the rear of Expo Center, next to the Back to the Future ride, this food court offers American, Chinese, German, Italian and Greek fast food. The advantage of this eatery is evident to families: everyone in the party should be able to indulge his or her own tastes in one place.

From the German selections, we liked the knockwurst platter ($6) with a side of red cabbage ($1) or potato salad ($1). Lovers of Italian food can select from a selection including jumbo shells ($6), pepperoni pizza ($4) and a large salad ($4).

Southern fried chicken ($6.95), barbecue pork sandwich platter ($6) and burgers head up the American section, while from the Greek menu you can select such tradi-tional specialties as Gyros ($6).

The Chinese offerings include a variety of stir fry dishes from vegetables ($2.50) to beef with peppers ($7). Sweet and sour chicken ($6) and shrimp lo mein ($6) also are included with the usual egg roll ($2) and fried rice ($2).

For dessert, black bottom pie ($2.50) from the American section and baklava ($2) from the Greek counter caught our eye. If that's not enough, check out the German black forest cake ($2), the Italian amaretto mousse ($1.75) or one of the frozen yogurt or ice cream offerings.

KEY

¶¶ = FAST FOOD

Y = PUB

🏠 = FULL-SERVICE RESTAURANT

¶¶ **Animal Crackers.** Hot dogs, burgers, chicken fingers and yogurt, $2-$5.50.

You'll find this quick food shop next to the E.T. Adventure at the edge of the Expo Center nearest to Hollywood.

Stop here for a hurried lunch or snack to keep you going on to the next section. The best of the lot, we think, is the smoked sausage hoagie ($5.40). You can add french fries ($1.50) or soft serve yogurt ($1.65) to the basic meal if you wish.

🏠 Y **Hard Rock Cafe.** American favorite fare from burg-ers to pies, salads and steaks. Entrees $8-$16.

Approach this interesting dining experience from inside the park via the walkway past the Bates Motel; visitors can also eat at the cafe without buying an admission ticket to the studios by entering from the parking lot side. (If you're coming from the studios, be sure to get your hand stamped at the gate so you can return to the park.)

The food here competes with a huge collection of pop memorabilia including original Beatles clothing, the huge motorcycle from the film, "Rebel Without a Cause," and "mom's" dress from "Psycho IV" (filmed at Universal Studios Florida). Notice the script of Psycho IV under the glass beside a number of autographed photographs.

You'll likely enjoy the unusual atmosphere and the good food, but don't plan on being able to carry on a normal con-versation while you eat. The background music here is loud, loud, loud rock and roll. For a little quieter atmosphere, ask for the fireplace room; the decor is nice and the sounds a little more subdued.

Appetizers are fairly ordinary, but carry interesting

Something old, some-thing new. The Psycho House set is an empty shell best seen by walking to the left of the park entrance to the Hard Rock Cafe. Note that the house has both an old and a new facade. An old and weathered side faces into the studios, while a freshly painted side faces Kirkman Road. "Psycho IV" was one of the first major motion pictures filmed at Universal Studios Florida, and the pro-ducers needed a new view of the house for flashback scenes as well as a dilapidated version for the updated story.

KEY

¶¶ = FAST FOOD

Y = PUB

🔺 = FULL-
SERVICE
RESTAURANT

---

names, including "Mom's chicken noodle soup" ($3.25), "Bordertown Guacamole & Chips" ($6), or "Love Me Tenders" ($5).

Salads include chef ($8), chicken ($8), or tortilla shell ($9). These can stand alone as meals, or lead into a complete lunch or dinner if you're really hungry.

Club sandwiches ($8-$9), barbecue platters ($9-$10), and burgers ($7-$10) are among the main offerings of the menu. If you want a little more to eat, try the Texas-T, a 16-ounce T-bone steak ($16) or one of the daily sea food specials that are priced according to the day's catch.

HOLLYWOOD

¶¶ Mel's Drive-In. Burgers, hot dogs, salads, chips and drinks in a 1950's diner, modeled after the eatery from "American Graffiti."

You can't miss Mel's. Just look for the garish, blue and pink building with its large neon sign on the corner of 8th and Hollywood Boulevard. Unless you are a child of the 50's you may not immediately appreciate the true beauty of the pink and white 1956 Ford Crown Victoria parked next to an absolutely cherry 1957 black Chevrolet out front.

Inside, a sock hop theme prevails, with period music and booths that promote more music with their individual juke box selectors. Check out the old 45 rpm records pasted to the wall and the pedal-pushers on the attendants.

Notice we didn't say "waitresses." Forget the personal table service you knew in the 50's, because you have to stand in line to retrieve your fast food here. You'll also have a lot of company in line at this popular place.

As for the food, the menu is authentically limited: "Mel's charbroiled double burger," $4; jumbo hot dog, $3, and a chili dog for $3.50. French fries, onion rings or a garden salad are all about $2. Finish up with cherry or apple pie ($2.50 plain; $3.50 a la mode).

¶¶ Café La Bamba. Find La Bamba on Hollywood Boulevard next to the Horror Make-up Show and across the corner from Mel's. Here you'll find attractive outdoor dining on glass-topped, circular tables with wrought iron chairs. The patio includes an attractive, bubbling fountain.

You can enter La Bamba through this patio or under the

large, green awning to the left of the patio. Inside you'll find a cool, tropical interior.

While you can choose a la carte offerings such as Tex-Mex and ranchero burgers ($4.50 with french fries) or chicken tostada salad ($7).

Separate bars are available for a variety of alcoholic and soft drinks.

When it is over, leave room for caramel custard flan or churros for dessert.

¶ Schwab's Pharmacy. A classic, old-time drugstore fountain drinks and treats, just waiting to be "discovered."

Hard to miss, on Hollywood Boulevard next to the Brown Derby Hat Shop. Look for the giant blue neon sign and walk into the bright, white drug store fountain area.

This is a typical 1950's drug store with a few booths and seating around a curved counter. Soda jerks in blue jeans, white shirts and classic paper hats take your order and prepare the treats while you watch. The walls are decorated with vintage photos from the original Schwab's in Hollywood and some of its famous patrons.

If you remember the 50's with its custom, hand-made ice cream treats (or even if you don't), you'll have a hard time selecting from the familiar Schwab's offerings. We liked the creamy, chocolate malt, made in the classic metal cup, poured into a thick, footed glass and topped with whipped cream and a cherry ($3). We also wished we had some room for one of the ice cream floats ($2) and sodas ($1). Sundaes ($2-$3) and cones ($2-$3).

SAN FRANCISCO/AMITY

¶ Boardwalk Snacks. Hot dogs, chips, fruit and drinks. For a quick, takeout snack or light meal on the go, stroll into the Boardwalk on the small wharf on Amity Avenue.

The shop offers a nautical theme with outdoor dining on picnic tables with a view of the lagoon.

Kids will love the traditional corn dogs—a meal on a stick—or a jumbo hot dog for $2.50. Chili or sauerkraut toppings are available for the hot dogs. Serious boardwalk fans will enjoy the cheese fries ($1.75-$2.50) and colorful cotton candy ($1.25).

KEY	
¶	= FAST FOOD
Y	= PUB
🏛	= FULL-SERVICE RESTAURANT

<table>
<tr><td>

KEY

Y⌐| = FAST FOOD

Y = PUB

**▲ = FULL-
SERVICE
RESTAURANT**

</td></tr>
</table>

▲ **Lombard's Landing.** Steak, pasta and seafood served in an elegant 1800's warehouse. Lunch entrees, $8-$13 for adults and $3.50-$5 for children. Dinner entrees, $13-$22 for adults and $5-$8 for children.

Located on the wharf next to the Pastry Company, Lombard's entrance is marked by a bright, blue awning. Outside, Lombard's looks like an 1800's warehouse; inside, the warehouse has been upgraded with jade green, simulated marble tables, fish fountains and aquariums. Notice the exposed iron work and wooden beams with bright copper bases.

The large "port hole" aquarium in the center of the rear dining room is not to be missed. And, while you select your food you can read the newspaper reproduction of the story of the great San Francisco Earthquake of 1906.

You can start lunch or dinner with a selection of three melons in honey ginger sauce ($6), shrimp cocktail ($7.50), or a "Fruits-of-the-Sea" bucket filled with clams, oysters and mussels ($13).

Entrees for lunch include fish and chips ($8), grilled chicken ($10), crab cakes ($10), New York Strip ($13) or chicken and chive fettuccine ($10) Children can choose from pasta with tomato sauce and meatballs ($3.50), chicken and noodles ($5) or a quarter pound hot dog ($4).

Many of the same entrees are available for dinner (though at higher prices), and in addition you can choose cioppino with lobster claws and other sea goodies simmered in tomato sauce ($19), grilled swordfish ($20), or stuffed veal ($15.50).

Whatever your choice for lunch or dinner, try to save room for dessert. The offerings include a chocolate brownie covered in ice cream and caramel sauce ($4), cream puffs ($3), selected pastries ($3.50) and ice cream ($2.50).

⌐| **Chez Alcatraz.** Quick seafood treats and drinks. Located over the water on the first wharf in San Francisco/Amity, this walk-up stand gives you a chance to sample shrimp cocktails ($3), clam chowder ($2), soft drinks or beer and wine ($3) while you watch the activities in the lagoon.

An interesting crab salad "Conewich" ($5) gives you a onehanded shot at seafood salad on the go, or you can try crab cocktail for $4.

Alcatraz offers outdoor seating on park-like benches, no tables.

¶¶ San Francisco Pastry Company. San Francisco-style pastries and sweets, plus espresso and capuccino.

At the front of Pier 27, on The Embarcadero across from Earthquake: The Big One. The European café design opens off of brick-paved streets and the patio overlooks the lagoon. Select your treats inside, then settle into the high-backed iron chairs at imitation marble tables and enjoy.

The Pastry Company artfully displays a variety of pastries and other desserts in a lighted case. In fact, once you move across the attractive tile floor and step up to the brass rail beside the display case, it will be hard to keep from overloading on the tasty offerings.

Our pick of the case is the chocolate or strawberry mousse or the fruit tart ($2.50). But you can't go wrong with the fudge supreme ($1.50), cheese cake ($2), or the eclair ($2). The smell of espresso ($2.25) and capuccino ($2.50) add to the atmosphere.

¶¶ ⅄ Pier 27. Barbecue, hot dogs, clam chowder, beer and chips.

You'd almost have to know this little eatery was here, or find it by accident, tucked into the back of Golden Gate Mercantile on Pier 27.

Draft ($2.50) and imported bottled beer ($3.50) complement the limited but rather nice selection of barbecue pork sandwiches ($3.75), clam chowder ($2) or hot dogs ($2.50).

You sit on high, padded stools at square tables you may share with others after selecting your food from the service counter.

PRODUCTION CENTRAL

🏛 Studio Stars Restaurant. Salads, pasta, seafood and chicken. Entrees $7.50-$16.50.

You'll find the Stars next to the Murder She Wrote Mystery Theatre on 57th Street. The attractive, modern entrance is under a pink awning. A large polygon skylight in the center of the dining room gives an open, bright atmosphere to the restaurant. Notice the large color transparencies of Universal stars that line the walls. Some outdoor dining under a covered patio is available.

When things get crowded, request one of the smaller "sunrooms" off of the main dining room at either side of the entrance for a possibly quieter, less hurried meal.

KEY	
¶¶	= Fast Food
⅄	= Pub
	= Full-Service Restaurant

KEY

〼 = FAST FOOD

Y = PUB

⛺ = FULL-
     SERVICE
     RESTAURANT

The food includes appetizers, sandwiches and full entrees to fit a variety of dining moods. For something light, try the chicken and walnut salad sandwich ($8), or the studio club ($8.50). The Florida seafood salad ($8.50) is also a good choice. The aged pepper sirloin steak ($13) is a good choice for beef lovers and if you like seafood, sample a variety in the Florida seafood fare ($16.50).

NEW YORK

Y ⛺ Finnegan's Bar and Grill. Traditional Irish fare including stews, meat pies, $5.50-$14.

Finnegan's occupies a prominent position on 5th Avenue across the street from Kongfrontation. In movie-set style, the corner Regal Café is just another entrance to Finnegan's.

This is a typical New York City community bar, complete with brick-paved sidewalk and awning-covered entrance. The neon signs in the windows add to the festive, "saloon" atmosphere. The ceilings are high and accented with hanging lights and slowmoving fans.

Appetizers include Cornish Pasti, a pastry shell filled with meat and potatoes ($4.75), and Edinborough Scotch Eggs, hard boiled eggs wrapped in country sausage and fried ($4.50). Both are served with beet and onion salad. Potato skins ($6) and chicken wings ($5) also are offered on the "Starters" menu.

The "Blarney Baguette" sandwich puts roast beef and corned beef together on a crusty roll ($6.75), and you have your choice of blue cheese, Swiss or cheddar on a sirloin burger ($6) or a plain sirloin burger ($5.75) to round out the sandwich offerings.

For a real meal, we recommend Yorkshire Beef, roast sirloin and vegetables wrapped in a giant yorkshire popover ($12), or the traditional Irish stew ($8). Meat and chicken pies ($7-$8) and fish and chips also are available.

What would an Irish Pub be without a selection of luscious libations? Finnegan's is no exception. Select from soft drinks, sparkling water, juice or coffee, or try something heartier from the bar, such as Guinness Stout, Harp Lager, or Bass Ale ($2.50 per half pint; $4.25 for a full pint).

Cherry or apple cobbler with Irish whiskey sauce provide the perfect end to the perfect Irish meal.

〼 Louie's Italian Restaurant. Italian antipasto, pizzas, salads and more.

Located right on Universal's 5th Avenue at Canal Street,

Louie's offers a wide selection of Italian specialties from antipasto to pizza, soups to salads, plus pasta and ices. If you find Mamma Lugina's you've also found Louie's. To get the most out of each establishment, Universal designers sometimes put more than one facade on an establishment.

The dining area here is very large and open with studio-type lighting. The high ceiling and large front windows give an open, bright atmosphere. Two serving lanes offer the same fare on either side, but veteran Louie's visitors say the left side usually is shorter (Do most people automatically seek the right side because they are right handed? Who knows.)

The portions are large and the food fresh. Pizza is available by the slice ($2.70) or by the pie ($13.50). The pizza is large and has very thick crust. When you buy a whole pie, you get an extra slice. Round tables seat five or six.

For a variety of Italian treats, try the antipasto misto ($6). Add soup ($2.50) and a small caesar salad ($4) and you have a complete and filling meal. For a heavier entree, we recommend the spinach tortellini ($6.75) or lasagna ($5.95).

ATTRACTIONS & RESTAURANTS

✳ = MUST SEE

✳ **1** Kongfrontation®
✳ **2** E.T. Adventure®
3 Amity
✳ **4** Earthquake®–The Big One
✳ **5** The Funtastic World of Hanna-Barbera™
6 Production Tour
✳ **7** Alferd Hitchcock: The Art of Making Movies
8 Ghostbusters™
9 "Murder She Wrote®!" Mystery Theatre
✳ **10** Animal Actors Stage
✳ **11** Nickelodeon Studios™
12 Screen Test Home Video Adventure℠

✳ **13** Gory, Gruesome & Grotesque Horror Make-Up Show
✳ **14** Back To The Future®... The Ride℠
15 An American Tail® Theater (Seasonal)
16 Wild, Wild, Wild West Stunt Show℠
17 Studio Stars Restaurant
18 Mel's Drive-In
19 Café La Bamba

20 Louie's Italian Restaurant
21 Hollywood Boulevard
22 San Francisco / Fisherman's Wharf
23 New England
24 New York Street Sets
25 International Food Bazaar
26 Hard Rock Cafe®
27 World Expo
28 Jaws

Main Gate

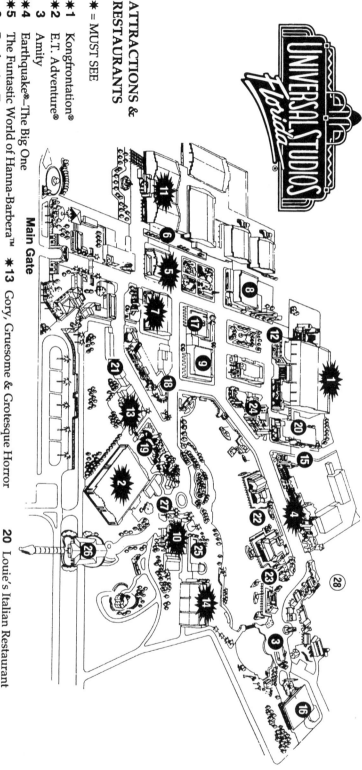

Sea World

Four-fifths of the earth's surface is water, and four mil-lion Orlando visitors a year swim upstream to Sea World, the world's most popular marine life park.

Located 10 minutes south of downtown Orlando and 15 minutes from Orlando International Airport, at the inter-section of I-4 and the Bee Line Expressway, Sea World is open every day. Call (407) 351-0021 for daily hours.

Sea World has a decidedly different feel from Walt Disney World and many other attractions in central Florida. Most of the scheduled events take place in outdoor theaters that seat 3,000 to 5,000 people. With rare exceptions you don't wait in line here; you simply walk into the theater 15 or 20 minutes before the event and pick a seat. When the theater is full, you are told to return for another scheduled show. (One notable exception to this will come with the opening of the Mission Bermuda Triangle simulator ride, which will probably result in significant waiting lines.)

Whereas other parks warn you against eating and drink-ing during presentations, at Sea World you will frequently see walking vendors hawking cold drinks, snacks and souvenirs like at a baseball game.

Sea World estimates it will require about eight hours to see the entire park. We recommend that you see all of the shows first and then spend remaining time visiting areas that are not regulated by the clock. If you really want to see it all, plan on arriving at opening time (usually 9 a.m.) and staying through dusk.

One very interesting effort by Sea World is the free,

Behind the scenes. A 90-minute, guided walking tour offering a backstage look at Sea World sells for about $6 for adults and $5 for children (plus an admission ticket). You'll see the park's breed-ing, research and train-ing facilities and have a chance to meet a few species not seen in any of the shows. The tour includes VIP seating at the "Shamu: New visions" show. Make reservations at the Information Counter to the left of the park entrance.

MUST-SEES

Window to the Sea

Shamu: New Visions

Hotel Clyde and Seamore

Terrors of the Deep

Mission: Bermuda Triangle

Manatees: The Last Generation?

Shamu Breeding & Research Pool

THE POWER TRIP

Begin your Sea World tour by stopping at the information counter to the left of the entrance gate. Ask for your own personalized park map and show schedule. This computer print out will guide you through an efficient schedule based on your time of arrival.

Notice that many of Sea World's shows and events occur only a few times each day. Decide which of these you definitely want to see (See our "MUST SEE" suggestions above), then work the schedule.

We recommend that you see the scheduled shows in the order they occur from your arrival time; then spend the rest of your day viewing continuous view exhibits. This may sound inefficient, but the Sea World property isn't all that large; you can crisscross a few times if you need to.

Here's one scenario: go straight to the Sea World Theatre for the **Window to the Sea** presentation to get a good orientation to the park. Next, move quickly to the new **Manatees: The Last Generation?** exhibit area. From there it's an easy jog to the Whale and Dolphin Stadium in the North East corner of the park for the **Whale and Dolphin Discovery** program. Depending on your time of arrival, you may have time to pass through the **Penguin Encounter** after the Discovery show. Penguin Encounter is a "continuous view" event; after this brief look you can come back if you want to.

After viewing the **Hotel Clyde and Seamore** show, pass by one of the lagoon-side restaurants for a sandwich on your way across the lagoon to the Atlantis Water Ski Stadium for the **Gold Rush Ski Show.** Don't worry if lunch takes a little longer than you'd like; simply sit dockside and you can see the start of the ski show from the back side of the lake.

After the water show, move into the Shamu Stadium (on the same side of the lagoon) for **Shamu: New Visions.** Before or after the show, depending on the timing, visit the **Shamu Breeding & Research Pool** (due to open about Spring of 1994).

Now relax a little. Make your way back across the lagoon for **Terrors of the Deep.** Check out the current show and schedule in the Nautilus Showplace. Pass by a couple of the "touch and feed" pools such as Stingray Lagoon or the Dolphin Community Pool. Take time for rest and snacks, a walk through the Tropical Rain Forest (beside the dolphin pool), and leave time for the **Shamu Night Magic** finale.

computer-prepared map offered at the information desk to the left of the main entrance.

This map is keyed to your time of arrival and includes a suggested itinerary to help you see as much of the park as possible without time conflicts. The schedule of events and show times is based on your arrival time.

Where possible arrive for any presentation at least 15 minutes ahead of the show time. This gives you the best chance at getting the seat you want and it lets you view the "Pre-show" activities offered at all events. Most shows are 20 to 25 minutes. We found that you can usually make the next show on your computer-suggested schedule, even if there are only 5 or 10 minutes between shows.

Admission prices in 1993 were about $33 for those over the age of 10, and $29 for visitors between 3 and 9. An excellent deal for visitors with a second day available are two-day passes good any time within a seven-day period; they cost just $5 more than daily tickets.

A Three-Park Daily Combo ticket includes one-day passes to Sea World, Busch Gardens in Tampa and Cypress Gardens in Winter Haven, and sells for about $78 for adults and $61 for children. A two-day pass good at Sea World and Busch Gardens goes for about $60 for adults and $49 for children; a two-day pass for Sea World and Cypress Gardens sells for $51 for adults and $40 for children. Finally, there are yearly passes to Sea World, for $59.95 for adults and $49.95 for children. Seniors receive about a 15 percent discount on all tickets.

The popular Guided Tour at the park is $5.95 for adults and $4.95 for children. Parking is $4 per car. Tickets for the Luau dinner are $29.63 for adults, $20.09 for juniors from 8 to 12, and $10.55 for children from 3 to 7.

WOW **Mission: Bermuda Triangle.** Here's the safest way we know of to explore the mysteries of the Bermuda Triangle, the infamous graveyard of ships and planes. Climb on board Sea World's newest major attraction, a high-tech simulator of a voyage beneath the sea.

Aboard the scientific research submarine "Neptune," passengers try to unwrap the mystery of the Bermuda Triangle. You won't be able to answer with certainty what has happened to the more than 100 ships and planes that have vanished in the 500,000-square mile triangle of ocean marked by Bermuda, Puerto Rico and Florida. But you can imagine what it would be like to join a fact-finding expedition

The missing bookstore. Visitors who may have come to Sea World several years ago often made a special trip to the huge Harcourt Brace Jovanovich children's and science bookstore just outside the gates of the park. HBJ, which used to own Sea World, sold out to Anheuser-Busch and closed the bookstore, alas.

Three simulators, with waiting. There are three simulator cabins in the Bermuda Triangle building, each seating 59 people. The attraction accommodates up to 1,800 guests per hour when all three simulators are in operation. Handicapped access is provided. High definition video laser disk projectors provide the visual stimulation, backed up by 1,200 watt, 6-channel laser disc sound systems. Each cabin moves six ways—yaw, pitch, roll, heave, surge and sway. Sometimes the cabin moves as much as nine feet, and in some directions it moves at speeds up to 24 inches per second.

in a submersible watercraft.

Aboard the Neptune you will investigate The Puerto Rico Trench—one of the Triangle's deepest places. The simulator cabin pitches, lunges, rocks and tilts in sync with the view from the forward "window," which is really a large rear projection screen. The sub shudders as it seems to plunge into the ocean and spiral deeper and deeper. Depth gauges spin wildly as the craft leaves daylight behind.

Among the "discoveries" you make on this ride is the U.S.S. Cyclops, a navy ship that vanished without a trace in 1918.

The experience is a lot like flying. You will feel surprisingly real sensations of acceleration and increased gforces.

Shamu's Happy Harbor. A 3-acre playground with a colorful Caribbean theme, including favorite "get wet" activities, a large sand play area, and crawlable, climbable places that reach as high as four stories.

Youngsters meet a crew of seaworthy playmates, including Virgil Pelican and his sidekick, a tennis-shoed pink flamingo.

Actually, this new harbor—opened in the summer of 1992—is a good place for the whole family to relax from the rigors of a full Sea World tour. There are shaded benches and the Coconut Grove Fruit Company food cabana where parents can rest while children climb a four-story tower, check out a 35-foot-tall crow's nest lookout, enjoy the ball crawl or try to reach the top of the vinyl mountain.

Lock and run. Pay lockers are located to the right of the entrance next to Key Hole Photo. Leave things here you don't want to carry all day.

If all of this is too rambunctious for your young ones, they can explore "Boogie Bump Bay," a special area for small ones that includes bubble bikes, a mini-ball crawl, an air bounce, a fence maze, and many other activities appropriate to their size.

A schooner funship stands in the middle of the harbor, waiting to be boarded. The boat is surrounded by cargo net climbs suspended over water. The vessel is defended by water cannons whose targets are anyone careless enough to wander within range.

A smaller playground has been at Sea World for awhile. **Cap'n Kid's World** is located at the far North end of the park beside Stingray Lagoon. A smaller pirate ship, ground mounted and shipboard water cannon, a ball crawl and radio-controlled cars are part of the fun here.

Anheuser-Busch Hospitality Center. Sea World is owned by brewer Anheuser-Busch (which also owns Florida attractions Cypress Gardens, Busch Gardens and Adventure

Island) and the new Hospitality House offers a bit of the corporate message (conservation and sensible drinking themes)–along with free samples of the company's beers.

Set amid tropical lagoons and lush foliage, the center includes a display of antique brewery equipment, including a turn-of-the-century Studebaker wagon used for hauling more than six tons of Budweiser beer behind a team of Clydesdale horses.

Adults can sample Anheuser-Busch products including Budweiser and Michelob beers. A separate counter offers soft drinks at the going Sea World price of about $1.40 to $1.70.

An outside terrace offers a quite, shady spot for sampling and resting and also provides a good view of the associated gardens, waterfalls and the Clydesdale paddocks close by.

SHOWS

WOW **Window to the Sea.** A must-see, first-see if possible. It's a multi-media overview of the Sea World park, including a tour of the facilities and a description of the naturalist's philosophy.

The show opens with multi-colored, dancing water fountains that move in time with music. When the curtain rises behind the water fountain you see a computer room set with aquariums, consoles and large display screens.

In a simulation of a global video linkup, the moderator introduces researchers who are participating in Sea World projects around the globe. In an interview with biologist Dr. Jeanie Clark, for example, the Alvin deep sea submersible is introduced and we see the "discovery" of new deep-sea creatures.

All of the interviews are on tape, of course, but the production is so well done you'll feel that a whole crew of world-renowned researchers is standing by to talk with you live.

Whale & Dolphin Stadium. The Whale and Dolphin Discovery show is presented in a stadium facing a large tank; before and after the show, you can walk up to the glass on the tank, nose to nose with the dolphins, but visitors are asked not to touch or slap the side.

Dolphins are real show business types and they seem to love to perform for an audience. On the trainer's command they "dance" in time to the music or stand up in the water to take a "bow" after they have done well.

You'll see dolphins swimming, flipping and splashing in a variety of stunts with their trainers and with a volunteer

Bigfoot. Think your feet are tired at the end of the day? A Clydesdale horseshoe measures 20 inches end-to-end and weighs about five pounds.

Clod reins. The driver of an eight-horse hitch pulling a beer wagon like the ones at Sea World must wrestle more than 40 pounds of reins to control the horses.

Whale wisdom. Whales are aquatic mammals and not fish, though they are good swimmers. Killer whales can remain submerged up to 12 minutes before surfacing for air. Newborn killer whales weigh about 300 pounds. Star of the show Shamu is 17 feet long and weighs about 5,000 pounds.

Watered down. The first four rows of the stadium, especially toward the center of the arena, are the wet seats. The views from anywhere are good, but the best seats are mid-stadium within the first ten rows.

Sea food. Each dolphin eats about 20 pounds of fish a day, much of it as part of a performance reward during the show. Dolphin skin feels like a wet inner tube. These sea creatures like to be touched and rubbed.

Rock fish. The show opening involves sea lions and an otter who appear to perform all by themselves. They're not that smart: their trainers are actually hidden behind rocks high up on the set. Look carefully and you will be able to see fish for the animals fly out of the rocks where the trainers wait.

from the audience. Among our favorite feats are Dolphin Power-boating, when two dolphins push a trainer around the tank by placing their noses on the bottom of his or her feet, and Dolphin Water Skiing, when the trainer, riding with one foot on each dolphin, holds a loose harness around each animal and goes for a ride.

Perhaps the most spectacular trick is the Bouncing Trainer, when the whale surfaces with a trainer balanced on its nose, pushing him or her about 20 feet into the air.

In addition to dolphins, this show features a pair of "Pseugorca," or false killer whales. Their beautiful, solid black color and smooth features make them unusual performers. These fast swimmers and fun performers are up to 25 feet long.

WOW Hotel Clyde and Seamore. If your hotel in Central Florida is anything like the cozy little inn run by sea lions Clyde and Seamore, we'd suggest you move on down the road. Sea World's aquatic clowns introduced their new fun-silly show in 1993 at the 3,000-seat Sea Lion and Otter Stadium, one of the most popular attractions at the park.

The humans in this show are more than mere characters: they are skilled animal handlers who are chosen for both their animal knowledge and their acting skill.

Depending on the time of day (and time of year) you visit this stadium, you may be facing the sun during this show. A portion of the stadium is covered. Sit in the upper rows of the deck to find a little shade.

We'd suggest you arrive at this show at least 15 minutes early to watch the mime pre-show, among the more popular presentations at Sea World. Be prepared for some outrageous, spontaneous situations.

Gold Rush Ski Show. On the 17-acre lagoon facing the 5,200-seat Atlantis Water Ski Stadium, early American history comes to life in this action-packed and sometimes wacky production. The world-famous Sea World performers display daring trick skiing, long-distance jumping and graceful water ski ballet. This is a high energy, flashy show that usually plays to a full house.

This show includes some sometimes silly or heavy-handed humor; put up with it to see the spectacular ski exhibition. The best part of this show is the "water ski duel," described in a song that is a take -off of the Charlie Daniels song, "The Devil Went Down To Georgia." The good guys and the bad guys "ski for broke" in a sequence of jumps and send up to four skiers somersaulting at over 90 miles an hour. The impressive finale is a 13-person pyramid.

The ski crew waits after the show to pose for pictures and to sign autographs.

Backstage at the ski show. After you've seen this show once, come back for the next showing, but view it from the gift shop in the middle of the walkway over the lagoon. Here you can see some of the backstage preparations for events like the three-tiered 13-skier pyramid.

Shamu: New Visions. Narrated by actor James Earl Jones, this is the showpiece of Sea World. Presented in the 5,200-seat Shamu Stadium just down the hill from the Atlantis Water Ski Stadium and on the same side of the lagoon, this show is built around a five-million gallon saltwater tank that is home to the entire Shamu family of killer whales, including Baby Namu.

Sea World has spent 25 years researching and studying killer whales and this program gives you a tantalizing look at a little of what they have learned.

A high resolution video screen allows guests to get close up to the whales and their trainers; four television cameras-including one under water–follow the action.

Lion school. How do the trainers make a sea lion appear to talk? Watch for a trainer's inconspicuous snapping together of thumb and forefinger. This clues the sea lion to move its mouth while a recorded voice makes it appear to talk. Also, listen for repeated sentences that may include hidden vocal commands.

The pre-show entertainment for this show also is popular. Questions about killer whales are flashed on the video screen, and the cameras scan the audience seeking the right answer. You hold up fingers or nod your head to answer the questions. With luck, your much-larger-than-life face will fill the stadium screen.

During this show you'll see whales leap, jump and swim, interacting with the audience and with the trainers. A highlight of the show is when Shamu leaps onto a platform in the center of the water stage and waits while a trainer selects a small child to sit on his back. The video cameras help bring this part of the show up close to you.

Notice that the whales seem to be enjoying themselves, both before the show and during it. They cavort and play, bringing a light hearted mood to the stadium.

The late evening show–performed only in high season–**Night Magic at Sea World,** show Shamu and friends in a different light as they perform under the stars in a laser and fireworks spectacular.

Shamu Breeding & Research Pool. Due to open some-time early in 1994, this addition to Shamu Stadium will offer one of the world's largest marine mammal facilities, a breeding and nursery area including underwater viewing of killer whales. Sea World claims the most successful breeding program in the world for these animals; six calves have been born and raised at the various Sea World parks since 1985.

Manatees: The Last Generation? Also new for 1993 is a three-and-a-half acre attraction that winds through a river-like setting, filled with the gentle manatee giants as well as turtles, fish (including tarpon, gar and snook) and birds. A seamless, 126-foot-long acrylic panel permits underwater views. Nearby is a Nursing Pool built for manatee mothers and their babies.

The area includes the **Manatee Theater,** which presents a special film using "Bi-Vision" technology that uses stunning underwater footage to make it seem as if the viewer is completely surrounded by manatees.

There is also the **Alligator Habitat,** a marsh display of creepy crawlers, fish and turtles. The **Bird Habitat** is home to great egrets, white ibis, green herons and other species of birds.

Pacific Point Preserve. Opened in 1993, this is a recreated naturalistic setting for California sea lions and harbor and fur seals, including beaches, waves and coastal rock.

Nautilus Showplace. This covered, outdoor theater houses seasonal shows from Chinese acrobats to theater groups. Check the daily schedule to see if there is a show of interest on the day of your visit.

Hawaiian Village. The "Hawaiian Rhythms" troupe performs songs and dances of the Polynesian isles on the beach at Atlantis Lagoon.

If you're the uninhibited type, you can join hula dancers–male and female–on the stage for an impromptu hula lesson.

CONTINUOUS VIEWING EXHIBITS

A number of Sea World exhibits are open all day without scheduled events. You can enter them for a quick walk through or a leisurely study.

Terrors of the Deep. A unique collection of dangerous sea creatures. You will find yourself immersed in the secret hiding places of menacing eels, venomous fish,

He's the one with the mustache. The first four rows of the Clyde and Seamore show are designated as a Splash Area, but you probably won't get wet from a splash there; watch out for the Walrus, though. He likes to spit water at the audience.

Whale water. Shamu puts on a wet and wild show: The first 14 rows, up to the second tier of seats, stand an excellent chance of getting doused with 55-degree salt water.

The best seat in the stadium–if you don't mind getting wet-is in the first 6 rows. Here you will be able to see under the water through the glass wall of the tank, as well as the show up above. If you prefer to stay dry, sit toward the front of the second bank of seats, in the middle of the stadium. You'll have a good view of the video screen and of the platform where the whales frequently beach themselves during the show.

hungry barracuda and...sharks. The creatures in this exhibit all can be potentially dangerous, it is true, but the message of this exhibit is clear: "Respect them, don't kill them."

The first aquarium in this exhibit focuses on eels–more than 500 of them in a 10-foot-deep tank full of artificial coral that looks like the real thing but is easier to maintain.

One of the really interesting facets of this exhibit is the acrylic tunnel at the bottom of the aquarium that allows you to walk through the tank to view the "terrors." Among the creatures you'll see are moray eels (some more than six feet long), spotted morays, and purple-mouthed eels. Grouper, snapper, lookdowns and jacks–predatory fish native to the same ecosystems inhabited by eels–also are housed in the habitat.

A high-tech system simulates the currents and wave action of the reef and a single light source is placed just so to simulate the sun.

After the walk through the first tunnel, you next encounter venomous lionfish and scorpionfish. The graceful lionfish will captivate you with their movement and the colors of the fins that hide their dangerous spines. The scorpionfish show their ability to camouflage themselves as they blend in with the sand and wait for an unsuspecting meal to swim overhead.

The final stop on the journey comes when you descend 15 feet below the surface to the territory of the shark through a six-inch-thick clear acrylic tube. You'll travel the 125-foot-long shark-filled habitat on a people mover, as dozens of nurse, brown, bull and sand tiger sharks swim overhead and in front.

Penguin Encounter. The largest and most technically advanced exhibit of its kind, it is the home to hundreds of penguins (from the Antarctic) and alcids (from the Arctic). The science center goes beyond entertainment to educate guests about the need to protect and preserve polar life.

So realistic that it even snows inside, this exhibit moves you past living Arctic and Antarctic displays on a 120-foot people mover. Tempered glass provides an unobstructed and unobtrusive view above and below the water of stately king penguins, gentle gentoos and bounding rockhoppers.

At the alcid exhibit, you come face-to-face with more than 100 puffins, buffleheads, smews and murres from the

Arctic. While not related to penguins, they are considered their ecological counterpart.

After the ride past the live exhibits you enter an exhibit hall with many fascinating, lighted displays. Press on the kid-sized hand prints within each display to hear a recorded message about what you are seeing.

Tropical Reef and Caribbean Tide Pool. More than 1,000 tropical fish live in the 160,000 gallon exhibit, the largest South Pacific coral reef display in the United States. The Caribbean Tide Pool gives you close up views of tropical fish and invertebrates such as sea urchins, crabs, starfish and anemones. Seventeen smaller aquariums contain exhibits including sea horses, octopi and clown fish.

Stingray Lagoon. Walk right up to a shallow pool full of stingrays of varied size and shape. These fascinating creatures swim close to the edge of the pool where you can easily rub their rubbery skin and feel their flappy fins. You can purchase food to offer them for a nominal fee; wash basins beside the exhibit give you a place to clean up before you move on.

Watch out! At least one stingray usually swims with one fin out of the water, splashing everything–and everyone–in sight.

Sky Tower. This 400-foot needle tower can be seen from miles around Sea World, marking the park location and helping you find your way in. Once inside the park, you can ride a sit-down, circular elevator to the top for a panoramic view of Sea World and much of central Florida.

Admission to this ride is not included in the daily park pass. The elevator may not operate some of the time–during heavy winds or other bad weather, for example.

Take your Sea World map on this ride; it will help you orient yourself to the layout of the park as well as other attractions in the area such as Disney World, which you can see from your rotating, 400-foot perch. The entire ride takes about five-and-a-half minutes.

Sea World officials say there is rarely a long line at this ride, even though you must buy a separate ticket and wait your turn for the elevator. We estimate the average wait is between 5 and 10 minutes.

EATING YOUR WAY THROUGH SEA WORLD

In this section we offer a quick reference to Sea World restaurants. While we give price ranges, you should con-

Whale school. Many of the whale's actions are prompted by trainers' hand signals. For example, when the trainer holds up an open hand toward the audience, the whales face the audience and open their mouths. Also listen carefully for the faint sound of high-pitched training whistles during the show.

KEY

⦀ = Fast Food

Y = Pub

⛰ = Full-Service Restaurant

sider these approximate because food prices change. All Sea World restaurants offer a range of Pepsi soft drinks from about $1.40 to $1.65. Some also offer hot or iced tea, coffee and beer. A souvenir soft drink mug is available for $3.

In general, Sea World food offerings are rather more simple than you will find at Epcot or Universal. Menus are more limited (fewer different offerings at each restaurant), but the food generally is of high quality and the portions are large. Two new fast food eateries, **Buccaneer Barbecue** and **Mango Joe's** are planned for opening in 1992.

⛰ **Bimini Bay Cafe.** Seafood sandwiches ($7-$8) and platters ($10-$13). Entree Salads and fruit, $6-$8. Child's sandwich plate, $4. Domestic & Imported Beer $2.50.

Pleasant polynesian or tropical atmosphere with bright "sunshine" colors. Tasteful decor feels like a hotel or resort restaurant.

Child's plate is grilled cheese or turkey sandwich with a slice of fruit and a drink.

For a different appetizer, try the Key West conch chowder (About $3.00).

Glass-enclosed dining room overlooks Atlantis Lagoon and offers a cool get-a-way for lunch.

Outside the Bimini, beside the Hawaiian Rhythms show, you'll find a large kiosk that offers drinks and very light snacks. Buffalo wings or fish fingers, $6; french fries, $2. Coffee, beer and mixed drinks. A small stage nearby sometimes holds a performer for entertainment while you relax.

⦀ **Spinnaker Cafe.** Hamburgers and sandwiches, $5-$6. Interesting salads and desserts, $2. Separate non-smoking section.

Large inside dining room decorated in blue and white. Sea motif includes ships lanterns and flags. This is a large dining area with high ceilings and tiered sections to help separate guests.

The California Light (offered in several places throughout Sea World) is a turkey breast sandwich with sprouts and cheese. The clam chowder is acceptable ($3), and the fruit salad is a cool alternative to hamburgers.

The real forte at Spinnaker, however, is desserts. Select from Black Forest cake, Key Lime pie, cheesecake, strawberries and cream, and other delectables ($2).

⦀ **Pizza 'N Pasta.** Pasta and pizza dishes. $5-$6. Domestic beer, $2. Separate non-smoking area.

Enter this attractive restaurant via a weathered wooden boardwalk that overlooks a small, landscaped lagoon full of flowering shrubs and trees. Sea birds are everywhere around this area, which extends around three sides of the restaurant. Tropical blue umbrellas with round tables. Indoor seating also available.

For a full taste of this restaurant's italian offerings, try the Italian sampler platter, or order eggplant parmesan, spaghetti, pizza or salads.

This is a large restaurant with tile floors inside that produce a "live" sound. When the room is full with families and their children it is very loud. Weather permitting, outdoor dining is preferred.

At the outside corners of this restaurant, find **Frosted Fruit Coolers** and **Soft Serve Ice Cream**. Ice cold fruit flavored drinks range from $2 to $5; soft serve ice cream treats are $2 to $3.

🍴 **Hot Dogs 'n Spuds.** Hot dogs and baked potatoes. $3-$4.

Outdoor fast food in an attractive and pleasant "woodsy" setting. Umbrella seating on a wooden patio at one end of the rain forest.

Nothing exciting on the menu here, but you get a full belly for a low price. Hot dogs are "foot long" offerings and the baked potatoes are relatively large. Cheese or chili toppings are available with either.

🍴 **International Sandwich Shop.** Sandwich platters with potato salad and pickle, $6.

This walk up, outdoor restaurant shares patio seating with the Hot Dog 'n Spuds restaurant at the end of the tropical rain forest. Round tables covered with large umbrellas seat six. An attractive stone wall and small waterfall give a pleasant outdoor mood. Try the chicken salad croissant, or the turkey and smoked ham club for an interesting sandwich treat.

🏠 **Aloha! Polynesian Luau Dinner and Show.** Polynesian Luau and show. $28 adults, $19 ages 8-12, $10 ages 3-7.

An exciting south Seas adventure. Seating begins at 6:35 p.m. and is limited. Reservations required. Call (800) 227-8048 or (407) 351-6000, Ext. 195, or stop by the information desk to the left of the main Sea World entrance. Sea World sometimes offers a discount coupon for this dinner on the back of your parking ticket.

KEY

🍴 = Fast Food

🍸 = Pub

🏠 = Full-Service Restaurant

KEY

 = Fast Food

 = Pub

= Full-
Service
Restaurant

Meal varies, but usually consists of salads, seafood, pork and chicken, rice, vegetables and dessert. One cocktail or beer is included in the price of the meal.

Pancho's Tacos. Tacos and salads. $3-$4. Domestic beer, $2.

Covered tables on an attractive "southwest" patio offer outdoor dining near the Stingray Lagoon. This is a cool place to relax and snack during your Sea World travels.

For a hungry appetite, try the Super Taco with refried beans and rice, or order from a la carte offerings: beans, rice, fries and tacos. The taco salad is a filling choice with minimum caloric impact.

The Smokehouse. Chicken and ribs. Entrees $5 - $7.

Picnic style barbecue platters served with chicken or ribs, coleslaw and role. Umbrella seating available dockside overlooking the Atlantis Lagoon. Building has a weathered, "seaside" appearance; umbrellas are an attractive yellow. Pleasant place to rest and eat. You even have a "back door" view of the ski show from the lagoon-side seats.

You can watch chicken and ribs being grilled through a large window beside the serving line. The chicken and ribs are slow hickory smoked, then grilled just before they are served. The chicken will have a slight pink color inside.

You will be drawn to this restaurant by the smell of wood smoke and barbecue sauce during meal times. Stacks of split hardwood outside the restaurant add to the atmosphere.

Haagen-Dazs Ice Cream. Ice cream and coffee. $1.50-$3.

Classic ice cream parlor and cool patio beside a lagoon. Round tables seat four. Birds and trees outside. Variety of ice cream and frozen yogurt. We favor the strawberry sundae or Waffle cones for under $3.

The Haagen-Dazs frozen ice cream bars here sell for slightly less than they do at the outdoor carts located throughout Sea World.

Waterfront Sandwich Grill. Hamburgers and Sandwiches. $4-$6. Child's plate, $4.

Adjacent to Atlantis Lagoon, behind The Smokehouse. Shares dockside seating with The Smokehouse. Good view of the Sky Tower and Atlantis Lagoon. Attractive nautical decor. Separate smaller rooms inside hold closely placed, fixed tables that seat four each. Another opportunity to try Sea World's California Light Platter ($6). The child's platter is a turkey sandwich with fruit salad and a cookie for $4.

🍴 **Chicken 'n Biscuit.** Fried or baked chicken. $4 to $6. Child's menu. Domestic beer $2.

This is one of the largest fried chicken restaurants you'll ever see. A huge indoor dining room flanks the multi-line walkup serving area. Order your chicken fried or baked. Two-piece and three-piece dinners are offered with french fries and a roll. The child's meal consists of one drumstick or two wings, french fries and a cookie.

The indoor seating is somewhat close together, and when crowded the restaurant is a little noisy. Outside seating is very spacious. Round tables seat six easily; wide spacing with umbrellas. Attractive patio with fountain and large flower boxes.

Sea World
Orlando, Florida

ATTRACTIONS & RESTAURANTS

✳ = MUST SEE

✳ **1** Mission: Bermuda Triangle
2 Shamu Happy Harbor
3 Anheuser-Busch Hospitality Center
✳ **4** Window to the Sea
5 Whale & Dolphin Stadium
✳ **6** Clyde and Seamore
7 Gold Rush Ski Show
✳ **8** Shamu: New Visions
9 Night Magic at Sea World
10 Nautilus Showplace
11 Hawaiian Village
✳ **12** Terrors of the Deep

13 Penguin Encounter
14 Tropical Reef
15 Stingray Lagoon
16 Sky Tower
17 Bimini Bay Cafe
18 Spinnaker Cafe
19 Pizza 'N Pasta
20 International Sandwich Shop

21 Aloha! Polynesian Luau Dinner & Show
22 Pancho's Tacos
23 Dockside Grill
24 Treasure Isle Ice Cream
25 Waterfront Sandwich Grill
26 Chicken 'n Biscuit
27 Buccaneer's Smokehouse
28 Mango Joe's
****29** Manatees: The Last Generation?
30 Pacific Point Preserve
****31** Shamu Breeding & Research Pool

MAIN ENTRANCE

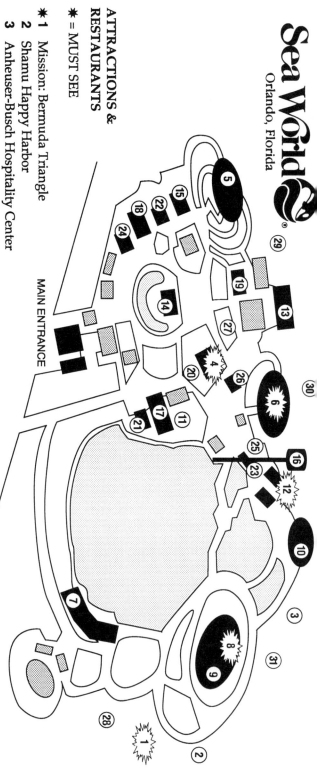

Elsewhere in Central Florida

CHAPTER 14
Spring Training Baseball/
Church Street Station / Cypress Gardens
Cape Kennedy, Spaceport U.S.A.

Spring training is an experience for the serious fan and the casual observer. You are so close to the superstars of baseball, the young hopefuls trying for a one in a million spot on a major league roster and the greats of yesteryear soaking up the spring sunshine as coaches. Listen to the enthusiastic chatter of the ball players–talk of "taters" (home runs) and "hacks" (swings) and "beep" (batting practice).

There are two parts to Florida's Grapefruit League: the training and the not-quite-prime time practice games. Pitchers and catchers arrive in Florida in mid-February to work themselves into shape with exercise and steadily lengthening throwing sessions. The rest of the team usually arrives around March 1. In general, the teams can be found at their practice fields each morning until early afternoon; check with the spring training sites before heading out. At most parks there is no admission charge for the workouts, and you will be able to wander in and among the superstars.

Most teams invite many of their upper-level minor league players as well as promising rookies to their camps; you'll see uniform numbers as high as 99.

Practice games begin about March 7, and most of the early games take place in the afternoon. Toward the end of the season, in early April, some games may be scheduled under the lights. Teams tend to concentrate on playing nearby neighbors to cut down on travel time; some of the games are "split squad," meaning that half of the large pre-season roster may be playing elsewhere at the same time.

Ticket prices range from about $4 to $8. You can usually obtain tickets as late as the day of game, except for the more popular matchups, like Yankees-Mets or Mets-Red Sox.

If you're a golfer, you might want to check out a course near one or another of the training camps; many players and coaches share that sport and can be found on the links in the afternoon.

Once the big-leaguers depart, they leave behind their minor league farm teams who play a full summer season in the Florida League.

There are three minor league stadiums that are very close to Orlando:

Kansas City Royals. Baseball City Stadium, Baseball City Sports Complex. I-4 and U.S. 27, SW Orlando. (813) 424-2500.

Houston Astros. Osceola County Stadium, S.R. 192, Kissimmee. (407) 933-2520.

Detroit Tigers. Joker Marchant Stadium, 2301 Lakeland Hills Blvd., Lakeland. (813) 682-1401.

Fifteen other teams are elsewhere in Florida, all within a day-trip's drive: The **Boston Red Sox** were planning to leave their long-time home in Winter Haven for new digs in Fort Myers in 1993. Baseball boosters in Winter Haven were seeking a new tenant as this book went to press.

The **Los Angeles Dodgers** play in Holman Stadium in Vero Beach on the Atlantic Coast, south of Orlando. The **New York Mets** hold camp in Port St. Lucie, nearby.

In West Palm Beach, you will find the **Montreal Expos** and the **Atlanta Braves** sharing Municipal Stadium there. Further south, the **New York Yankees** play in Yankee Stadium of Fort Lauderdale.

Gulf Coast teams include the **Cincinnati Reds** in Plant City, the **Baltimore Orioles** and **St. Louis Cardinals** in St. Petersburg, the **Philadelphia Phillies** in Clearwater and the **Toronto Bluejays** in Dunedin.

Gulf Coast teams below Tampa include the **Pittsburgh Pirates** in Bradenton's Pirate City, the **Chicago White Sox** in Sarasota, the **Texas Rangers** in Port Charlotte and the **Minnesota Twins** and new neighbors the **Boston Red Sox** in Fort Myers.

BASKETBALL

The **Orlando Magic** of the National Basketball Association play to packed houses at the Orlando Arena, 4600 W. Amelia St.

Call (407) 649-3200 for ticket information.

KENNEDY SPACE CENTER/SPACEPORT USA.

Spaceport USA is the visitor center at Kennedy Space Center, home launch base of America's Space Shuttle, and the fifth most popular attraction in Florida. It's also one of the best tourist bargains anywhere.

Parking and admission to all indoor and outdoor space exhibits are free. The Ambassador, a full-size replica of the Space Shuttle, accurate down to the switches in the cockpit, has been on display at various times. The award-winning film, "The Boy from Mars" is shown for free in the 500-seat Galaxy Theater.

An optional two-hour bus tour of Launch Complex 39 includes the massive Vehicle Assembly Building, the Space Shuttle launch pads and an authentic Saturn V moon rocket. Also available are tours of the historic Cape Canaveral Air Force Station. Under construction for winter 1994 is a full-size replica of a shuttle craft.

Note that the tour route may be altered or even cancelled when rockets are being prepared or launched.

Also offered are two spectacular IMAX movies, shown on the huge screen of the

MAX Theater. Shown are the 37-minute "The Dream is Alive," which shows astronauts living and working in space, and the 42-minute "Blue Planet," which offers an environmental view of the Earth from 200 miles up.

The IMAX film format produces an image ten times larger than conventional 35mm film used in theaters. To share a view of Earth few humans have experienced, crews from five Space Shuttle missions were trained to operate the cameras.

In 1991, the Astronauts Memorial was dedicated to honor the 15 American astronauts who gave their lives in the line of duty (including the crew of the Challenger and the Apollo 1 spacecraft as well as others killed in training accidents.) The 42-foot high "space Mirror" is set by a quiet lagoon near the entrance to the spaceport.

The exhibit area is free. In 1993, prices for the bus tour were $7 for adults and $4 for children between 3 and 11. Tickets for each IMAX movie were $4 for adults and $2 for children.

The park tends to be less busy on weekends than weekdays, and is open every day of the year except for Christmas Day, from 9 a.m. to dusk. Some areas may be off-limits on launch days.

Located off SR405, NASA Parkway, seven miles east of U.S. 1. From Orlando, take SR528 (The Beeline) to SR407, about one hour total driving. From Atlantic Coast Florida, take Exit 78 off I95.

CYPRESS GARDENS

One of America's oldest tourist attractions, Cypress Gardens was established in 1938 off U.S. 27 near Winter Haven, Fla., about 45 minutes from Orlando. The famed botanical gardens include more than 8,000 varieties of plants from 75 countries. The accredited zoo includes **Critter Encounters**, a petting zoo for all ages; **Hug Haven**,

a special-care nursery for baby and tiny animals; **Fly Free!**, a display of native and exotic birds; **Ocean and Wading Bird Exhibit**, a display in cooperation with non-profit wildlife agencies finding and rehabilitating injured birds; an educational **Alligator/Snake-Handling Dem-onstration**, and an **Exotic Bird Revue**, which features performances by stars including Barney, the jeep-riding macaw.

But the park is perhaps best know for **The Greatest American Ski Show**, a water ski extravaganza which showcases high-powered boat races and ski-jumping feats. Other entertainment includes a magic show and an

elaborate model railroad, **Cypress Junction.** Other highlights include **Souther**
Crossroads, a replica of an antebellum town featuring shops and restaurants; th
All-American Rose Garden with displays of more than 500 varieties, and an elec
tric boat ride through the manmade canals that wind through the 223-acre park

CHURCH STREET STATION

When you've maxed out on rides and exhibits at Disney World, take a short driv
into Orlando for a visit to Church Street Station. This is a restored historical sec
tion of the city set up for live entertainment, shopping, and dining.

Actually, Church Street Station–located in one block of Orlando's downtown Churcl
Street–is two facilities at once. You'll see one Church Street Station if you go dur
ing the day, and a completely different and exciting facility after the sun goes dow
and lights come up.

Church Street Station consists of several show rooms, a number of restaurant:
and some interesting shopping. During the day, you can enjoy a leisurely lunc
or brunch at Lili Marlene's Aviator's Pub and Restaurant (Inside Rosie O'Grady'
saloon), or across the street at the Cheyenne Saloon Restaurant. For lighter and quick
er fast food fare, try the food pavilion inside the Church Street Exchange, a sma
covered mall with interesting shops and food.

If you really want to shake off the dus
of the day–well, then, come to Churcl
Street at night. There's a cover charg
(about $12) for access to all the activ
ities with discounts for children. Wha
you get is six continuous shows fron
rock and roll classics and bluegrass, t
Dixieland jazz and can-can girls.

The mood is high energy with musi
cians roaming through the dinin
areas or performing on stage. Th
rooms generally are crowded, noisy
active and fun. This is one plac
where you don't have to choose on
restaurant or bar, you can "hop
around all evening for food, drink anc
entertainment.

Church Street Station is open ever
day from 11 a.m. to 2 a.m.

To get to Church Street Station
take I-4 toward Orlando. Exit or
Anderson Street and follow the blue signs to Church Street Station. Open park
ing is available under the I-4 roadway, but you must pay in advance and if yor
overstay your promised time, you will get ticketed. A better choice is to follow th
parking garage signs to the covered parking. You'll walk a little further, but you'
avoid a ticket.

CHAPTER 15
Other Area Attractions

Flying Tigers Warbird Air Museum. An impressive collection of American warplanes in working condition or undergoing restoration by mechanics and artisans. The private collection includes a B-17 "Flying Fortress" bomber, P-51 "Mustang" fighter and antique biplanes. Tour guides take you through the hangars. Open every day. At Kissimmee Airport, off S.R. 192 on Hoagland Blvd. (407) 933-1942.

Vintage Bi-Plane Tours. Soar over central Florida in a lovingly restored WACO open cockpit biplane. Three tours are available, including a 45-minute trip that includes aerial reconnaissance of Walt Disney World, Universal Studios, Sea World, Kissimmee and more. At Kissimmee Airport, off S.R. 192 on Hoagland Blvd. (407) 870-8687 or (800) 472-8687.

Pirate's Cove. A clever Pirate-theme 36-hole golf course with three locations in the Orlando area: 8601 International Drive in Orlando, 2845 Florida Plaza Blvd. in Kissimmee, and I-4 at Lake Buena Vista (Exit 27) in Lake Buena Vista.

Gatorland. You probably already have an idea of the stars of this place. The park includes an alligator breeding marsh, a three-story observation tower, the Gatorland Express Railroad and the Gator Jumparoo Show and the "Cracker Style" Gator Wrestlin' show. After 40 years in "alligator aquaculture," Gatorland also offers a line of alligator boots, belts, wallets and meat. Located at 14501 S. Orange Blossom Trail (S.R. 441) in Orlando. (800) 777-9044.

Water Mania. Catch a wave at this water park right on U.S. 192 in Kissimmee, in and among many of the off-site hotels. The slides are not as artfully decorated as those at Typhoon Lagoon, but still wet and fun. There's the Banana Peel 2-person raft plunge, the Rain Forest children's water playground and the Anaconda family raft ride. Open year-round except for early December. Located at 6073 W. Irlo Bronson Highway. (407) 396-2626 or (800) 527-3092.

Green Meadows Farm. A 50-acre working farm dedicated to educating children and adults about farm animals. Includes a two-hour guided tour with introductions to more than 200 animals including pigs, cows, goats, sheep, donkeys, chickens, rabbits, turkeys, ducks and geese. Everyone gets to milk a cow and children can go for pony rides and a tractor-pulled hayride.

The farm is one of eight similar operations around the company, the brainchild of Bob and Coni Keyes of Waterford, Wisc. It began in Wisconsin when that farm began to allow visitors to come and pick vegetables and raspberries. It expanded from that to allow urban youngsters to get up close to farm animals.

There are now Green Meadows farms near Houston, Texas; Elmhurst, Ill.; Orange, Calif.; Roseland, N.J., and Floral Park, N.Y. Additional farms are planned for San Diego, Calif. and Westland, Mich. Green Meadows in Kissimmee opened in 1988.

Take I-192 east toward Kissimmee and turn right at Poinciana Blvd.; go 5 miles to the farm. Open every day but Thanksgiving and Christmas. (407) 846-0770.

Airship Shamu. A passenger-carrying blimp that offers tours of the Orlando area. Reservations suggested. Departs Kissimmee Municipal Airport, off U.S. 192 in Kissimmee. (407) 870-7426.

Virgin Lightships. Three blimp tours, including a Champagne Evening Cruise for two passengers. Departs Kissimmee Municipal Airport, off U.S. 192 in Kissimmee. (407) 841-8787.

Wet 'n Wild. It's all in the name, in this large water park. Attractions include Der Stuka, claimed to be the highest, fastest water slide in the world; Knee Ski, a cable-operated ski tow around a half-mile lake course; the Black Hole, a 500-foot twisting, turning journey through darkness, time and space; the Surf Lagoon wave pool, and the Kids Playground, with smaller versions of the park's most popular rides. At 6200 International Drive, just off I-4. (407) 351-9453. Open year-round except for most of January and early February.

Mystery Fun House. A houseful of surprises including the Forbidden Temple, an Egyptian tomb, a miniature golf course, a video arcade and the "Ultimate Lazer Game–Starbase Omega." Across from the maingate of Universal Studios at 5767 Major Blvd. in Orlando. (407) 351-3355.

Fun 'n Wheels. The wheels include a Ferris Wheel (in Orlando), bumper cars, boats and small race cars; other fun includes miniature golf (in Orlando) and bumper cars (in Kissimmee.) Two locations: International Drive at Sand Lake Road in Orlando (407) 351-5651, and U.S. 192 at Osceola Square Mall in Kissimmee, (407) 870-2222.

Elvis Presley Museum. Said to be the largest collection of "official" Elvis items on exhibit outside of Graceland. Includes Elvis' Rolls Royce, Mercedes limo, a piano from Graceland, one of his guitars and 300 other such items. If this is what you're looking for, here's a fine example. Located at Old Town in Kissimmee, on U.S. 192. (407) 396-8594.

King Henry's Feast. Dine in the Great Hall and be entertained by dueling knights, magicians and performers on stage. Your meal, which includes tankards of beer, wine or soft drinks, is brought by singing serving wenches. Open every day. Located at 8984 International Drive, Orlando. (407) 351-5151.

Mardi Gras. A two-hour carnival extravaganza including dancers, singing, specialty acts and a Dixieland jazz band. Includes dinner. Open every day. Located at Mercado Mediterranean Village, 8445 International Drive, Orlando. (407) 351-5151.

Medieval Times. Come to dinner as the guests of the royal family in the 11th Century. The feast includes spectacular pageantry, dramatic horsemanship, wordplay, falconry, sorcery and a jousting contest. Located on U.S. 192 near the intersection with Route 441 in Kissimmee. (407) 396-1518 or (800) 327-4024.

Sleuths Mystery Dinner Show. Step into the scene of the crime. Mix with the characters, search for clues and help track down the culprit. You'll also eat dinner. Performed daily. Located at 7508 Republic Drive, off International Drive behind Wet 'n Wild. (407) 363-1985.

Fort Liberty. Step back into the Old West. The dinner show, hosted by Miss Kitty, features western specialty acts, native Comanche Indians and the comical soldiers of E Troop. Also featuring the Brave Warrior Adventure Wax Museum and a Wild West Trading Post. Located at 5260 U.S. 192 in Kissimmee. (407) 351-5151.

Arabian Nights. An unusual combination of performers and acts in one of Central Florida's largest live dinner shows, including more than 100 horses in a 1,200 seat indoor arena. Busiest days are Thursday through Sunday. Located at 6225 W. rlo Bronson Hwy. (U.S. 192) east of the intersection with I-4 in Kissimmee. (407) 239-9223.

Weeki Wachee Spring. Mermaids abound at this water park on the Gulf Coast. Presentations include an underwater version of the original Hans Christian Andersen story, "The Little Mermaid," as well as a Wilderness River Cruise, a Birds of the World Show and a petting zoo. North of Tampa on U.S. 19 at the intersection with S.R. 50. Open year round. (800) 678-9335 or (904) 596-2062.

Silver Springs. Cruise on glass-bottom boats, travel back in time on a Lost River Voyage or take a Jeep Safari into the jungle where the original "Tarzan" movies were filmed. Approximately 72 miles from Orlando; take exit 69 off I-75 to S.R. 40 East. (800) 274-7458.

Bok Tower Gardens. Florida's historic bell tower, centerpiece of a magnificent garden, is at Florida's highest point–all of 295 feet. The 57 bronze bells are as large as 12 tons. The 128 acres of gardens include thousands of azaleas, camellias, magnolias and other flowering plants as well as more than one hundred species of birds. Located in Lake Wales, about 55 miles south of Orlando, off U.S. 27 to Alt. 27. (813) 676-1408.

Lion Country Safari. The nation's first drive-through zoo when Lion Country opened in 1967. The park includes more than 1,000 wild animals from all over the world, including giraffes, chimpanzees, eland, bison, elephants, rhino, zebra ostrich and antelope, wandering free over hundreds of acres. Other areas include a petting zoo and an amusement area that includes paddleboats, a boat ride and an old-time carousel. A KOA campground is nearby. Open every day from 9:30 a.m. to 5:30 p.m.; convertibles must be exchanged for available rental cars to drive through the preserve. Located in West Palm Beach, off exit 99 of the Florida Turnpike (407) 793-1084.

CHAPTER 16
Shopping: The Florida Mall
192 Flea Market / Altamonte Mall
Mercado

The Florida Mall. Berk Linsey, Dillard's, Maison Blanche, Sears and 170 specialty shops. Located at the intersection of Sand Lake Road (S.R. 482) and South Orange Blossom Trail (Hwy. 441). (407) 851-6255.

192 Flea Market. A full-time, free admission market with as many as 400 dealer booths under one roof. Disney souvenirs, jewelry, crafts, clothing and more. Located at 4301 W. Vine St. (U.S. 192) in Kissimmee. (407) 396-4555.

Altamonte Mall. Burdine's, JC Penney, Jordan Marsh, Maison Blanche, Sears and more than 165 specialty shops. Located north of Orlando, east of I-4 on S.R. 436 in Altamonte Springs. (407) 830-4400.

Mercado. When is a mall not a mall? When it is Mercado, a small but interesting shopping and dining area between Disney World and Orlando on International Drive. Just as Disney's creative roller coaster packaging makes Space Mountain an above average ride, the Mercado "package" makes this mall a different sort of shopping experience.

You can find about what you'd expect at a mall here: small jewelry shops, handmade crafts, designer clothes, sporting goods, a beach store, a pet shop, and more. Unlike most big city malls, however, Mercado doesn't use large, name brand department stores as cornerstones. Rather the anchors that hold this mall together are interesting restaurants: the Mardi Gras Dinner Attraction, The Butcher Shop Steakhouse, José O'Day's Mexican Restaurant, Bergamo's Italian Restaurant, Charlie's Lobster House, and Damon's–The Place for Ribs.

Inside an open courtyard is surrounded by shops and outdoor seating in a southwest "mission" atmosphere. If you don't want to take time for a world class meal at one of the cornerstone restaurants, check out the village cafés for quick meals from the United States and around the world.

At night, the grounds and shops are alight with twinkling lights, and free entertainment is presented in the courtyard.

Basically, Mercado is a shopping mall. That said, we can also say it is unusuall enough to warrant your attention as an interesting break in your vacation day.

How to get there: From Disney World, take I-4 toward Orlando and exit on Sand Lake Road (East). Turn right (South) on International Drive and you'll find Mercado on the left in about half a mile. Look for the tall mission tower and pennant.

Busch Gardens Tampa

CHAPTER 17
Busch Gardens

Busch Gardens opened as a hospitality center for the Anheuser-Busch brewery in Tampa in 1959, showcasing a collection of exotic birds and some of the Busch family's collection of African animals. In 1971, as the era of Florida as theme park began, the company began a massive expansion of Busch Gardens.

Today, the park is like stepping onto the African veldt-albeit a veldt with a monorail circling above and some of the most outrageous modern roller coasters and other rides on the horizon.

Busch Garden is a welcome getaway from the concrete of Walt Disney World and environs, drawing three million visitors a year to its 300 acres, home to more than 3,400 animals, including 74 species of mammals, 218 species of birds and 60 species of reptiles.

The map of Florida looks so huge to many visitors that the thought of a drive from Orlando to Tampa seems like a day's drive; it's not. Measured from the intersection of I-4 and I-192, it's 70 easy miles at 65 mph to the gates of Busch Gardens Tampa, about 75 minutes.

The busiest times of the year are similar to those of the Orlando attractions: June to Labor Day and Spring and Easter Breaks. Other times of the year bring large crowds of foreign visitors, including plane loads from South America and Brazil. Lines, though, rarely approach anything like those at Walt Disney World or Universal Studios Florida.

In 1993, ticket prices were $29.95 for adults and $23.95 for children from three to nine. (An increase in prices was

Here are the vital specs for Kumba, one of the largest and fastest steel roller coasters in the country.

Track Length: 3,978 feet
Maximum Speed: 60 mph
Maximum G-Force: 3.75
Maximum Drop: 135 feet
Length of Ride: 2:54
Capacity: About 1,700 riders per hour.

MUST-SEES

Kumba/The Scorpion/ The Python
(Roller coaster fans)

Myombe Reserve: The Great Ape Domain

Questor

Tanganyika Tidal Wave

Congo River Rapids

Claw Island

Stanley Falls

Moroccan Palace Theater
(Ice show fans)

The Monorail

THE POWER TRIP

Begin your Busch Gardens tour by studying the schedule of entertainment you will be handed at the gate; some shows are put on numerous times during the day. Other presentations may be scheduled only once or twice. Adjust your Power Trip to include any must-see shows.

If you are a roller coaster fan, arrive early and head directly for the Congo and join the line for the new **Kumba** coaster. While you're in the neighborhood, you can also check out **The Congo River Rapids.** We like all three of the major water rides at Busch Gardens; you might want to leave a dry sweatshirt in a locker for the occasional chilly day. Now try the awesome **Python** roller-twister-coaster. When you're through, the majestic tigers on **Claw Island** will probably seem tame, but they're certainly worth a visit.

Of the two remaining water rides, **Stanley Falls** may be more fun but the **Tanganyika Tidal Wave** is more dramatic. What the heck: ride 'em both.

If you are not in the mood for an immediate upside down rattle and roll, you can instead start your day by bearing right from the entrance toward Crown Colony to visit **Questor.** Once you return to earth, backtrack to the Skyride and Monorail station. We'd recommend a trip on the **Monorail** to explore the Serengeti Plain.

At busy times of the year, we'd advise you to now press on through Nairobi without stopping and head for the thrill ride areas, stopping in Timbuktu. If you've got the stomach for it you've got to ride **The Scorpion;** it'll set you up for even more of a wild ride later on. If a show is planned that matches your schedule, visit the **Dolphin Theater** now.

At this point you will have ridden on all of the major rides. Now take a second, more leisurely circuit of the park and visit the animal exhibits and shows and finish with the **Skyride** and **Trans-Veldt Railroad.**

being contemplated for the fall.) Also worth considering are Annual Passports and combination tickets for Busch Gardens, Sea World and Cypress Gardens.

FROM ORLANDO: Take I-4 West about 60 miles to Tampa. Exit to I-75 North and then take the Fowler Ave. (Exit 54) off ramp and follow signs to the park.

MOROCCO

Morocco. A recreation of the exotic city of Marrakesh, featuring unusual architecture and a wide range of demonstrations of Moroccan crafts, snake charmers and the "Mystic Sheiks of Morocco" marching band.

Marrakesh Theater. Two shows alternate daily: "Listen to a Country Song," which features a revue of country music from the early days of country gospel through the Grand Old Opry and into the contemporary sound; also performed is "Latin, Latin!"

Sultan's Tent. A snake charmer performs daily.

Moroccan Palace Theatre. "Around the World on Ice," performed several times daily in this 1,200-seat arena. Midday shows fill up within 20 minutes of show time.

Serious shoppers only. Busch Gardens offers a plan for visitors who want a quick shopping spree at one of the native craft stores or souvenir shops just inside its gates. Buy your ticket, go forth and shop and be back at the Guest Relations booth within 30 minutes and you will be given a refund of your ticket. (You'll have to pay for parking, though.) We're told that some visitors make a mad dash from the gate to the Smokehouse restaurant for take-out ribs or chicken.

Serious shoppers may enjoy a visit to the brass store just past the ticket booths; an artisan/importer from Morocco offers an impressive display. And, if you like to pay to carry someone else's corporate slogan or ad campaign, check out the **Rabat Label** store, where you can buy just about any article of clothing or sporting equipment with one or another Anheuser-Busch logo on it.

NAIROBI

WOW **Myombe Reserve: The Great Ape Domain.** Busch Garden's newest habitat, featuring six lowland gorillas and eight common chimpanzees in a tropical forest setting. Gorillas include Lash, a 14-year-old 330-pound silverback male who was hand-raised by surrogates at the Cincinnati Zoo after his mother died. Also resident is a social group of five gorillas on a long-term breeding loan from Emory University in Atlanta, Ga.

Visitors enter the three-acre habitat through dense foliage to a clearing with a glass wall where they can observe the

chimps; passing through a bamboo thicket, guests will come upon the gorillas at the base of a mountain between waterfalls in a simulated tropical rain forest. (On cool days, boulders near the viewing areas are heated to draw animals.)

Although most people's idea of a gorilla has been shaped by the violent "King Kong" myth, field studies show that gorillas are no more dangerous than any other wild animal. Adult males are fiercely aggressive only in defense of their breeding rights and family groups. They feed mainly on leaves, stems and fruit and rarely travel very far from their home.

Nairobi Station, Trans-Veldt Railroad. The train offers some of the best close-up views of the animals on the Serengeti Plain between the Nairobi and Congo stations. Other portions of the track offer a tourist's eye on the back sides of The Python and The Scorpion coasters. The train is a 3/4-scale replica of an actual African steam engine and cars; the engine is an unusual combination of energy sources, using propane gas to boil water for steam that powers an electric generator for the wheels.

Animals. As close as you can get to some of the animals, and some special treats for the children. You'll find an unusually attractive **Petting Zoo,** but don't overlook the fascinating **Animal Nursery,** home to Busch Garden's newest and littlest bird and animal employees, set in a replica of a yesteryear African hospital. The **Elephant Wash** is just what it sounds like: ponderous pachyderms stand still for showers several times a day; nearby is a small enclosure where guests can climb onto a seat on the back of an elephant for a short ride.

CROWN COLONY

Questor. Set sail on a truly amazing adventure in this spectacular high-tech simulator voyage along with the eccentric inventor Sir Edison Fitzwilly on a harrowing mission in search of the elusive Crystal of Zed. You'll bore down through the earth, dodge stalagmites in a dark cavern and blast back to the watery surface just in time to plunge over a raging waterfall—all this without leaving your seat or even moving very far. Be warned, though, that passengers will experience more G-force than a roller coaster drop.

The somewhat fanciful waiting area includes pipes marked "coolant to flaxilator," a meter for the Jurbilium

Respect the animals. Please don't throw anything into the animal preserves. Plastic objects—like straws or drink lids-could be lethal playthings.

First captive breedings In North America: Road antelope, steinbok, Zanzibar duiker, slender-horned gazelle, marabou stork, Festive Amazon, yellow-collared macaw, Patagonian conure, Jardine's parrot, Maximilian's parrot, yellow-billed hornbill and Lear's macaw.

Animal hospital. The veterinary clinic includes operating rooms, an X-ray, laboratory and recovery areas, as well as brooder rooms for birds.

capacitor (energy units measured in Jurbs) as well as blueprints and drawings of Fitzwilly's invention.

We found the ride somewhat similar–although a bit goofier-to the Star Tours simulator at the Disney-MGM Studios. There are two, identical simulators, each seating 60 travelers for a four-minute ride. On busy days, we'd suggest heading for Questor early or late in the day.

The Skyride. An open cable car ride from the Crown Colony to the Congo and back, passing above the Serengeti Plain and then deep into deepest, darkest amusement parkland with good views of The Scorpion and the Congo River Rapids. A lovely way to see the park on a lovely day; the ride can be a bit chilly at times, and is shut down in inclement weather.

WOW **The Monorail.** An ultra-modern train that hangs from an overhead single rail for a nearly silent ten-minute cruise in and among the zebras, rhinos, ostriches and other animals of the Serengeti Plain. The track drops down low for close-up views of some of the residents.

Educational programs. Busch Gardens includes summer Zoo Camp sessions for school children, Summer Safari programs for children and adults and behind-the-scenes tours of the zoo for families and groups. Inquire at the Guest Relations booth for information.

The driver of the train, which can carry about 72 persons in its six air-conditioned cabins, will fill you in on all sorts of things you always wanted to know–like the fact that more people are killed each year by river hippos than by crocodiles.

Animals. Some of Anheuser-Busch's famous corporate symbols can be visited in their stables at the **Clydesdale Hamlet.** The largest adult males can be as large as six feet at the shoulder and weigh a ton or more.

SERENGETI PLAIN

Serengeti Plain. The largest open area of the park, an 80-acre natural setting featuring more than 800 animals in free-roaming herds of camels, elephants, zebras, giraffes, chimpanzees, rhinoceros, Cape Buffalo, gazelles, Greater Kudus and hippopotamuses. Ride the Monorail for the closest views; the Trans-Veldt Railroad also circles the Plain, while the Skyride passes overhead.

TIMBUKTU

WOW **The Scorpion.**™ It goes up to the top of its tower, then down and to the left at 55 mph before entering a full 360-degree loop into a series of corkscrew descents that put you on your side.

Carousel Caravan. A most unusual merry-go-round, featuring desert camels and Arabian horses.

The Phoenix. A dry boat ride that gives new meaning to the term "rock and roll." The platform moves forward and then backward with increasing power until riders make a complete pass up and over the top.

Other rides here include **The Sandstorm,** an aerial whip; **The Crazy Camel,** a collection of **Children's Rides,** an **Electronic Arcade** and a group of carnival **Games of Skill.**

Dolphins of the Deep Show. Bud and Mich, with their sea lion sidekick (and their trainers) demonstrate their speed and agility in an entertaining show at the Dolphin Theatre.

CONGO

The Kumba™ coaster includes a Diving Loop, which plunges riders into a loop from a height of 110 feet; Camelback, a maneuver which creates three seconds of weightlessness while spiraling 360 degrees; a 108-foot vertical loop, the world's largest; and a Cobra roll which turns passengers upside down as they twist around a spectator bridge.

The Python.™ Only at a park like Busch Gardens would a roller coaster like The Python have to settle for second place status behind Kumba. The Python includes wicked twists and turns and a 360-degree *double* spiral and cars reach speeds of more than 50 mph.

The Congo River Rapids.™ Riders sit in a 12-passenger circular air raft and are let loose on a churning whitewater trip in an artificial river with rapids, logs and other boats in the way. We'd tell you to sit at the back of the boat to avoid getting soaked, but the darned thing keeps turning around. The ride won't get your heart pounding quite as fast as one of the flume trips, but it's still a lot of fun.

Skyride Congo Station.

Congo Station Trans-Veldt Railroad. Disembark only.

Congo Cal's Video Ventures. Sophisticated video equipment will allow you to come home with a VHS tape in which you will fly across Africa on the wing of a plane, battle a giant spider and drop over the edge of a mighty waterfall. The process is similar to one used at Universal Studios. The Busch Garden tape will cost you about $20.

Animals. Visit **Claw Island** to get as close you may ever want to a rare white Bengal tiger.

STANLEYVILLE

Stanley Falls Log Flume. Over the edge of a 43-foot plastic cliff in a hollowed-out log. Lines build at midday; visit early or late in the day to avoid long waits.

KEY	
🍴	= FAST FOOD
🍸	= PUB
🏛	= FULL-SERVICE RESTAURANT

WOW **Tanganyika Tidal Wave.** Go for a pleasant little cruise through lush, tropical foliage. Sounds relaxing . . . that is, until your boat plunges over the edge to fall 55 feet into a splash pool. The result is a huge wave–really huge–that wets the passengers but can really *soak* observers standing in the wrong place on the walkway below.

For a great view of the tidal wave, climb the bridge and stand within the glass-walled tunnel. If you are riding, the back of the boat gets wet the least.

Animals. Orangutans.

Stanleyville Station Trans-Veldt Railroad.

Stanleyville Theater. Variety show presented several times daily.

Zambezi Theater. Improvisational comedy presented several times daily in season.

BIRD GARDENS/BREWERY

Bird Gardens/Brewery. The brewery was the reason Busch Gardens was started in 1959, and Bird Gardens is its oldest area. Its lush foliage includes nearly 2,000 exotic birds and birds of prey, representing 218 species and including one of the largest managed flocks of Caribbean flamingos. The koala exhibit features Koobar and Mueseli, on loan from the San Diego Zoo.

Dwarf Village and **Children's Play Area.** A shaded playground with little rides for little folk.

Busch Gardens Bird Show. Several performances each day of a show that includes macaws, cockatoos and birds of prey in free-flight demonstrations.

Brewery Tour. A quick and somewhat disappointing peek at the brewing process at Anheuser-Busch's large brewery. Be sure to check out the eagles along the left side of the outdoor escalator. The smell within the brewery is wonderful–if you like beer, that is. Samples of Busch products are available across the park at the new Crown Colony Hospitality Center.

Hospitality House Stage. A musical variety show including ragtime jazz piano.

Animals. Some of the park's most famous species are on display here, at **Flamingo Island, Eagle Canyon** and the **Koala Display.** Eagles on display alongside the brewery include golden and American bald eagles. The koala habitat also includes Dama wallabies and rose-breasted cockatoos.

KEY

¶¶ = Fast Food

Y = Pub

 = Full-
   Service
   Restaurant

EATING YOUR WAY THROUGH BUSCH GARDENS

MOROCCO

|Y| **Boujad Bakery.** An exotic place to grab breakfast or a sweet at any time of the day. Check out the gigantic blueberry and other types of muffins; also sold are impressive turnovers and pastries for $2 to $3 each.

|Y| **Zagora Cafe.** An exotic outdoor bazaar setting for unexotic burgers ($3.50-$4.50), onion rings and turkey sandwich platters ($5.50). Breakfast is served until 11 a.m.

|Y| **Ice Cream Parlor.**

CROWN COLONY

🏠 **Crown Colony House.** A lovely new 240-seat restaurant with spectacular views of the Serengeti Plain from its glasswalled Veldt Room. Another interesting location is the Library, stocked with antique books and a collection of photographs from Colonial days in Africa. A piano player entertains during meals.

Featured is the Crown Colony's Famous Family Style Chicken Dinner. Platters of batter-dipped chicken, cole slaw, soft yeast rolls, dressing, mashed potatoes and gravy, garden vegetables and cranberry relish. $8.95 per person; age 12 and under, $3.95. Other offerings include broiled Florida grouper, $12.95; medallions of veal in marsala sauce, $11.95 and chicken, turkey and fried grouper sandwiches for about $7. Children's meals include drumstick platters or spaghetti and meatballs, for about $4.

There are only 12 tables next to the windows in the Veldt Room, and they go fast. No reservations are accepted. The least crowded times are before noon, and from 4 to 5:30 p.m.; each day a throng heads for the restaurant about 12:15 p.m. when the midday ice show lets out.

|Y||Y| **Anheuser-Busch Hospitality Center.** Pizza, sandwiches and free samples of beer and snacks made by Anheuser-Busch companies.

TIMBUKTU

🏠 **Festhaus.** In the center of the large hall is an elevated bandstand, home of the Bavarian Colony Dancers and Band. The show harks back to the early German settlers in Africa who made their home in Timbuktu. Also seen on the stage is the International Show, which features music and performances from around the world. 1,200 seats.

Offerings include German sausage sandwich, roast turkey sandwich platter, corned beef and sauerkraut and a sausage sampler platter, with prices ranging from $4 to $6. A range of Anheuser-Busch beers is offered.

[¶] **Oasis.** Fruit juices and churros.

STANLEYVILLE

[¶] **Stanleyville Smokehouse.** Slow-smoked chicken, beef and ribs, served with french fries and cole slaw. Prices range from $5 to $7.50; a good deal is the $6.95 combo platter.

[¶] **Bazaar Cafe.** Bar-B-Q beef sandwich platters at $5 and salads for $2.

BIRD GARDENS/BREWERY

[¶] **Hospitality House.** Pepperoni and chef's combo pizzas, at $3 to $4 per slice. Tampa sandwiches–salami, turkey, cheese and salad on a roll–sell for about $5.50.

ADVENTURE ISLAND

Although the tidal wave and rafting expeditions at Busch Gardens are guaranteed to dampen your hairdo, if you want to get really wet, you may want to head around the corner to Adventure Island.

The 22-acre water park, also owned by Busch Entertainment Co., offers giant speed slides, body flumes, diving platforms, inner tube slides, a wave pool, water games, a white sand beach and volleyball courts.

Attractions include **Calypso Coaster,** a spiraling snake-like ride down an open flume in an innertube or raft for two; **Rambling Bayou,** a slow float along a rambling river around bends, under bridges and through a man-made rain forest; the **Caribbean Corkscrew** takes riders from a four-story tower down a fully enclosed, twisting translucent tube; **Water Moccasin** is a triple-tube water slide which cascades riders downward through a spiral before dumping them in a pool; **Tampa Typhoon** is a free-fall body slide which drops from a height of 76 feet before it levels out in a slick trough, and **Gulf Scream,** a speed slide in which riders can go as fast as 25 mph down a 210-foot fiberglass slide.

Paradise Lagoon is a 9,000-square-foot swimming pool fed by waterfalls; built into the surrounding cliffs are 20-

foot-high diving platforms, a cable drop, a cannonball slide and tube slides. The **Endless Surf** is a 17,000 square foot pool with mechanically produced three- to five-foot waves for body and rubber raft surfing.

New in 1992 was **Fabian's Funport**, a children's play area designed for the youngest visitors.

Adventure Island is open from the end of March daily until after Labor day, and weekends into October. Adult admission prices were about $16 in 1992, and $14 for youngsters from 3 to 9. Season passes are also available. Call (813) 987-5660 for schedules.

BUSCH GARDENS®
TAMPA BAY, FLORIDA

32

CONGO

SERENGETI PLAIN

TIMBUKTU

STANLEYVILLE

BREWERY

NAIROBI

CROWN COLONY

BIRD GARDENS

MOROCCO

✶ = MUST SEE

MAIN ENTRANCE

ATTRACTIONS & RESTAURANTS

1 Marrakesh Theater
2 Sultan's Tent
✶3 Moroccan Palace Theater
4 Rabat Label Store
✶5 Myombe Reserve:
   The Great Ape Domain
6 Train Station
✶7 Questor
✶8 Skyride and Monorail Station
✶9 The Scorpion™
10 Carousel Caravan
11 The Phoenix
✶12 The Python®
✶13 The Congo River Rapids™
14 Congo Train Station
✶15 Claw Island
✶16 Stanleyville Falls Log Flume

✶17 Tanganyika Tidal Wave
18 Stanleyville Station
19 Stanleyville Theater
20 Zambezi Theater
21 Dwarf Village Children's Play Area
22 Hospitality House Stage
23 Boujad Bakery
24 Zangora Cafe
25 Crown Colony Restaurant and
   Hospitality Center
26 Anheuser Busch Hospitality Center
27 Festhaus
28 Oasis
29 Stanleyville Smokehouse
30 Bazaar Cafe
31 Hospitality House
*32 Kumba

Appendix

A. Navigating in Orlando / Kissimmee

Interstate 4 Exits in Kissimmee/Orlando Area

23   Highway 27/Haines City. To Baseball City and Cypress Gardens.

25A   U.S. 192 East. (Irlo Bronson.) Motel strip toward downtown Kissimmee.

25B   U.S. 192 West. (Irlo Bronson.) Main gate of Walt Disney World. Motel strip.

26A/26B

    S.R. 536 to Epcot Center and Disney Village.

27   S.R. 535 to Kissimmee and Lake Buena Vista.

27A   Sea World. Central Florida Parkway Eastbound (toward Orlando) only.

28   528 East (Bee Line) to Sea World, Orlando International Airport and Kennedy Space Center. (Toll road.)

29   S.R. 482 to Orlando, Orlando International Airport and International Drive.

30A   Highway 435 South/Kirkman Road. Universal Studios.

30B   Highway 435 North/Kirkman Road. Universal Studios.

31   Florida Turnpike south to Miami or north to Wildwood.

33A   Hwy. 441, 17-92 (South Orange Blossom Trail).

36   East-West Expressway. (Toll road.)

38   Anderson Street, Orlando. Church Street Station.

40   Robinson Street, downtown Orlando.

41   Amelia Avenue, downtown Orlando.

B. Handicapped Access to Walt Disney World

Walt Disney World has done an exceptional job of making its facilities open to persons with special needs, including those in wheelchairs or with hearing or sight impairments. Nearly every attraction, exhibit, restaurant and shop is accessible; persons with handicaps will have to decide if the demands of a particular ride is beyond your abilities. The facilities at Epcot Center and the Disney-MGM Studios Theme Park are even more friendly than those at the Magic Kingdom.

Similar accommodations are offered at Universal Studios, Sea World and other area attractions. For more details, consult Guest Services at one of the parks.

In this chapter, we'll highlight some of the most important things to know about access to Walt Disney World. Disney also publishes "The Disabled Guest's Guide Book," available free at information centers.

PARKING

Magic Kingdom.

The Handicap Parking Lot is located at the front of the lot at the Transportation and Ticket Center. When you come to the Auto Plaza stay in the far right lane to obtain a special dashboard pass. After you park, proceed to the motor tram for a ride to the Transportation and Ticket Center where you can take the monorail or ferry to the entrance to the park itself. Wheelchairs may be folded and placed on the tram.

Epcot Center. The Handicap Parking Lot is to the right of the main entrance of the park. Stay in the far right lane when approaching the Auto Plaza and then take the road on the right.

Motor Trams are available to take you to the entrance; wheelchairs may be folded and placed on the tram.

Disney-MGM Studios Theme Park. Handicap Parking is available near the main entrance to the park. Stay in the far left lane when entering the Auto Plaza and take the road to the left. Motor trams are available to take you to the main entrance; wheelchairs may be folded and placed on the tram.

WHEELCHAIR RENTAL

Guests may bring their own wheelchairs or motorized vehicles, or can rent them for a minimal daily charge plus deposit. Quantities are limited and are available on a first-come, first-served basis. A limited number of three-wheel convenience vehicles may be rented at Epcot Center.

Rentals are available at the following locations:[1] in the Magic Kingdom at the **Transportation and Ticket Center** and just inside the Main Entrance at the stroller and wheelchair shop beneath the railroad station;[2] at Epcot Center inside the Entrance Plaza on the left, at the Gift Stop to the right of the ticket booths, and at the International Gateway, and at the Disney-MGM Studios Theme Park just inside the main entrance on the right at Oscar's Super Service.

LEADER DOGS

Guests using leader dogs are allowed in most areas of Walt Disney World. Some attractions, though, may not be suitable for a dog.

TRANSPORTATION

Ferryboats. Ferryboats provide easier access for guests in wheelchairs than do monorail trains between the Transportation and Ticket Center and the Magic Kingdom.

Monorail. Connecting the Transportation and Ticket Center with the Magic Kingdom, Epcot Center, Disney's Contemporary Resort, Disney's Polynesian Resort, and Disney's Grand Floridian Beach Resort. Use the ramps to the boarding area and seek the assistance of an attendant.

At Epcot Center, Disney's Polynesian Resort and Disney's Grand Floridian Beach Resorts, use the elevator to the monorail platform on the second floor.[3]

Buses. Many of the buses which connect all areas of the Walt Disney World Resort are equipped with wheelchair lifts, and special arrangements for unusual wheelchairs can be made by consulting dispatchers at the parks, the Transportation and Ticket Center or the Guest Services desk at the various resorts.

REST ROOMS/FIRST AID

Most of rest rooms within the Magic Kingdom, and all at Epcot Center and Disney-MGM Studios Theme Park are designed for access by wheelchairs. For special needs or to seek assistance from a registered nurse, visit the following locations:

Magic Kingdom. First Aid, near The Crystal Palace.

Epcot Center. The Odyssey Restaurant Complex.

Disney-MGM Studios Theme Park. Guest Services Building.

---

[1] If you plan to visit more than one park on the same day, be sure to have the deposit ticket for the wheelchair validated at the return station before leaving the first park you visit. You will then be able to rent another wheelchair at the next park without paying a second time or leaving a second deposit.

[2] Visitors to Walt Disney World may find it slightly easier to navigate the park in a counter-clockwise direction, starting at Tomorrowland and heading toward Advertureland. Heading that way puts you on a fairly consistent slightly downward slope.

[3] The monorail platform at Disney's Contemporary Resort is not accessible to wheelchair guests; wheelchair guests there and elsewhere within Walt Disney World can ride special buses with lifts.

SPECIAL SERVICES
Persons with impairment of sight can borrow portable tape players and descriptive cassettes at the following locations:
Magic Kingdom. City Hall.
Epcot Center. Earth Station.
Disney-MGM Studios Theme Park. Guest Services Building.
At Epcot center's Earth Station information counter, persons with hearing problems can borrow personal translator units which amplify the audio in selected attractions. Written descriptions of most attractions are also available.

Translator units with audio tapes in Spanish, French and German are also available at Earth Station.

> According to Disney policy, a person with a handicap may be accompanied through the disabled guest entrance by one other person in his or her party; all others in the party must go through the regular entrance and wait in line.
>
> In the following listing of highlights, attractions marked with a 🚶 symbol require disabled guests to leave their wheelchairs and walk a short distance, or be lifted out of their chairs and placed into a ride with the assistance of another member of their party. Attractions marked with ♿ symbol do not require visitors to exit their wheelchair.
>
> Virtually every area of Walt Disney World is accessible to the handicapped. Following are some specific hints for the most popular attractions at the park.

MAGIC KINGDOM
MAIN STREET, U.S.A.

🚶 **Walt Disney World Railroad.** A 21-minute round trip excursion on a real steam engine train circling the park. To enter from Main Street, U.S.A., wheelchair users should enter through the exit ramp gate located on the right of the center entrance of the train station. Wheelchairs may be folded and stored on the train, or left at the station for round trips. Guests who must remain in their wheelchair may board and disembark from either the Frontierland or Mickey's Birthdayland Railroad Stations.

🚶 **Main Street Vehicles (Fire Engine, Horseless Carriage, Horse-drawn Trolley.)** Folding wheelchairs can be placed in the vehicles for a one-way, 3-minute trip.

TOMORROWLAND

♿ **Mission to Mars.** A 20-minute theater presentation with some vibration effect. Enter to the right of the turnstiles. Wheelchair brakes should be locked; not recommended for leader dogs.

♿ **American Journeys Circle-Vision 360.** Use the regular entrance; an attendant can advise the best placement of the wheelchair to view the 20-minute film.

⚲ Dreamflight. A slow-moving vehicle. Contact an attendant for assistance.

⚲ StarJets. A short but somewhat dizzying ride that circles high above Tomorrowland. Approach the exit gates on either side of the gantry and obtain assistance from an attendant to board the elevator. An attendant on the upper level will assist with loading. Not recommended for leader dogs.

♿ Carousel of Progress. A 21-minute show in which a theater rotates slowly around a central stage; wheelchair brakes should be locked. Seek assistance at entrance ramps.

⚲ WEDway PeopleMover. A slow, 10-minute tour above Tomorrowland. Riders must be able to walk from steeply ascending moving ramp to a vehicle via a moving turntable.

⚲ Skyway. The stairs at the Tomorrowland Station are difficult, and disabled guests are requested to board the Skyway at the Fantasyland Station for a 10-minute round trip.

⚲ Space Mountain. A high-speed, turbulent 3-minute roller coaster ride that takes place within a darkened building. Guests required to wear back, neck or leg braces may not ride; pregnant women are advised not ride; leader dogs should not be brought on board, and sight-impaired guests must be accompanied by another member of his or her group. There is also a minimum height requirement for riders. Riders must also be able to walk across high catwalks and down a series of ladders in case of an emergency evacuation. Guests in wheelchairs may choose to visit just the pre-show and post-show areas.

⚲ Grand Prix Raceway. Head for the "Grandstand Entrance" sign and wait by the gate on the left side for assistance from an attendant. If visitors are unable to steer and depress a gas pedal, another member of the party must accompany the guest. There is also a minimum height requirement for guests driving Grand Prix race cars.

MICKEY'S BIRTHDAYLAND

♿ All attractions, shops and refreshment stands are accessible to guests in wheelchairs.

FANTASYLAND

⚲ Mad Tea Party. A 2-minute spinning teacup ride. Wait at the exit to the right of the operator's control booth and wait for assistance. Individuals with impaired trunk muscle control are advised they will not be able to support themselves in a sitting position because of centrifugal force.

⚲ 20,000 Leagues Under the Sea. Guests must be able to negotiate a steep nine-riser staircase consisting of nine stairs and maneuver through a narrow passageway within the submarine. Wait at the exit to the far right of the attraction and notify an attendant.

⚹ **Mr. Toad's Wild Ride.** Proceed to the far left or far right side of the attraction and wait while other members of the party go through the line; notify the attendant for assistance. The 3-minute moving ride is not recommended for leader dogs.

⚹ **Snow White's Adventures.** Same instructions as with Mr. Toad's Wild Ride.

♿ **Magic Journeys.** Enter the theater and stay to the far left; an attendant will direct guests to a special seating area for the 25-minute presentation.

⚹ **Peter Pan's Flight.** Contact an attendant for assistance. A 2-minute suspended vehicle ride.

⚹ **Dumbo, The Flying Elephant.** Wait with another member of your party at the exit to the left of the operator's console. When the ride has completely stopped, guests may board with the assistance of a member of your party; not recommended for leader dogs.

⚹ **Cinderella's Golden Carrousel.** Wait outside an exit gate close to the entrance and have another member of the party notify the attendant that you are waiting to enter. Guests must be seated on one of the Carrousel horses.

♿ **It's A Small World.** Enter through the exit area, to the far left of the entrance and proceed down the ramp to the unload dock. An 11-minute boat ride.

⚹ **Skyway.** Go through the exit to the unload area. Leave wheelchair at the Fantasyland Station for the 10-minute round trip ride. Stairs at the Tomorrowland Station are not accessible to disabled. Not recommended for leader dogs.

LIBERTY SQUARE

⚹ **The Haunted Mansion.** Enter through the exit area on the far right side. The corridor will wind back to the unload area, where an attendant will assist. An 8-minute ride.

♿ **Liberty Square Riverboat.** Locate the exit ramp on the left side of the Riverboat landing and proceed to the dock area for assistance. A 15-minute ride.

⚹ **Mike Fink Keelboats.** Locate the exit ramp on the left side of the Keelboat landing and proceed to the dock area for assistance.

♿ **The Hall of Presidents.** Enter the lobby through the door to the right of the main entrance and seek assistance for the 24-minute presentation.

FRONTIERLAND

⚹ **Big Thunder Mountain Railroad.** A high-speed, 4- minute turbulent roller coaster-type attraction. Guests required to wear back, neck or leg braces may not ride; pregnant women are advised not to ride; leader dogs should not be brought on board, and sight-impaired guests must be accompanied by another member of his or her group. There is also a minimum height requirement for riders, and guests must be able to walk or be carried a short distance. Locate the exit at the far right side of the attraction. Continue on to the loading area, staying on the left side of the pathway and seek assistance in boarding.

♿ **"Diamond Horseshoe Jamboree".** Reservations for this 1 hour, 15 minute Old West Vaudeville Show are required; make them early in the day at the Hospitality House, acrose the street from City Hall, on Main Street, U.S.A. Locate the ramp by the Tricornered Hat Shoppe to the right of The Diamond Horseshoe Jamboree and seek assistance at the door to the right of the main entrance.

♿ **Country Bear Jamboree.** Enter from the far left, approaching a side door near the Frontier Trading Post and notify an attendant.

♿ **Frontierland Shootin' Arcade.** Use the ramp to the left of the arcade; two gun positions can accommodate wheelchairs.

🚶 **Tom Sawyer Island.** Open until dusk. Enter through the right exit. Maneuvering on the island itself may be difficult for some disabled persons because of stairs, bridges, steep inclines and narrow caves. Guests may choose to take a raft ride to the island and back.

ADVENTURELAND

🚶 **Pirates of the Caribbean.** Seek the assistance of an attendant at the turnstiles. Folding wheelchairs may be lifted into the boat; a nonfolding chair may be exchanged for a folding one at the entrance. The boat ride includes a sequence with a drop down a short, steep waterfall.

♿ **Tropical Serenade.** Enter at the left side of the turnstile entrance area and seek assistance.

🚶 **Jungle Cruise.** Go down the wheelchair pathway next to the exit of the Swiss Family Treehouse and seek assistance from an attendant in boarding.

🚶 **Swiss Family Treehouse.** Not accessible to guests unable to walk up and down stairs.

EPCOT (FUTURE WORLD)
SPACESHIP EARTH

🚶 **Spaceship Earth.** Contact a host or hostess at the entrance for assistance. Guests ride in slow-moving cars up a steep incline and then descend backward for the return; not recommended for leader dogs.

♿ **Communicore East.** The following exhibits and presentations are directly accessible to guests in wheelchairs: Epcot Computer Central; TravelPort, and Energy Exchange. Seek assistance from an attendant for the following: Backstage Magic and Electronic Forum.

♿ **Communicore West.** The following exhibits and presentations are directly accessible to guests in wheelchairs: FutureCom; Expo Robotics; Sunrise Terrace; Epcot Outreach, and Epcot Teacher's Center.

UNIVERSE OF ENERGY

♿ **Universe of Energy.** Seek assistance to be directed to a special seating area in the moving theater. Guests in motorized convenience vehicles must transfer to an available wheelchair for this 45-minute ride.

WONDERS OF LIFE

🚶 **Body Wars.** A high speed, 5-minute turbulent ride through the human body in a simulator. Wheelchair guests must transfer into a ride seat. Guests should be in good health, free from neck or back injuries, heart problems and motion sickness. Due to the motion of the ride, good upper body strength is needed; an extra restraint, fitted over the shoulders, may be requested. Sight impaired guests must be accompanied by another member of his or her party. The ride is not recommended for pregnant women, and for leader dogs. Contact an attendant at the entrance for assistance.

♿ **Cranium Command** and **The Making of Me.** Contact an attendant for assistance at the entrance to either of these 12- minute shows.

♿ **Anacomical Theatre.** Special seating areas are labeled.

WORLD OF MOTION

♿ **World of Motion.** Contact an attendant in front of the entrance. Some vehicles in this 16-minute moving ride have been modified to accommodate wheelchairs. Guests in motorized convenience vehicles must transfer to an available wheelchair.

THE LAND

Entrance is on the upper level; guests in wheelchairs may use the elevator to the left of The Land Grille Room to reach attractions on the lower level.

♿ **Listen to The Land.** (Lower level.) Some of the boats in this 14-minute ride have been designed to accommodate wheelchairs. Guests in motorized convenience vehicles must transfer to an available wheelchair. Contact an attendant at the boat exit area behind the fountain for assistance.

♿ **Harvest Theatre.** (Upper Level.) Seek assistance from an attendant to enter the theater for this 19-minute presentation.

♿ **Kitchen Kabaret.** (Lower Level.) Seek assistance from an attendant.

♿ **The Land Grille Room.** (Upper Level.) One level of this revolving restaurant is accessible by wheelchair. Reservations required.

♿ **Harvest Tour.** Reservations for this guided tour of the Greenhouse and Aquacell areas may be made near the Broccoli and Co. shop on the lower level.

JOURNEY INTO IMAGINATION

♦ **Journey into Imagination.** Partial mobility is required to enter this 13-minute ride. See assistance from the attendant at the entrance.

♿ **Image Works.** "Hands on" activities on the second floor. Use the elevator for access.

♿ **Magic Eye Theater.** Seek assistance from an attendant to use the special seating area for this 18-minute 3-D film presentation. In 1992, the theater was showing **Captain EO**, starring Michael Jackson.

THE LIVING SEAS

♿ **The Living Seas.** All areas of the exhibit, including a theater, exhibits, a shop and Sea Base Alpha, an underwater environment for observation are wheelchair accessible.

♿ **Coral Reef Restaurant.** One level is accessible by wheelchair; reservations are required.

EPCOT (WORLD SHOWCASE)

TRANSPORTATION

♿ **FriendShips.** Traverse the World Showcase Lagoon to and from World Showcase Plaza and Germany or Morocco.

♦ **Promenade Buses.** Buses circle the lagoon, stopping at several locations along the Promenade. Wheelchairs must be folded and placed on the bus.

MEXICO

Enter using the ramp to the right of the pyramid. All exhibits and the San Angel Inn Restaurante are accessible to wheelchairs.

♿ **El Rio del Tiempo.** Some boats for this 9-minute ride have been designed to accommodate wheelchairs. Enter through the exit area of the boat ride and seek assistance from an attendant. Guests in motorized convenience vehicles must transfer to an available wheelchair.

NORWAY

♦ **Maelstrom.** Seek assistance from an attendant to board. Boats move up a steep incline, which eventually move backward and then plunge down a short waterfall. Riders must be able to maneuver down stairs in an emergency evacuation.

CHINA

♿ **Wonders of China.** Seek assistance from an attendant in placement of the wheelchair for the best viewing of the 19-minute film which is projected in a 360 degree arc.

GERMANY

♿ The restaurant and shops are accessible by wheelchair.

ITALY

♿ The restaurant and shops are accessible by wheelchair.

JAPAN

♿ **Bijutsu-kan** cultural exhibit and Mitsukoshi Department Store is accessible by wheelchair.

♿ **Restaurants.** Access to the second level dining and lounge areas is through the elevator to the left of the front entrance of the Mitsukoshi Department Store.

THE AMERICAN ADVENTURE

♿ **The American Adventure.** Use the elevator for access to the second-floor theater; seek assistance from an attendant.

MOROCCO

♿ The restaurant and shops are accessible by wheelchair.

FRANCE

♿ **"Impressions de France."** Enter through left door and keep to the left side of the entrance hallway. Seek assistance from an attendant to locate the special seating area.

♿ **Restaurants.** Seek assistance from an attendant at Chefs de France. Bistro de Paris requires guests to walk up and down a staircase.

♿ **Shops.** All shops are accessible by wheelchair except the second level of Plume et Palette.

UNITED KINGDOM

Restaurant and Pub. Seek assistance from an attendant.

♿ **Shops.** All shops are accessible by wheelchair except the upper level of Lords and Ladies.

CANADA

♿ **O Canada!** Enter along the path to the far right side of Canada through Victoria Gardens and past Le Cellier. Seek assistance from an attendant to find the best place to view the 17-minute film.

♿ **Restaurant.** Use the same entrance as for the film for this Buffeteria food service.

DISNEY-MGM STUDIOS THEME PARK

♿ All shops and restaurants at Disney-MGM Studios Theme Park are accessible by wheelchair.

HOLLYWOOD BOULEVARD

♿ **The Great Movie Ride.** Seek assistance from an attendant at the entrance to the Chinese Theatre. Guests in motorized convenience vehicles may need to transfer to an available wheelchair for this 22-minute moving theater ride.

LAKESIDE CIRCLE

🦽 **SuperStar Television.** Seek assistance from an attendant at the entrance. Guests who want to volunteer to participate onstage should ask the attendant for additional information.

🦽 **The Monster Sound Show.** Seek assistance from an attendant at the entrance.

BACKLOT ANNEX

🦽 **Indiana Jones Epic Stunt Spectacular.** Seek assistance from an attendant at the entrance.

🚶 **Star Tours.** Stay to the left at the entrance and ask assistance from an attendant. Guests must be able to leave wheelchairs and enter a seat in the starspeeder. This ride is not recommended for pregnant women or leader dogs. There is also a minimum height and age requirement.

BACKSTAGE STUDIO TOUR

🦽 **Backstage Studio Tour.** A 2-hour ride and walking tour. Seek assistance from an attendant at the entrance. Guests in motorized convenience vehicles may need to transfer to an available wheelchair. Guests can stay on board the motor tram and return to the start without walking.

🦽 **The Magic of Disney Animation.** Seek assistance from an attendant at the entrance.

🦽 **Restaurants.** To reach The Catwalk Bar, use the elevator in the Soundstage Restaurant.

Coupons

Look to your left, look to your right. One of you three people on vacation in Florida is paying the regular price for attractions, hotels, meals and shopping. One of the three is paying above regular price. And one pays only discount prices.

Which one would you rather be?

We've already written about strategies to obtain the lowest prices on airfare, about the cheapest and best times to visit and about how to negotiate for just about everything you'll need on a vacation trip.

Now, we're happy to present a special section of discount coupons from the Orlando and surrounding area. A careful reader of this book could save several hundred dollars on a trip to Central Florida using just a few of the coupons.

Of course, it is difficult for us to assign a single value to these coupons, since we don't know how many days you will travel, how many people are in your party and what time of the year you will come to Florida.

We used the following model to assign a value to the coupons: a family of four, occupying one room, on a one-week visit in high season, who order from the middle range of restaurant menus. Based on that formula, we estimate the total value of coupons in this book at more than $3,000!

A few things to bear in mind about these coupons:

* The authors do not endorse any of the businesses whose coupons appear here, and

* The presence of a coupon in this section does not in any way affect the authors' opinions expressed in this book.

Nevertheless, we hope you'll use the coupons. Let us know how you are received when you use them, and give us your opinions of these merchants—and others—in Central Florida.

The Ultimate

Word Association, Inc.
Box 2779 Nantucket, MA 02584

The Ultimate

ECONOGUIDE

Word Association, Inc.
Box 2779 Nantucket, MA 02584

$2.50 OFF
ADMISSION

Limited six guests per coupon

Orlando, Florida

Make contact with another world!

Sea World of Florida, the world's largest most popular marine life park is a window to the wonders of the ocean. Guests experience exciting shows, such as Shamu: New Visions® ; Mission: Bermuda Triangle℠ , an adventure ride; Shamu's Happy Harbor℠ , a three-acre play - area and *Manatees: The Last Generations?*℠ a new experience featuring the world of the manatee.

Not valid with other discounts or on purchase of multi-park/multi-visit passes or tickets. Present coupon before bill is totaled. Redeemable only at time of ticket purchase. Photocopies not accepted.
7007 Sea World Drive, Orlando, FL 32821

Valid through 3/31/95 Code 3731/3732

MERCADO MEDITERRANEAN SHOPPING VILLAGE

Redeem this at Mercado for a coupon book worth $200 in values! Redeem at either Mardi Gras Dinner Attraction 10 a.m.-10 p.m. or the Visitor Information Center 8 a.m.-8 p.m.

* *Over 60 unique specialty shops*
* *Five major restaurants*
* *Home of Mardi Gras Dinner Attraction*
* *English pub & frozen drink bar*
* *Free nightly entertainment*
* *International Village Cafes*
  Offer expires 12/31/94.

MEDITERRANEAN VILLAGE
**Open 10 a.m. to 10 p.m. Daily
Restaurants/Bars stay open later**

**8445 South International Dr.
Orlando, FL 32819   (407) 345-9337**

Value # American Tourister ® INC.
FACTORY OUTLET
40-70% off

SHONEY'S
America's Dinner Table ®

10% OFF
BREAKFAST, LUNCH OR DINNER

at Orlando area Shoney's. Offer expires 12/31/94.

218

The Ultimate

Word Association, Inc.
Box 2779 Nantucket, MA 02584

The Ultimate

ECONOGUIDE

Word Association, Inc.
Box 2779 Nantucket, MA 02584

The Ultimate

Word Association, Inc.
Box 2779 Nantucket, MA 02584

The Ultimate

Word Association, Inc.
Box 2779 Nantucket, MA 02584

The Ultimate

Word Association, Inc.
Box 2779 Nantucket, MA 02584

The Ultimate

Word Association, Inc.
Box 2779 Nantucket, MA 02584

The Ultimate

Word Association, Inc.
Box 2779 Nantucket, MA 02584

222

The Ultimate

Word Association, Inc.
Box 2779 Nantucket, MA 02584

The Ultimate

Word Association, Inc.
Box 2779 Nantucket, MA 02584

The Ultimate

ECONOGUIDE

Word Association, Inc.
Box 2779 Nantucket, MA 02584

224

The Ultimate

ECONOGUIDE

Word Association, Inc.
Box 2779 Nantucket, MA 02584

The Ultimate

ECONOGUIDE

Word Association, Inc.
Box 2779 Nantucket, MA 02584

The Ultimate

ECONOGUIDE

Word Association, Inc.
Box 2779 Nantucket, MA 02584

The Ultimate

Word Association, Inc.
Box 2779 Nantucket, MA 02584

The Ultimate

Word Association, Inc.
Box 2779 Nantucket, MA 02584

The Ultimate

Word Association, Inc.
Box 2779 Nantucket, MA 02584

The Ultimate

Word Association, Inc.
Box 2779 Nantucket, MA 02584

INTRODUCTORY OFFER

$1 OFF

STARBASE OMEGA.

"The Ultimate Lazer Game"

(Not good in conjunction with any other discount.) Just minutes from
Walt Disney World and Sea World in Florida Center. Open daily 10 am-11 pm.

5767 Major Blvd. Orlando, FL 32819 (407) 351-3355

Coupon ID #160 Offer Expires 12/31/94

F L A M I N G O   I N N

$24 PLUS TAX, UP TO TWO PEOPLE, $3 EXTRA PERSON

New Motel

AAA APPROVED
801 E. Vine Street (HWY 192) Kissimmee, FL 34744
(1/4 Mile east of Jct. 441 & 192)

Limited availability. Rate $24 Up to 2 persons, Extra person $3. Valid dates: 1/5 - 2/6, 4/21 - 6/10, 8/25 - 12/20.
All other dates: $34 up to 2 persons, Extra person $3

Exclusion dates: 12/21 - 1/3

Minutes from +attractions * Pool, free refrigeratiors * Health Club * Remote Controlled cable TV with HBO, ESPN
* Microwave * Discount attraction tickets available * Luxury rooms at economic prices

Tel: (407) 846 -1935
US and Canada Reservations only 1-800-780-7617
FAX: 407-846-7225
Expirations 12/31/94

10% OFF

ANY ADULT BUFFET

(with coupon, not available with any other discount)

Billy the Kid's features its famous buffet served with a western flair (includes BBQ
Ribs and Chicken, Shrimp, Ham and Country Fried Steak and Gravy, Salad Bar and
Dessert Bar with Unlimited Ice Cream). So look for the covered wagon and rustle
yourself over for a great meal. Offer expires 1/30/95

5051 W Hwy 192, Kissimmee, FL 34746 (407) 396-6532
located on Rt 192, 1/2 mile west of S.R. 535 in the midway center

228

The Ultimate

ECONOGUIDE

Word Association, Inc.
Box 2779 Nantucket, MA 02584

The Ultimate

ECONOGUIDE

Word Association, Inc.
Box 2779 Nantucket, MA 02584

The Ultimate

ECONOGUIDE

Word Association, Inc.
Box 2779 Nantucket, MA 02584

The Ultimate

Word Association, Inc.
Box 2779 Nantucket, MA 02584

The Ultimate

ECONOGUIDE

Word Association, Inc.
Box 2779 Nantucket, MA 02584

The Ultimate

Word Association, Inc.
Box 2779 Nantucket, MA 02584

The Ultimate

Word Association, Inc.
Box 2779 Nantucket, MA 02584

The Ultimate
ECONOGUIDE
Word Association, Inc.
Box 2779 Nantucket, MA 02584

The Ultimate
ECONOGUIDE
Word Association, Inc.
Box 2779 Nantucket, MA 02584

The Ultimate
ECONOGUIDE
Word Association, Inc.
Box 2779 Nantucket, MA 02584

The Ultimate
ECONOGUIDE
Word Association, Inc.
Box 2779 Nantucket, MA 02584

The Ultimate

Word Association, Inc.
Box 2779 Nantucket, MA 02584

The Ultimate

Word Association, Inc.
Box 2779 Nantucket, MA 02584

The Ultimate

ECONOGUIDE

Word Association, Inc.
Box 2779 Nantucket, MA 02584

The Ultimate

Word Association, Inc.
Box 2779 Nantucket, MA 02584

The Ultimate

Word Association, Inc.
Box 2779 Nantucket, MA 02584

The Ultimate

Word Association, Inc.
Box 2779 Nantucket, MA 02584

The Ultimate

Word Association, Inc.
Box 2779 Nantucket, MA 02584

The Ultimate

Word Association, Inc.
Box 2779 Nantucket, MA 02584

The Ultimate

Word Association, Inc.
Box 2779 Nantucket, MA 02584

The Ultimate

Word Association, Inc.
Box 2779 Nantucket, MA 02584

The Ultimate

Word Association, Inc.
Box 2779 Nantucket, MA 02584

The Ultimate

Word Association, Inc.
Box 2779 Nantucket, MA 02584

The Ultimate

ECONOGUIDE

Word Association, Inc.
Box 2779 Nantucket, MA 02584

The Ultimate

ECONOGUIDE

Word Association, Inc.
Box 2779 Nantucket, MA 02584

The Ultimate

Word Association, Inc.
Box 2779 Nantucket, MA 02584

The Ultimate

Word Association, Inc.
Box 2779 Nantucket, MA 02584

The Ultimate

ECONOGUIDE

Word Association, Inc.
Box 2779 Nantucket, MA 02584

The Ultimate

Word Association, Inc.
Box 2779 Nantucket, MA 02584

244

The Ultimate

Word Association, Inc.
Box 2779 Nantucket, MA 02584

The Ultimate

ECONOGUIDE

Word Association, Inc.
Box 2779 Nantucket, MA 02584

The Ultimate

ECONOGUIDE

Word Association, Inc.
Box 2779 Nantucket, MA 02584

The Ultimate

Word Association, Inc.
Box 2779 Nantucket, MA 02584

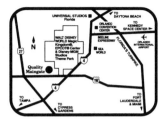

The Ultimate

Word Association, Inc.
Box 2779 Nantucket, MA 02584

The Ultimate

ECONOGUIDE

Word Association, Inc.
Box 2779 Nantucket, MA 02584

The Ultimate

Word Association, Inc.
Box 2779 Nantucket, MA 02584

The Ultimate

Word Association, Inc.
Box 2779 Nantucket, MA 02584

The Ultimate

Word Association, Inc.
Box 2779 Nantucket, MA 02584

The Ultimate

Word Association, Inc.
Box 2779 Nantucket, MA 02584

The Ultimate

Word Association, Inc.
Box 2779 Nantucket, MA 02584

The Ultimate

Word Association, Inc.
Box 2779 Nantucket, MA 02584

The Ultimate
ECONOGUIDE
Word Association, Inc.
Box 2779 Nantucket, MA 02584

The Ultimate
ECONOGUIDE
Word Association, Inc.
Box 2779 Nantucket, MA 02584

The Ultimate
ECONOGUIDE
Word Association, Inc.
Box 2779 Nantucket, MA 02584

The Ultimate
ECONOGUIDE
Word Association, Inc.
Box 2779 Nantucket, MA 02584

252

The Ultimate

Word Association, Inc.
Box 2779 Nantucket, MA 02584

The Ultimate

Word Association, Inc.
Box 2779 Nantucket, MA 02584

The Ultimate

Word Association, Inc.
Box 2779 Nantucket, MA 02584

The Ultimate

Word Association, Inc.
Box 2779 Nantucket, MA 02584

The Ultimate

Word Association, Inc.
Box 2779 Nantucket, MA 02584

The Ultimate

Word Association, Inc.
Box 2779 Nantucket, MA 02584

The Ultimate

Word Association, Inc.
Box 2779 Nantucket, MA 02584

The Ultimate

Word Association, Inc.
Box 2779 Nantucket, MA 02584

The Ultimate

Word Association, Inc.
Box 2779 Nantucket, MA 02584

The Ultimate

ECONOGUIDE

Word Association, Inc.
Box 2779 Nantucket, MA 02584

The Ultimate

Word Association, Inc.
Box 2779 Nantucket, MA 02584

The Ultimate

ECONOGUIDE

Word Association, Inc.
Box 2779 Nantucket, MA 02584

The Ultimate
ECONOGUIDE
Word Association, Inc.
Box 2779 Nantucket, MA 02584

The Ultimate
ECONOGUIDE
Word Association, Inc.
Box 2779 Nantucket, MA 02584

The Ultimate
ECONOGUIDE
Word Association, Inc.
Box 2779 Nantucket, MA 02584

The Ultimate
ECONOGUIDE
Word Association, Inc.
Box 2779 Nantucket, MA 02584

The Ultimate

ECONOGUIDE

Word Association, Inc.
Box 2779 Nantucket, MA 02584

The Ultimate

ECONOGUIDE

Word Association, Inc.
Box 2779 Nantucket, MA 02584

The Ultimate

ECONOGUIDE

Word Association, Inc.
Box 2779 Nantucket, MA 02584

The Ultimate

ECONOGUIDE

Word Association, Inc.
Box 2779 Nantucket, MA 02584

The Ultimate

ECONOGUIDE

Word Association, Inc.
Box 2779 Nantucket, MA 02584

Index

How to Write to the Author

About the author

Corey Sandler has written more than 40 non-fiction books on a wide range of topics–from video games to high-tech computers to speechwriting. A former correspondent for The Associated Press, he also served as a reporter for Gannett Newspapers and as editor-in-chief of magazines published by Ziff-Davis Publishing Co. and International Data Group.

Sandler lives and works on Nantucket island, 30 miles off the coast of Cape Cod, Massachusetts, with his wife Janice and children William and Tessa.

How to Write to the Author

We'd love to read your inside tips and hints and any comments on the attractions and businesses we've written about here. Please send your comments to:

Ultimate Unauthorized Econoguide
WORD ASSOCIATION, INC.
P.O. Box 2779
Nantucket, MA 02584